Western Lore
and Language

Western Lore and Language

A Dictionary for
Enthusiasts of the
American West

Thomas L. Clark

= University of Utah Press =
= Salt Lake City =

LIBRARY OF CONGRESS CATALOGING-IN-PUBLICATION DATA

Clark, Thomas L.
    Western lore and languague : a dictionary for
enthusiasts of the American West / Thomas L. Clark.
        p.   cm.
    Includes bibliographical references.
    ISBN 0-87480-510-4 (alk. paper)
    1. English language—West (U.S.)—Slang—Dictio-
naries. 2. West (U.S.—Social life and customs—Dictionaries. 3. Americanisms—West (U.S.)—Dictionaries.
I. Title.
PE2970.W4C58   1996
427'.978—dc20   96-12089
                                                        CIP

Contents

Preface

What Is *The West*?

It is a geographical region if you are a citizen of the Mountain, Pacific, or Alaskan time zones. It is a state of mind if you are a cowboy, a surfer, a climber, a logger, a computer maker, a movie fan, a Pacific fisherman, an avid skier, a citizen of the Pacific Rim. The English words that came into the language in western North America are like those that enter the language in any geographical region: the borrowings and neologisms are determined by the land, the occupations, and pastimes of the inhabitants. The needs of the people living with unique encounters of vegetation, landscape, and fauna require words like *sego lily, wash,* and *roadrunner.* The occupations of westerners require new words like *Silicon Valley, skid row, outrider.* The pastimes of westerners have required the adoption of new meanings like *malibu board, ace in the hole, Iditarod.* Encounters with other cultures give us new English words like *fry bread, arroyo, avocado.*

The West can represent wide-open spaces, freedom of mind, freedom of expression, freedom of action, even the Marlboro Man image—all reflected in the language of the West. Westerners seem to relish the notion that they are less restricted than people from other parts of the country. They generally are enamored of states' rights, freedom from gun control, and the ability to move anywhere at anytime. The Sagebrush Rebellion gets enough press from time to time to let others know that westerners will allow themselves a certain amount of aggravation, but the limit can be reached by centralized bureaucracies, whether emanating from Washington, D.C., or Ottawa.

Talking "western" means using the words that have come into the English language in western North America. The area includes the region of the Mountain time zone: Alberta, Montana, Idaho, Wyoming, Utah, Colorado, Arizona, New Mexico, and west Texas.

The rest of the West is California, Nevada, Oregon, Washington, British Columbia, the Yukon Territory, and Alaska. Many speakers of English who wound up in Alaska came from the ranches and oil fields of the western states.

Now, Hawaii *is* the westernmost state, but the English spoken in the islands is heavily peppered with Hawaiian, Asian, and Polynesian words (*aloha, wahine, haole, luau, mele kalikimaka*). Should they be included within the scope of "western talk"? No. Western talk is restricted to English used in western North America.

Texas covers both the south and the west. (Some folks who live near El Paso say that Texas covers most of the habitable universe.) Separating west Texas talk from south Texas talk is my chore as editor to deal with. Making the choice for inclusion or exclusion comes from long experience with dialects, advice from others in the field, survey of the sources, and, finally, the domain of the word.

Border Spanish (Tex-Mex, Tejana, Spanglish) would certainly flavor a book of western talk, as would California Mellow, Old West (such as stagecoach, early mining, sawmill vocabularies), or New West (such as vocabularies associated with Esalen, western skiing, vineyard cultivation, Hollywood, surfing, enviromania, Silicon Valley, Valley Girl vapidity, Pacific Rim).

All the words and phrases included in this work originated in the West or are associated mainly with the West. The following entries (1) originated in the West (*forty-niner, Silicon Valley, skookum, quaking aspen*), (2) are used mainly in the West (*butte, Spanish sword, spider crab*), or (3) are associated with the West (*mesa, rodeo, puncher*).

Some examples of these three categories:

1. *arroyo*—a word borrowed from Spanish in the 1840s directly into the English of the American Southwest, and still used almost exclusively in the Southwest.

Silicon Valley—part of the Santa Clara Valley, southwest of San Francisco, where many of the high-technology semiconductors used in computers are designed and manufactured. Referring to the silicon wafers used in the semiconductors, the term for the region was first used by Don C. Hoefler in a series of articles in *Electronic News* in the early 1970s. Hoefler, in turn, said the name was suggested to him by Ralph Voerst.

2. *butte*—a Middle French word known in the eastern United States as early as the seventeenth century, but, according to the *Dictionary of American Regional English,* used almost exclusively in the West today in the daily language of westerners.

3. *rodeo*—a word borrowed from Spanish in the 1830s, originally referring to a roundup of cattle, later to mean a series of riding and roping contests. Rodeos have been held nationwide, even in Madison Square Garden, but the word and what it stands for are still mainly associated with the West.

wrangler is traced back to the sixteenth century in England with the sense of "disputant." William Shakespeare has Henry V refer to himself as a "wrangler" for the throne of France. But the word developed a new sense in the American West in the 1880s, first as "horse-wrangler," then as a cowboy who worked with livestock on a ranch. The *Oxford English Dictionary* (*OED*) has a separate entry for it as a word from the "American West."

This book is not a survey of a regional dialect. Dialect studies include phonological and syntactic components that are not found here. The pronunciation differences are profound, from El Paso to Vancouver, British Columbia. The regional dialect in terms of accent ranges from southern to northern. But the vocabulary is the key to the constitution of western English. The pronunciation differences between, say, west Texas and western Washington are the subject of an entirely different study.

Nor is this a book specifically dedicated to "cowboy lingo," "wrangler speech," or "trailhand talk"—that particular set of phrasings and sayings that writers of western novels trade in. There are already a number of those kinds of books.

Format of Entries	The **main entry** is the word or term itself, in straight alphabetical order. That is, hyphens and spaces are ignored, as are symbols not spelled alphabetically.

The **main entry** is the word or term itself, in straight alphabetical order. That is, hyphens and spaces are ignored, as are symbols not spelled alphabetically.

If required, the **pronunciation** is next. A simple newspaper style of pronunciation is used for ease of use by nonspecialists.

The part of speech of the word or term is next:

n = noun
v = verb
adj = adjective
excl = exclamation
adv = adverb
poss = possessive form
phr = phrase

The **definition** is given next. If the term has more than one western application, that is numbered consecutively. No attempt has been made to list meanings in terms of frequency of use.

If the term has an identifiable, specific **source,** that is given next. But, as is the case with most food terms, the words normally began to appear in western publications sometime after the word had been adopted into spoken English.

The **etymology,** or history of the word is presented next, if known. Occasionally, a fanciful, or folk etymology will be recorded. These folk etymologies—fanciful explanations of how a word came about—are clearly identified as being fanciful, not factual.

If possible, the **date of first occurrence** is provided next. Sometimes it is possible to narrow a term to a general time frame, such as the 1930s or the early 1800s.

The **editor's comments** are presented last. Such comments may have to do with folk etymologies or cultural notes.

Domains of the Vocabulary

Western words and terms come from a variety of domains that are dependent on geography, language contact, occupations, and activities that are particular to this region of North America.

The names of flora are manifold and diverse. The extremes of altitude account for vegetational terms related to the highest mountains and the lowest deserts on the continent. Some of the oldest, biggest, and smallest forms of vegetation are to be found in the bristlecone pine of mountain peaks, the redwoods of the coast, the bellyflowers of the desert. Listing every instance of vegetational names, or faunal names for that matter, would require a much larger book. I have, therefore, included the most common terms and those that reflect naming practices: the scientists, explorers, railroaders, and ranchers who gave their names to specific plants and animals.

Language contact accounts for a significant number of borrowings into English. Spanish has been the largest contributor to English in the West. But other languages have also made significant contributions. Japanese has contributed more than other Asian languages, but regional vocabularies of English in areas where a high concentration of immigrants has settled have also profited from borrowings. Many of these borrowings remain regional, but a few, usually food terms, become nationally recognized. Vietnamese, Thai, Mandarin, Cantonese, and other Asian languages have contributed in this fashion. But other languages have concentrations of groups of people who contribute to a vocabulary on a local level. Although a number of people around Fresno, California, trace their roots to Armenia, and a large number of people in Nevada, northern California, and southern Idaho trace their ancestry to the Basques of Spain, few, if any, English words are to be traced to these two groups.

Among Native American languages in the region, Navajo, Hopi, Kwakiutl, Yahi, and Haida have had minimal impact on the vocabulary except for a few regional terms. Most of the contributions of these groups, including Piute, Gosiute, and other Uto-Aztecan languages, have been placenames. Nahuatl is the exception. That language gave a number of terms to the Spanish, who in turn contributed them to English: words like *tomato, chocolate, avocado.*

Much of the vocabulary entered the general language from occupations and activities in the West. The computer, mining, and logging industries contributed, as did sheep and cattle ranching, commercial fishing, and legalized gaming. A number of old-time gamblers contributed their language in the West, but so did other people who pursued a variety of interests, from skiing, surfing, and rodeo to sportfishing and river rafting. In each case, certain vocabulary words moved from the realm of the specialist into the general vocabulary.

Sources

Dictionaries are derivative by nature. And this dictionary is no different. It is not constructed on historical principles. That is, each entry in this book comes from one or more of the sources listed in the Bibliography at the end of the book. Because this dictionary is more in the mold of general commercial dictionaries, details of the sources of items are not listed in the text. Rather, the space is devoted to breadth of coverage and definitions written in a more leisurely (and space-consuming) fashion. But no dictionary is created from scratch by the person whose name appears on the title page. This section credits the many sources used in the creation of this book: newspapers, dictionaries, oral histories, and books about western North America.

Newspapers

The archives, files, and electronic databases for nearly twenty newspapers were part of the reading program for the preparation of this book. All the entries identified from these sources were checked against appropriate dictionaries. In many cases, the items found in the newspaper reading program were antedated by material found in the dictionaries. But, more than any other source (with the exception of the oral collection), the newspapers gave the flavor of the terms in a western context. The newspapers are listed alphabetically in the Bibliography at the end of the book.

One newspaper requires special mention. The *San Jose Mercury-News* (*SJM*) has excellent library facilities. Gary Lance made both print and electronic archives completely accessible. The paper has had full-text electronic accessibility since June 1, 1985. Many word searches of that source were more successful than similar searches on NEXUS.

Dictionaries

Walter Avis gave major credit for the success of his *Dictionary of Canadianisms on Historical Principles* (*DC*) to the earlier work and methods of Mitford Mathews, whose *Dictionary of Americanisms on Historical Principles* (*DA*) has served as a model for specialized dictionaries since 1951. Indeed, most of the items from the Pacific Northwest, British Columbia, the Yukon Territory, and Alaska were checked against Avis's book, then again against *DA*. In final analysis, *DA* was the most-consulted work among the dictionaries.

Another major dictionary, and one of inestimable assistance, is the still uncompleted *Dictionary of American Regional English* (*DARE*). My association with this large project dates from 1965, when field-workers were being organized to drive around the country and collect data in personal interviews. In 1966 I drove my "word wagon" around Ohio collecting material and sending it back to Madison, Wisconsin, where Fred Cassidy and the rest of the staff were collating information, overseeing a large reading program, and constantly searching for funding for the project. One of the organizations involved in the project was the American Dialect Society. I was very proud to be president of that organization the year the first volume of *DARE* appeared.

Through the years, Frederic Cassidy and Joan Hall have been most gracious in providing information from the files of *DARE* and have treated me with every kindness when I was actually able to go visit the archives. They make a special point of assisting researchers in every way possible.

More recently, an index to the first two volumes (letters A–H) was produced, which organized the entries according to region. This index was helpful in locating western terms. The people at *DARE* headquarters are constantly working to make their information more accessible.

Other specialized dictionaries and word lists played a role in the making of this book. Surfing terms were checked against Trevor Cralle's *Surfin'ary* (*SURF*), probably the most freewheeling dictionary ever produced. Russell Tabbert's *Dictionary of Alaskan English* (*DAK*) was indispensable for tracking the many terms Native Americans have contributed to English. Unlike dictionaries that use a completely alphabetical listing, *DAK* divides the lexicon by topic. The reader is given a very good feel for the various domains treated: climate, food, drink, clothing, plants, and so on.

Gambling terms played an important part in the development of the culture of the West. My *Dictionary of Gambling and Gaming* (*DGG*) was useful for checking terms. But the Nevada Oral Collection (see below) probably played a more important role.

Other dictionaries listed in the Bibliography were important to greater and lesser degrees. The magnificent *OED* is necessary to every lexicographical endeavor. I have been fortunate in enlisting the aid of Elizabeth Knowles, of the Oxford staff, for information on particularly western North America items. The *Random House Dictionary of the English Language,* second edition, unabridged (*RHD*), was extensively used and amazingly useful. *Merriam Webster's Collegiate Dictionary,* tenth edition (*W10*) sat at my right hand at every stage of the manuscript.

Wordbooks

Word lists, glossaries, and other word sources are important to a study such as this. Works like Bright's *A Word Geography of California and Nevada* (*BR*) were important in building the initial list of terms. Ramon Adams's *Western Words* (*WW*) was also checked for words relative to rodeo, cowboys, and such. But, similar to its contribution to the second volume of *DARE,* *WW* contributed in only a few instances. McConnell's *Our Own Voices* and McCulloch's *Woods Words* were useful for terms from the Pacific Northwest, both logging and general vocabularies. Slatta's *Cowboy Encyclopedia* (*CE*) is a contemporary treasure for rodeo. And the *Barnhart Dictionary Companion* (*BDC*) is indispensable in analyzing the origin and distribution of new words in English.

Oral Collections

The major oral collection of tapes and surveys and interviews of western language is the Nevada Language Survey. Initiated in 1971, this survey has tracked western language for twenty-five years. The Nevada Oral Collection (*NOC*) was a major source for *DGG* and played an important role in this collection. Other unpublished collections were from the files of *DARE* and from George Kobayashi, curator of the California Room at the Martin Luther King, Jr., Public Library in San Jose, California. Mr Kobayashi has been especially helpful in aiding the understanding of terms from various Asian languages. New food terms are especially prolific, due to the many new cuisines emanating from California.

Other works that had an effect on the development of this book are listed in the Bibliography. In some cases, information from them was instrumental in establishing dates of use or, more often, frequency of use in western English. This last point is especially important because many words listed here did not originate in the West, but are considered mainly western or *most frequently used* in the West.

Indispensable Assistance

No collection can be achieved by a single individual in these modern days of the information highway. Great assistance was provided by Michael J. Wise. Beginning in 1991 on this project, he spent more than three years working on data collection, dictionary comparison, and, toward the end, writing definitions.

Personnel from the Dickinson Library at the University of Nevada, Las Vegas, also contributed to this work, including Susan Jarvis, Elmer Curley, and Kathleen War. The University of Nevada, Las Vegas, Research Council assisted this project with a grant.

Others who contributed to the project include stalwarts from *OED*'s many offshoots: Elizabeth Knowles, in Oxford, who headed off many a fruitless chase, and Linda M. Jones, from the Waterloo (Canada) project to computerize *OED,* who provided lists of file names of westernisms. Allyn Partin contributed with information about westernisms from Hollywood and the movies. Russell Tabbert, author of *DAK* was most kind in clarifying domains and frequency of items. An entire crew from the best newspaper in the Western Hemisphere also contributed. *SJM* contributors include Gary Lance, Jeffrey Klein, Bob Hucker, and (to her surprise) Joanne Jacobs, whose sense of westernisms matches H. L. Mencken's sense of Americanisms.

A great deal of work was done on short notice by those making and finding illustrations: Margaret Brander, Sasha Tate-Clark, Tim Clark, Jeanne Clark, David Monteith, Wesley Niles, Donald Baepler, James Deacon, Kelley Stevens, Liz Smith, Diane Brenner, Mina Jacobs, Donna Barrow, Debbie Sanders, John Lyman, David Millman, and Tom Dyer. Finally, I must thank Steve and Kristin, Thom and HM, who produced three of my very dearest friends, grandchildren Johnathon, Max, and Claire, children of the West and inheritors of it.

A

aarigaa

■ /ah REE gah/ excl Also spelled *ahregah, aarrigaa, adegah, arriga.* In Alaska, an expression borrowed from Inupiaq meaning 'good, fine'. People in Alaska have a vocabulary peppered with borrowings from various native Indian languages and dialects as well as from the early Russian settlers.

Aaronic Priesthood

■ /air ON ik ~/ n In the hierarchy of the Mormon church (**Church of Jesus Christ of Latter-day Saints**), a category for males who are progressing through the three stages of deacon, teacher, and priest. Since the 1830s all men of good standing in the church have been expected to enter the priesthood, go on a mission, then marry. See also **Melchizedek priesthood.**

abalone

■ n Any of a variety of mollusks found along the California coast. The inside of the shell is lustrous, giving rise to the occasional name "bastard pearl." (Monterey Indian *aulun* via Spanish *abulón*)

abalone

■ v To collect abalone. The verb form was developed in California by Californians in the 1960s. Californians are responsible for many of the developments in new verbs that spread eastward.

"Sign near beach: Restricted Area: Keep Out. No Fishing or Abaloning." —1975 *DARE*

Abert's

■ poss Lieutenant J. W. Abert, a U.S. soldier and scientist who was stationed at forts in the Southwest during the 1850s, gave his name as the first element to certain birds and animals in the Southwest: *Abert's finch, Abert's pipilo, Abert's squirrel, Abert's towhee.*

abogado

■ n A lawyer or advocate. Common usage in Southwest, where the ratio of lawyers to citizens is about the same as what infects the rest of the country. (Spanish)

above

■ postnoun modifier Also called **above discovery.** In the Yukon and Alaska, this term designates strike claims on a stream other than the first. The first strike on a stream is the "discovery claim," the next strike upstream is called "number one above," or "number one above discovery." From the 1890s, gold rush patrons were falling all over each other and claiming sites just above or below one another, hoping that the gold flakes would shift a few feet and pay out like a lottery jackpot. Compare **below** postnoun modifier.

abra

■ n A narrow pass or defile between mountains or mesas. (From 1890s, Spanish)

absinthe bush

■ n Also spelled *absynth, absanth*. The sagebrush or prairie sage. Not, I think, the kind of absinthe that makes the heart grow fonder. (From 1840s, French)

ace in the hole

■ n An effective strategy, argument, or resource held in reserve during a discussion or negotiation. Originally, this term was for the first card dealt face down in stud poker should it be an ace. If no pairs appeared in the other hands, the ace in the hole would take the pot.

acequia

■ n Also spelled *sequia*. Also called **irrigation acequia.** A man-made ditch created for **irrigation.** The term is Spanish, used from the 1840s in Texas, the 1890s in Utah, where Mormon pioneers refined irrigation systems to a high art and made the desert bloom with vegetables rather than wild flowers. See also **zanja.**

Acoma

■ n The name of an Indian tribe and a pueblo in New Mexico. The Acomas are part of the Keresan language family. The native name means 'white-rock people', and was first written in the 1890s. The adjective *Acomanian* dates from the same time.

Adam-and-Eve

■ n Also called **chamise-lily.** A western wildflower called "dogtooth violet" elsewhere. (From 1890s)

add-on

■ n In Kodiak, Alaska, an addition built onto a house trailer that has been made immobile is called an add-on. See also **wanigan.** (From 1980s)

adios

■ excl Good-bye, farewell. This cheerful call has been used from the 1830s. From Spanish, literally, 'to God', in the sense "God be with you" and, in English, "good-bye." The term is likely to be heard as often as the Italian *ciao,* the Japanese *sayonara,* or the Spanish *hasta la vista.* The extended form is "Adios, amigo."

adobe

■ n 1. In the Southwest, since the 1820s, a crude cement made from sun-dried clay. Houses made from adobe have very thick walls, are cool in summer, and retain heat in the winter. The style has become so identified with the Southwest that *faux adobe,* an external plaster, is regularly lathered over the Sheetrock in new housing developments, along with the imitation red-tile roof that looks like sections of sewer pipe cut in half lengthwise. See also **cahon,** 1. 2. Also since the 1820s the term has been used as the first element in compounds: *adobe block, adobe brick, adobe house.* 3. Since 1900, the term has been used as the first element in reference to the peso: *adobe dollar.* See also **dobe.**

aerial

■ n A surfer's maneuver, sometimes thought of as "hotdogging," in which the surfer and board are above the water for a short time, usually performed by turning into the wave and going up and over the top of it. As a result of the maneuver, the **hotdogger** may be rewarded with a cheer, but more often is rewarded with a **wipeout.**

A-frame barrel

■ n In surfing, a wave that peaks in the middle and forms two breakers going to the left and to the right.

agarita, agrillo, agrito, algeredo

■ n See **barberry.**

ahkio

■ n Also called **pulk.** A light cargo sled used in Alaska, somewhat resembling the front half of a canoe, usually made of fiberglass or aluminum, pulled by dogs, people, or snowmobiles. The term is from Lappish via Finnish, and was first used in English in writing in the 1950s.

airtight

■ n A canned meat, fruit, or vegetable. (From 1890s; now mainly rural)

ajo

■ /AH ho/ n 1. Also called **ajo lily.** The desert lily, *Hesperocallis undulata* found in Arizona and California, whose edible bulb was used as onion or garliclike flavoring by Indians (from 1880s, Spanish *ajo* 'garlic'). See also **false garlic.** 2. A plant from the genus *Allium* common to the Southwest.

alacran

■ n A type of scorpion found, but mostly avoided, especially in Texas. (From 1830s, Spanish)

Alabama wool

■ n Among old-time loggers, beginning around the 1950s, clothing made of cotton, especially underwear.

aladik

■ n Also spelled *alodik, alotuk, aladaxs.* A fried bread found in Alaska, usually served in place of toast or with powdered sugar or jam as a dessert. The tradition is a carry-over from Russian *alad'i* 'thin pancakes' via Alaskan native languages, including Atkan Aleut, Dena'ina, and Central Yupik. First recorded in the 1970s, the term is much older in the oral tradition. See also **Eskimo doughnut.** Compare **fry bread.**

alameda

■ n A public walkway, promenade, or road with alamos or other trees lining both sides. The term is used as a place-name in California and widely used in the West as a street name. (From 1830s, Spanish)

alamo

■ n Also **alamo tree.** Any of several poplar trees, such as the cottonwood. The famous Texas fort, defended to the death by Sam Houston, Davy Crockett, and others, was built near a grove of these trees. (From 1850s, Spanish)

Alaska

■ n Also spelled *Alaeksu, Alachschak, Alaschka, Alaxa.* Forty-ninth state of the Union. Known as "Russian America" until bought by the United States in 1867. Settled in 1784. A territory from 1912 until it became a state in 1959. Capital: Juneau. The name *Alaska* is derived from the Aleutian word meaning 'mainland', to distinguish these inhabitants from those on the islands. The meaning of the word seems to lose something in translation, which is literally, "the object toward which the action of the sea is directed." Also known as **The Great Land.** See also **Walrussia.**

Alaska blackfish

■ n A small dark fish, five to eight inches long, and known for its hardiness. It requires little oxygenated water and actually survives light freezing! It served as an oily subsistence food for many years in Alaska and Siberia. Its genus name *Dallia pectoralis* honors William H. Dall, a naturalist who studied the fish in the 1870s and who called the fish by its common name.

Alaska candy

■ n Narrow strips of salmon cut lengthwise, salted, dried, and smoked. Yum. Introduced by Alaska Natives, the palatal delight has been called by various names since the 1950s. See **squaw candy** for a complete listing.

Alaska cedar

■ n Also called **Alaska cypress, Alaska ground cypress.** The common yellow cedar *Chamaecyparis nootkatensis,* prized for cabinetry in the Northwest. (From 1880s)

Alaska cotton

■ n In Alaska, any of a variety of grasses of the genus *Eriophorum,* with a single stem topped by a white tuft. (From 1930s)

Alaska jay

■ n Also called **Alaskan jay.** A common northern gray jay with dark cap, *Perisoreus canadensis.* Since the 1880s, this raucous, often pesky bird has had many names throughout its northern and western North American range. The western-related names appear to be Alaska jay and **camp robber,** though it is known in other areas as *camp bird, Canada jay, carrion bird, deer hunter, elk bird, gorby, gray jay, grease bird, lumberjack, meatbird, moosebird, old logger, pork bird, tallow bird, venison bird, whiskey jack, white-headed jay, woodman's ghost.*

Alaska king crab

■ n Also called **king crab, red king crab, Japanese spider crab, spider crab.** A large crab, up to fifteen pounds and five feet across, found in Alaskan waters. The legs have been particularly favored restaurant fare since the 1920s. The commercial success of crabbers and the insatiable appetites of crab lovers have given rise to a variety of terms for similar crabs. See also **blue king crab, brown king crab, golden king crab.** Compare **queen crab, Tanner crab.**

Alaskan

■ adj Of or pertaining to Alaska. (From 1870s) The use of this term, ending as it does in a consonant, is unusual in place-name modification. Other state names ending in unstressed vowels (e.g., Nevada, Minnesota, California, South Dakota) are not spelled with a final -*n* when used in modification. Thus, Alaskan coast, but California coast; similarly, Nevada gambler, but Alaskan gambler.

Alaska Native

■ n An indigenous, non-European inhabitant of Alaska; an Alaskan of aboriginal ancestry. The term specifically distinguishes such a person from a "native Alaskan," a person born in Alaska of nonaboriginal ancestry. (From 1970s)

" . . . in current Alaskan usage the distinction is usually clear. *Alaska Native* (almost never *Alaskan Native*) is firmly established for designating aboriginal ancestry. This leaves *native Alaskan,* which is much less frequent, available to mean an Alaskan-born non-aborigine." —Russell Tabbert, *DAK* 1991

Alaskan high kick

■ n Also called **one-foot high kick, two-foot high kick.** A variation of the Eskimo game, **high kick,** in which a contestant grasps one foot, then jumps to kick a suspended object with the other foot. First recorded in the 1980s, the game is obviously much older.

Alaskan husky

■ n Also called **Eskimo dog, husky, mush dog, sled dog.** Any of the northern type crossbreed of dogs with a double coat, curly tail, and erect ears. Often used for pulling sleds on snow. First recorded in the 1970s. See also **Alaskan malamute, malamute.**

Alaskan jay

■ n (From 1880s) See **Alaska jay.**

Alaskan mackerel

■ n Also **Alaska mackeral.** This food fish is not a mackerel at all, but *Plerurogrammus monopterygius,* a greenish fish with dark blue bands over the back which tastes somewhat like mackerel. (From 1880s) The fish is known by a variety of names:

Atka fish, Atka mackerel, Attu mackerel, kelp fish, striped fish, yellow fish.

Alaskan malamute

■ n Also called **malamute.** A breed of working dog recognized by the American Kennel Club in 1935. The powerful deep-chested dog has a thick under-coat, with black, gray and white markings, white face with dark mask. The ears are short and erect, and the tail bushy and curled. See **Alaskan husky** for further information.

Alaskan turkey

■ n A jocular name for the sandhill crane, *Grus canadensis,* a large, slow-moving bird, reported to be edible. The term dates from 1940s, though few reports exist raving about the taste of the bird, giving rise to the speculation that it was caught not because it was so delectable but because it was so slow. A starving **sourdough** could stagger after it and dispatch it to the cooking pot.

Alaska pine

■ n In northwestern North America, a hemlock, *Tsuga heterophylla.* (From 1890s)

Alaska pollock

■ n Also called **pollock.** Sometimes spelled *pollack.* A codfish, about thirty inches long, inhabiting northern Pacific waters. The *Theragra chalcogramma* resembles other members of tomcod, the general cod found in the Atlantic, but is a different species. (From 1910s)

Alaska robin

■ n Also called **Oregon robin.** The varied thrush *Ixoreus naevius.* The bird ranges from the Columbia River Basin to Alaska. (From 1910s)

Alaska tea

■ n The low-growing evergreen *Ledum* used as a hot beverage in the North and Northwest. The plant goes by a number of local names, including **Greenland tea, Hudson Bay tea, Indian tea, Labrador tea, muskeg tea, swamp tea, Yukon tea.** (From 1930s)

alaskite

■ n Also spelled *alaskaite*. A medium- to fine-grained granite composed mainly of quartz and alkali feldspars, light in color. The rock was found in 1880s, but nowhere near Alaska. It was named after the Alaska Mine in Colorado, where it was first found.

alberca

■ n A water hole or watering place. Used mainly in west Texas. Cowboys adopted the term in the 1890s from the Spanish-speaking Mexicans, who first had it from the Arabic meaning of 'pond, pool'.

Alberta

■ n Canadian province. Settled in 1778, was made a district in 1882, and entered the confederation in 1905. Capital: Edmonton. Named for Princess Louise Caroline Alberta, daughter of Prince Albert and Queen Victoria. Her husband, the Marquess of Lorne, governor general of Canada from 1878 to 1883, gave the district its name.

albondigas

■ n Also called **albondigas soup.** A common vegetable soup with meatballs and chopped carrots, celery, potatoes, beans, cilantro. The term dates from the 1940s and is from Spanish *albondiga* 'meatball'.

alcalde

■ /al CAL dee/ n Also spelled *alcade, alcaide*. An old-fashioned term for a local official, now a reference to a somewhat important or self-important local person. In the 1860s in this sense, it was Spanish for "governor of a fort or castle."

Alcan

■ n Also **Alcan highway.** Informal term for the Alaskan Highway, specifically that segment from Dawson Creek, British Columbia, to Delta Junction, Alaska, built by the U.S. military during World War II. From the 1940s the blend of *Al*aska + *Can*ada has been used.

alegria

■ n A plant, often called **pigweed,** of the genus *Amaranthus paniculatus.* The leaves of the plant were chewed or crushed, yielding a red or crimson juice that was used as a cosmetic in the nineteenth-century Southwest. In the 1840s, many a **señorita** colored her lips for her **caballero.** I can think of no obvious connection between pigweed and señoritas.

Aleut

■ /AL yoot, AL ee oot/ n A member of the indigenous people of the Aleutian Islands, the western Alaska Peninsula, Kodiak Island, and Prince William Sound. The population was strongly influenced by Russian colonialism, adopting the Orthodox religion, foods, dress, and even Russian surnames. The term is from Chukchi *aliat* 'island' via Russian, and dates from the 1780s.

alforja

■ /ahl FOR juh, ahl FOR yuh/ n Also spelled *alfarga, alfarge, alfarky, alforche, alforga, alforge, alforka, alforki, alforkus, allforche.* A saddlebag; a widemouthed bag made of leather or canvas, suspended from a saddle or a mule pack. The term is somewhat old-fashioned; "saddlebag" is the more common term for any such container, whether designed for use on horse saddles or motorcycles. (From 1840s, Spanish)

aliso

■ n The common sycamore or plane tree *Platanus racemosa.* Also used for the common alder. (From 1860s, Spanish *aliso* 'alder tree')

alkali

■ n 1. A soluble salt found in soil or the ashes of some plants of negligible agricultural use. Frequently seen as a fine, very light-colored dust in western desert areas. 2. Since 1900: a person who has lived extensively in the West, especially as a prospector, cowboy, or desert dweller (see also **sourdough**). Many an old **waddy** is called Alkali Ed, Alkali Pete, or some such. 3. As the first element in a number of combinations relating to plant, water, and soil conditions in western areas: *alkali buttercup, ~ cordgrass, ~ desert, ~ dust, ~ flat, ~ lake, ~ spring, ~ sacaton, ~ sink, ~ spot, ~*

hardpan, ~ water, ~ weed. See also **salt grass** under **salt.**

alkalied

■ adj Affected by alkali, usually by living in an area saturated with alkaline soils and plants or having drunk its water. (From 1850s)

all-ee all-ee oxen free

■ excl A call used in the game of hide-and-seek to call players back to base at the conclusion of the game. Many variants of the call are used around North America, but this call is common to the West, sometimes with the variant **all-ee all-ee outs in free.** The term dates from the 1940s, but is found earlier in oral tradition.

alligator pear

■ n See **avocado.**

alpine

■ n The first element in the names of some plants and trees found in the Rocky Mountains: *alpine columbine, ~ fir, ~ forget-me-not, ~ hemlock.* (From 1920s) The term comes from association with an altitude and environment similar to the Swiss Alps.

amargosa

■ n Also spelled *amargoso.* Also *almergoso bark, amargoso bush.* A shrub found along the Rio Grande, whose bark is intensely bitter and often used as an astringent and tonic; the bark of the goatbush *Castela erecta.* Around Death Valley, the term is found frequently as a place-name, river name, valley name, even as an opera-house name. The term is Spanish and dates from 1870s.

amigo

■ n A friend. Less often, a female friend might be an **amiga.** The term came into English in the 1830s from Spanish.

amole

■ /uh MO lee/ n Any of a variety of plants used as a source of soap. The plants include a type of yucca, two types of agave (lechuguilla and *Agave schottii*), and roots from plants called **soapweed** and **soap plant.** The Nahuatl Indians donated a number of words to English, including this one, which arrived by way of Spanish in the 1830s.

anaqua

■ n Also spelled *anacua, anagua,* and spellings influenced by pronunciation: *knackaway, knock-*

away, nockaway. Also called **sugarberry.** A half-evergreen tree (*Ehretia anacua*) found along the Texas-Mexico border. The multiple-trunk tree bears a yellow-orange fruit said to be edible. (From 1880s, Nahuatl via Spanish)

andale

■ /UN duh lay, AHN duh lay/ excl Hurry; get going; rush; leave now, quickly. From 1930s Spanish, this term has been used by harried parents and partners for all manner of slugabeds. Often repeated several times for best effect.

angakok

■ n Also spelled *angekok, angatkuq;* the native spelling is becoming preferred: *angalkuk, angalkuq.* The Alaskan Eskimo shaman or medicine man. The term dates from the 1890s in English, was originally from Yupik and Inupiaq.

Angel City

■ n The full name of Los Angeles is *Reina de los Angeles,* "Queen of the Angels." From the 1970s, drivers of the big rigs, the eighteen-wheelers, have called to one another on their CB radios and used "Angel City" as a handle for the region from Anaheim through Long Beach to Santa Monica.

Angeleno

■ n Since the 1880s, a resident of Los Angeles. (From a combination: Los *Angeles* + *eno*)

angel's trumpet

■ n Any of several species of *Datura.* Related to jimsonweed (named after Jamestown, Virginia). This western variety is so called because of the shape of the white flowers. The plant is highly toxic, and some have suggested the name comes from the fact that anyone who eats from the plant may soon be hearing the trumpets of the angels. In the 1880s, the term applied to *Datura suaveolens;* in the 1950s, the term was extended to *Datura arborea;* in the 1970s, the term was further extended to *Datura stramonium.* Eating any of them can result in hallucinations and death, as several flower children learned during the late 1960s.

angle

■ v In surfing, to ride across the face of a wave rather than down the front of it toward the beach. (From 1940s)

Anglo

■ n A person who is not of Spanish or Indian descent; an **Anglo-American.** (From 1940s)

Anglo-American

■ n Originally, a white, English-speaking American who was not of Spanish or Indian descent. Now generalized to any English-speaking white person with European ancestry. (From 1830s)

angoras

■ n **Chaps** (q.v. for complete listing) made from angora goat hide with the hair worn on the outside. Very distinctive and flashy apparel affected by certain cowboys, though likely to cause curious looks when rained on or gotten wet—the smell becomes a bit gamy. (From 1940s) See also **chivarras, hair pants.**

angry acacia

■ n Also called **cat's claw.** A woody acacia that grows from ten to twenty feet high and carries sharp thorns. When disturbed, the leaves curl and give off an offensive odor. The range is Arizona, Nevada, and California. (From 1890s)

angyaq

■ /ANG yak/ n See **umiaq.**

anquera

■ /ANG kerra/ n The broad apronlike piece of leather sewn onto the back part, or cantle, of a western saddle. Sometimes highly decorated on show saddles and extending over the horse's rump. (From 1880s, Spanish)

antelope

■ n 1. The western pronghorn or prongbuck *Antilocapra americana,* first described in the papers of the 1803 Lewis and Clark expedition. The animal is so different from the European animal of the same name that a separate scientific family name was created for it, of which it is the only member. 2. In combinations of plant and animal names: (a) as the first element in *antelope brush, ~ chipmunk, ~ goat, ~ ground squirrel, ~ jack rabbit;* (b) as the last element in *American ~, buck ~, forked-horned ~, goat ~* (see **goat**), *Missouri ~, mountain ~, pronghorn(ed) ~* (see **berrendo**). 3. In miscellaneous combinations: *antelope dance,* a Hopi Indian ceremonial dance (from 1940s); *antelope range,* an area frequented by antelope herds (from 1840s); *antelope refuge,* a government-controlled range set aside for the protection of antelope herds (from 1940s); *antelope surround,* an ambush set in a **box canyon** or camouflaged corral for killing antelope driven into it (from 1840s).

antlerless moose

■ n A moose without antlers. Since the cows never have antlers and the bulls drop their antlers around November, a hunting season for antlerless moose after November is a hunt for moose of either sex. A hunting season for antlerless moose declared before November is specifically a hunt for female moose. (From 1960s)

Apache

■ n Any of a number of Indian tribes from the southerly group of the Athapaskan language family. Originally a name applied by the Zuni to the Navajo (from 1740s, Zuni 'enemy' via Spanish). Apache dancers, famed for their violent dances performed in Paris nightclubs in the early 1900s, took the name from the European perception of the Southwestern Apaches as "wild Indians."

Apache plume

■ n A shrub, *Fallucia paradoxa,* with white, rose-like flowers and reddish, feathery-tailed seed clusters that have a fancied resemblance to the feathered warbonnets of the Plains Indians. (From 1880s)

Apache state

■ n A nickname for **Arizona** (from 1890s). Also **Baby State** (from 1930s).

aparejo

■ /ap uh RAY ho/ n Also spelled *arapaho* (q.v.). A type of packsaddle, usually for a mule, made of leather or canvas, large enough to transport a child on each side. (From 1840s, Spanish)

aparejo grass

■ n A type of grass, either *Sporobolus depauperatus* or *Muhlenbergia utilis,* used to stuff the pads of **aparejos,** or packsaddles. (From 1890s)

apex

■ n In mining, the part of a vein closest to the surface. (From 1880s). As a verb from 1910, the term refers to a vein peaking near the surface.

appaloosa

■ /ap puh LOO suh, ap puh LOO see, ap puh LOOS/ n A breed of horse, generally white with dark spots over the rump or on other parts of the body and legs, with a sparse mane and tail. The origin of the name may be a conflation of two sources. Early reference to such a horse is from *Opelousa,* a Louisiana Indian tribal name, which in turn may be related to Choctaw *apolusa* 'mottled'. But in later years, such a horse was often associated with the Nez Perce tribe of the Palouse River country of western Idaho and eastern Washington. (From 1850s)

apple

■ n A nickname for the saddle horn on a western saddle. Also called **biscuit.** (From 1930s, a loan translation from Spanish *manzana* 'apple', used to refer to the saddle horn)

apple bird

■ n In the West, a type of woodpecker, *Asyndesmus lewisi.* (From 1910s) Not to be confused with two types of eastern birds often called by the same name, the cedar waxwing or hermit thrush.

arapaho

■ /uh RAP uh ho/ n A metathesized spelling of **aparejo** (q.v.), a type of pack saddle, probably from confused identification with the Arapaho Indian tribe. (From 1850s)

Arbuckle

■ n A greenhorn on a ranch; a **tenderfoot.** Somewhat old-fashioned. Arbuckle's was a mail-order company that supplied many western ranches, especially with its self-named brand of coffee and staples, from around 1900. The inference was that the foreman had gotten the tenderfoot from a mail-order catalog. (From 1930s) See also **cheechako.**

arch

■ n In logging, a derrick made of metal rods or the fork of a tree mounted on a tractor or on wheels, used for lifting the front end of a log clear of the ground to facilitate skidding it. (From 1940s) See also **high lead.**

arctic

■ n Usually plural. A rubber boot extending above the ankle and having buckles. Used mainly in the Rocky Mountains from the 1860s onward. When settlers finally began moving northward to Alaska and points closer to the Arctic Circle, a whole different type of footwear had to be developed.

Arctic haze

■ n In Alaska, a form of particulate pollution carried by winds from central Russia and eastern Europe. First called to the public's attention in the 1950s, the phenomenon occurs especially in late winter and early spring.

Arctic Slope ■ n Also called **North Slope, Slope.** The northern slope of the Brooks Range in Alaska, including the coastal plain to the Arctic Ocean. Though the term dates from the 1930s, the frequency of usage more recently is due to the development of oil reserves at Prudhoe Bay.

Arctic trout ■ n A general term for any trout or grayling found in the Arctic, but especially the **Dolly Varden,** less frequently, the **coho.** (From 1930s) See **salmon** n for a complete listing.

Area Fifty-One ■ n The worst-kept secret of the Nevada Test Site/Nellis Air Force Range/Tonopah Test Range in Nye County, Nevada. This is the area at which the secret weapons of the U.S. military are developed and tested. It was the site of the final testing stages of the Stealth bomber and Stealth fighter. Persistent rumors claim that even extraterrestrial beings have been housed at the site or that at least alien corpses have been processed there. The area is a favorite temptation for trespassers who want to snoop around a site that does not officially exist. (From 1970s)

Arizona ■ n Forty-eighth state of the Union. Settled in 1848, it became a territory in 1863 and a state in 1912. Capital: Phoenix. The name probably comes from the Pima or Papago *arizonac* or *aleh-zon* 'little spring', 'valley of the maiden', 'place of chastisement'. The name could also be derived from Spanish *arid*a 'dry' + *zona* 'country, area'. The early Spaniards may have changed the Indian name to fit their own pronunciation. Also called the **Baby State** because of its recent arrival in the Union (from 1930s). Also called **Apache State** (from 1890s).

Arizona ■ n Used as the first element in compounds identifying regional varieties of birds and plants found in other regions with slightly different variations: *Arizona arbutus, ~ bobwhite, ~ buckthorn, ~ cardinal, ~ cork fir, ~ crested flycatcher, ~ cypress, ~ gnatcatcher, ~ gourd, ~ hooded oriole, ~ jay, ~ junco, ~ longleaf pine, ~ pine, ~ screech owl, ~ song sparrow, ~ white pine, ~ woodpecker, ~ yellow pine.*

Arizona cloudburst

■ n A jocular reference to a sandstorm. (From 1960s)

Arizona nightingale

■ n A jocular reference to a mule, donkey, or **burro** (q.v. for a list of other names). The harsh bray of the animal invites such a comparison to a songbird. (From 1940s)

Arizona paint job

■ n A jocular reference to an unpainted, weathered, building; no paint at all. (From 1960s)

Arizona peacock

■ n Also called **California peacock.** A jocular reference to the **roadrunner.** (From 1950s)

Arizona ruby

■ n Also called **Navajo ruby.** A garnet stone found in igneous rock in the Southwest. (From 1890s)

Arizona tenor

■ n A jocular reference to a coughing tubercular. (From 1940s) Individuals with tuberculosis were often sent to dry desert environments as part of their treatment.

Arkansas wedding cake

■ n Among old-time loggers, a jocular term for corn bread. (From 1950s)

armadillo

■ n A burrowing mammal of the Southwest. This nocturnal animal stands about ten inches high and is about eighteen inches long with a twelve-inch tail. The banded, bony plates it uses for protection give the animal its name. Upscale Mexican restaurants in the Southwest sell "armadillo eggs," which are jalapeno peppers filled with cheese and deep-fried in a batter. (From 1570s, Spanish *armad* 'armed' + *illo* diminutive suffix)

armas

■ n pl Leather flaps attached to a saddle, designed to be pulled across the rider's legs when going through prickly brush on horseback. (From 1930s, Spanish *arma* 'weapon')

armitas ■ n pl A split, leather apron fastened around the waist of a cowboy. Leather thongs allow the two halves of the apron to be tied around the legs. The cowboy's legs are thus protected while going through brush on foot or on horseback. (From 1940s, Spanish *arma* 'weapon' + *ita* diminutive suffix)

armored tit ■ n Among old-time loggers, a jocular term for canned milk. (From 1950s)

arriero ■ n A muleteer; a person who owns or manages pack mules. Now used mainly for mule packers escorting people on canyon tours. (From 1820s, Spanish)

arroba ■ n A measure of twenty-five pounds. Used in relation to bulk items like flour, beans, rice, or potatoes. (From 1820s, Spanish)

arrow bush ■ n Also spelled *arrowbrush, arrowbush. Pluchea sericea,* a variety of shrub with relatively straight branches that can be used for making arrows. (*DA* and *DARE* differ in spelling the term. The *DA* form is used here since it is the older source.) See also **cachimilla.**

arroyo ■ n A water-carved channel with steep sides, with or without continuously running water. The sides are often five to fifty feet high and subject to flash floods after relatively little rainfall. (From 1880, Spanish) In more recently settled regions of the Southwest, the same feature of topography is called a **wash.** See also **gulch.**

arroyo grape ■ n The riverside grape *Vitis vulpina.* (From 1880s)

arroz con pollo ■ n Chicken cooked with rice, seasoned with garlic, saffron, pimentos, and salsa. English usage from the 1930s. Designed for a sit-down meal as opposed to quick snacks like **tacos** or **burritos.**

artillery ■ n 1. A jocular reference to personal weapons, especially handguns or pistols (from 1900). 2. A jocular reference to beans, especially among loggers, construction workers, railroaders, and ranchers (because of the flatulence beans create); also called **light artillery** (from 1930s).

aspen

■ n Also **aspen poplar.** Also called **quaking aspen** (q.v. for further information), **trembling aspen, quakenas.** A high-timber poplar found in the mountainous areas of the West. (From 1810s)

assessment work

■ n The amount of work required annually to maintain title to a mining claim. (From 1870s)

asshole

■ n In logging, a kink in a line or cable. (From 1950s)

atajo

■ /AT uh ho/ n Also spelled *hatajo*. A string or train of pack animals, mules or horses. Sometimes a group of horses, usually being herded or moved in a controlled fashion. (From 1840s, Spanish *hatajo* 'small herd, flock')

atigi

■ n Also spelled *artegi, artigi, attiga, attigi*. A hooded pullover garment common in Alaska and known elsewhere by the more common name, **parka.** (From 1870s)

Atka fish

■ n See **Alaskan mackerel.** (From 1900)

Atka mackerel

■ n See **Alaskan mackerel.** (From 1880s)

atlatl

■ /AT latl/ n A throwing stick, usually sixteen to thirty inches long, used to hurl a lance, spear, or harpoon. Used by a variety of Indians from central Mexico to northern Alaska. (From 1900, Nahuatl)

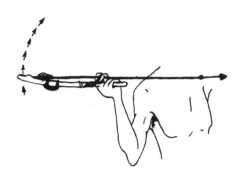

atole

■ n A thin gruel, mush, or porridge made of barley, corn, or maize. (From 1670s, Nahuatl via Spanish)

attle

■ n In mining, tailings or waste rock from the mine. (From 1940s, Cornish)

Attu mackerel

■ n See **Alaskan mackerel.** (From 1930s)

auger

■ n A conversation; a talk; an argument; a talker, especially an excessive one.

augur

■ v To converse, to argue, to talk in an animated fashion. Hence, **auguring.** (From 1910)

augurino

■ n A jocular reference to an imaginary creature that bores holes in irrigation ditches, allowing water to escape. (From 1940s)

avalanche lily

■ n A name for the dogtooth violet, especially in the Cascade Range. Its white flower appears early in alpine meadows near the edge of snow packs. (From 1910s)

avenging angel

■ n Old-fashioned. A name applied to an alleged enforcer or vigilante of the Mormon church, whose responsibility was to keep order according to civil law and church rules. The term carries connotations of secrecy and violence. (From 1900) See also **Danite, Destroying Angel.**

avocado

■ n The fruit of any of a variety of tropical trees of the genus *Persea*. The outer skin ranges from dark green to light green, smooth to leathery rough, the flesh is light green. Sometimes called **alligator pear.** (From 1830s, Nahuatl *ahuacatl* 'testicle' via Spanish *aguacate* 'avocado')

azote

■ /uh ZO tee/ n A switch or a whip; any long slender flexible tree branch that can be used as a whip. (From 1890s, Spanish)

azotea

■ /az oh TEE uh/ n A flat roof used as a porch or **patio** for taking the evening air, especially on a house built in the Mexican-Spanish style. (From 1840s)

B

baa-baa

■ 1. adj Descriptive of sheep or, more likely, of sheep's wool. In the 1920s, fashion conscious westerners were wearing baa-baa coats, leather jackets lined with sheep's wool. 2. n In the 1930s, the term became a noun and referred to a sheep, usually derisively. 3. excl Finally, in the 1940s, the term became an insult, whether shouted at a sheepherder or a cowboy.

babiche

■ /BAB eesh/ n Rawhide thong or threading material, especially a softer, lighter type made of caribou rather than steer hide. It was used in northern British Columbia and Alaska for fine work, such as lacing, snowshoe netting, tight joints on small boxes, bowstrings. (From 1880s, Algonquian *apapish* 'cord, thread' via Canadian French)

baby blue-eye

■ n (Plural in form, singular or plural in use.) A small, pale blue five-petal flower, *Nemophila menziesii;* sometimes called **bluebell** or **California bluebell.** (From 1880s)

Baby State

■ n A nickname for the state of **Arizona,** so called because it entered the Union after surrounding states (from 1930s). Also **Apache State** (from 1890s).

back corner

■ n Among loggers in the Pacific Northwest, the remote area of a logging operation. (From 1950s)

back East

■ adv The eastern part of the United States or Canada, not necessarily the East Coast. For most westerners, the term designates any part of the area from the Midwest (e.g., Nebraska, Kansas) eastward. For western Canadians, the term refers to any area east of Manitoba. More recently, westerners consider the area from eastern Texas eastward as "down South." (From 1870s)

badger fight

■ n Also called **pulling the badger.** A practical joke in the Southwest in which an inexperienced person is told there will be a fight between a dog and a badger. When the newcomer is taken to the site of the badger fight, a dog is present and a wash-tub is upside down on the ground with a long rope leading from under the tub. The newcomer is told to pull the rope toward the dog when another person lifts the tub. Attached to the rope, under the tub, is a chamber pot (in recent years, a bedpan). Similar to other practical jokes, such as a "snipe hunt." The term "badger" has been used throughout the United States since the turn of the century in reference to confidence games and scams. (From 1920s)

bad man

■ n In the "Old West," a desperado, outlaw, or senseless killer. Around the turn of the century, tall tales written in dime novels colored the image of the desperado and turned him into the romantic character of later movies. (From 1850s)

bad medicine

■ n A thing, event, or person that is clearly undesirable, traceable to the notion that, among Indians, "medicine" may be good or bad, but is usually inexplicable, though identifiable. (From 1810s)

bad water

■ n Water that has been contaminated by soluble salts; alkali water. The phenomenon is so common that the term is used in several place-names in the Southwest. (From 1850s)

baile

■ /BY lay/ n 1. An indoor social dance or ball in the Southwest, especially a dance at which traditional Mexican dancing is featured (from 1840s). 2. By transference, the hall at which a baile or any dancing takes place (from 1880s).

baile chango

■ /BY lay CHON go/ n Originally any dancing motion that was considered strange or odd. By transference, it came to mean beating on someone, as "Paco did a real baile chango on that guy's head. He beat him pretty bad." (From 1930s, Spanish, literally, 'monkey dance')

bairdi

■ n Also called **bairdi crab, opilio, queen crab, snow crab, spider crab, Tanner crab.** One of two crabs found in Alaskan waters that is included under the catchall of **Tanner crab.** *Chionocoetes bairdi* was commonly called **bairdi Tanner crab,** but that was soon shortened to bairdi crab, then simply to bairdi. The crab became commercially valuable as an alternate to the **Alaska king crab.** The bairdi crab was named after the first U.S. Commissioner of Fish and Fisheries, naturalist Spencer F. Baird (1823–1887), who also served as Secretary of the Smithsonian Institution. (From 1970s)

Baja bug

■ n A Volkswagen Beetle, or "bug," modified for driving on sandy beaches and carrying surfboards (from 1960s). Baja is the peninsula that stretches southward in Mexico, south of San Diego. The miles and miles of beaches constitute a playground of endless summer for surfers who spend more time catching waves than catching jobs.

bajada

■ /buh HOD duh/ n In the Southwest, a slope, especially an alluvial fan; a downgrade in the road or trail, often steep. (From 1860s, Spanish)

bake

■ v To ride a horse in such a manner as to overheat the animal. (From 1940s)

bakehead

■ n A fireman on a railroad engine. From the days when the fireman fed coal to the firebox in a steam locomotive. (From 1950s)

baldface

■ v In logging, to push a train of logs with the locomotive. The oncoming train car displays the white front of the ends of the freshly cut logs. (From 1950s)

bald-faced shirt

■ n Old-fashioned. A man's white dress shirt, often starched; in other places, a "boiled shirt." The term perhaps is derived from the white face of Hereford cattle; another possibility, however, is the potential pronunciation confusion with "boiled" (when pronounced /BALD/) and "bald-faced," a slang adjective meaning "without adornment, plain white." (From 1880s)

baldhead

■ n The rounded top, usually bare, of a mesa, plateau, or mountain. Common enough in the Southwest to figure in place-names, such as Mount Baldy. (From 1920s)

balloon

■ 1. Originally among tramps, then among loggers, a bedroll; a loose pack of blankets rolled and tied (from 1930s). 2. Also called **balloon Y,** a round-shaped railroad track used for turning the engines around (from 1950s).

banana belt

■ n A reference to any of a number of southerly regions where the climate is more temperate than where the speaker resides; in Alaska, the term refers to southern Alaska or the Aleutians; in Washington State, the term refers to the Palouse country of southeastern Washington; in Utah, the term refers to the St. George area of southern Utah; among loggers of the Pacific Northwest, the term refers to a mild winter, one with less snow than usual. (From 1890s)

banana yucca

■ n Also called **Mexican banana, datil.** A southwestern plant that produces edible fruit that has a bananalike appearance. The *Yucca baccata* fruit is eaten raw, roasted, or dried. The plant is found at elevations between three and eight thousand feet. (From 1930s) See also **Spanish bayonet.**

banco

■ n A section of land, sometimes a hundred acres or more, created on one side of the river when it suddenly cuts a new channel. The Rio Grande and the Colorado rivers are especially noted for creating such cuts of land, thereby changing the boundaries of states or countries in those cases where the riverbed determines a political division. (From 1880s, Spanish)

band

■ n A herd or drove of animals; a group of people, especially as an Indian band or band of Indians. Although the term has been in English since the fifteenth century, it came to be used extensively in the West in the 1820s in reference to groups of buffalo, cattle, sheep, horses, renegades, bandits, Indians, and Mormons. The kind of band that contains musicians is not a western term—not even a country-western band.

band

■ v To gather together into a flock or herd of sheep or cattle. (From 1870s)

bandito

■ n Used in the Southwest since the 1890s to refer

= 24 =

to a robber, outlaw, or bandit, especially a Mexican one. The term apparently had a negative connotation that caused the Frito-Lay people to drop their successful marketing campaign that featured the "Frito bandito." Feelings were hurt, and some people claimed the advertising hurt the image of people of Mexican heritage.

banya

■ n In Alaska, a structure housing a steam bath and dressing room. First introduced during Russian occupation, the structure and custom is widely known on Kodiak Island. (From 1890s, Russian)

bar

■ n 1. A horizontal line in a cattle brand, or the name of a ranch. For example, the Bar Cross ranch (in Nevada) uses a branding iron that looks like this: -+ (from 1890s). 2. A deposit of gold ore, usually near the surface. Now used mainly among prospectors (from 1850s).

barabara

■ /buh RAH buh rah/ n Old-fashioned. Also spelled *barabarra, barabba, barrabara, barrabkie.* Sometimes called **barabki.** In Alaska, a simple hut built partially or nearly completely underground. Used especially in the Aleutian Islands. (From 1860s, Russian *barabora* 'hut, hovel')

barberry

■ n Also called **agarita, agrillo, agrito, algeredo, chaparral berry, currant, hollygrape, mountain grape, Oregon grape, palo amarillo, wineberry.** A catch-all for plants found throughout the West and Southwest whose berries are used for jams, jellies, wines. This particular name has been in English since the fifteenth century, refers to the genus *Berberis,* and acquired its form through folk etymology with "berry."

barboquejo

■ /bar buh KAY ho/ n The chin strap or string on a cowboy's hat, especially the **sombrero** or a similar type with high, curved edges. (From 1940s, Spanish, probably oral much earlier)

barbudi

■ n Also spelled *barbood, barbooth, barboot, barbuti.* A dice game in which either shooter or player have an even chance to win. Played especially in areas with high concentrations of Greek or Jewish immigrants. The game is variously described as being Basque, Greek, or Jewish in background. (From 1950s, Turkish *barbut* via Canadian French *barbote*)

bar ditch

■ n Also called **bar pit, barrow pit** (q.v. for further information). The drainage ditch dug alongside a graded or paved road. Used mainly in Texas and New Mexico. The first element is perhaps a clipped form from "barrow," a mound of earth or dirt. (From 1940s)

barefoot

■ adj Descriptive of going without: a shot of alcohol without ice or mixer; coffee without cream or sugar; driving in snow without chains; surfing in cold water without a wetsuit; setting out on a day trip in the desert without water; driving a car without having insurance; starting up a business without much capital (especially in Silicon Valley); buying a house without a down payment, but with a balloon payment due in a few years. (From 1960s)

bark

■ n Among loggers, the outside of various foods: "spuds with the bark on" are potatoes with the skins on; "pie with the bark on" has a crust on top. (From 1920s)

bark a ride

■ v phr Among loggers, to skin the bark from one side of a log to make it slide more easily along a **skid road.** (From 1950s)

barkie

■ n In logging areas, small poles sold with the bark still attached. (From 1950s)

barn door

■ n An Alaskan sportfisherman's term for a very large halibut, usually ninety pounds or more. (From 1980s)

bar pit

■ n Also called **bar ditch, barrow pit** (q.v. for further information). The ditch along the side of a road. Used mainly in the Rocky Mountain region. The first element is perhaps a clipped form of "barrow," a mound of earth or dirt. (From 1940s)

barranca

■ /buh RAHN kah/ n A steep ravine or a deep gully; a large **arroyo.** Usually dry until it rains.

(From 1830s, Spanish) According to the Kingston Trio, "the lion still rules the barranca, and a man there is always alone."

barrel

■ n Also called **pipe, tube.** In surfing, the smooth inner portion of a breaking wave, especially one high enough to allow a surfer to ride at an angle inside the leading edge of the breaker. (From 1980s)

barrel cactus

■ n Any of a wide variety of Southwest succulents with spines and a squat, round appearance. Usually of the genera *Echinocactus* or *Ferocactus*. (From 1880s) For different types and names, see **beavertail cactus, beehive cactus, bisnaga, compass cactus, cottontop cactus, devil's head, devil's pincushion, eagle claws, Echinocactus, fishhawk cactus, fishhook cactus, globe cactus, hedge cactus, horse crippler, Indian melon, Mexican fireball, pincushion cactus, pineapple cactus, strawberry cactus, traveler's friend, turban cactus, turk's head.**

barrel stove

■ n Also called **Yukon stove.** In Alaska, a fifty-five-gallon steel drum placed horizontally on four cast-iron legs, with a door installed at one end and a stovepipe fitted at the other. Usually the upper part was removed and a sheet-metal top welded on to provide a flat cooking surface. (From 1970s)

barrio

■ n A Spanish-speaking community or neighborhood in a city in the United States, especially in the Southwest; a Latino or Chicano district. (From 1930s, Spanish)

barrow pit

■ n Also called **bar ditch, bar pit.** A drainage ditch built along a roadside. Used mainly in the Rocky Mountain region and the Pacific states. Occasionally a folk etymology appears, **borrow pit, borrow ditch,** from the mistaken notion that dirt is "borrowed" from one place and put in another. The term "barrow ditch" is not exclusively linked to the West, but is found in other parts of the country also. The term is perhaps from "barrow," an Old English word referring to an elongated mound of dirt. (From 1930s)

Basco

■ /BASS koh/ n Used as a nickname or term of affection for a person of Basque ancestry. There are many such people in northern Nevada, southern Idaho, and northwestern California. (From 1930s)

Basin State

■ n Also **Great Basin State.** A nickname for the state of **Utah,** which lies almost entirely within the **Great Basin.** (From 1850s) See also **Beehive State, Deseret.**

basket

■ n The part of a **dogsled** used in the Yukon and Alaska that is designed to carry the load. (From 1930s) See also **basket sled.**

Basket Maker

■ n The name of early inhabitants of the Southwest, prior to the use of pottery in the region. The name also designates the time period that these people flourished, from about A.D. 100 to 700. (From 1900)

basket sled

■ n The common **dogsled** of the North. It has a light frame made of hardwoods, with open latticework on the sides and back of the **basket,** held together with thongs or sinew. It is designed to traverse quickly and easily and is the most popular design for racing models. (From 1900)

bastos
■ n The leather lining or the skirt of a western saddle. (From 1880s, Spanish, *basto*)

batea
■ /buh TAY uh/ n A large, shallow **pan** used to wash dirt and gravel scooped up from streambeds in searching for gold. (From 1840s, Spanish *batella*) See also **washbowl**.

Battle-Born State
■ n A nickname for **Nevada**. Also **Sagebrush State, Sage Hen State, Silver Land, Silver State.**

bat wings
■ n pl Also called **batwing chaps**. Wide-legged **chaps** (q.v. for a complete listing) that fasten around a cowboy's legs by snaps. A flaring wing on the side gives them the batwing appearance. (From 1930s) Compare **Cheyenne cut.**

bayeta
■ n A hard-finish, wool-fiber yarn used especially by Navajos to weave blankets highly valued by traders and buyers in the Southwest. Such blankets

basket, basket sled

are sometimes called **bayeta blankets.** (From 1850s, Spanish *bayeta* 'baize')

bayo
■ n 1. A small reddish or bay-colored bean, especially used in northern California as a baking bean (from 1850s, Spanish). 2. Also **bayo coyote.** A bay or dun horse, usually with a dark stripe running down along the backbone (from 1850s, Spanish).

beach lovage
■ n See **wild parsley.**

beach-party film
■ n Any of a variety of movies celebrating teenage romance, surfing, and carefree Southern California living. (From 1960s) The first such movie was *Beach Party* in 1963, and featured former Mouseketeer Annette Funicello and Frankie Avalon.

beaner
■ n Also called **beano, bean eater.** A person of Mexican origin or ancestry. A derogatory term. From the fact that beans form an important part of the diet. (From 1910s)

bearberry honeysuckle
■ n Also called **fly honeysuckle, inkberry, pigeonberry, skunkberry.** A shrub of the honeysuckle family, *Lonicera involucrata,* which produces paired black berries, said to be poisonous. The flowers are yellow. (From 1930s)

bear claw
■ n A large sweet pastry, about six to eight inches across, shaped like a bear's paw, with indentations around one side representing claws. The pastry features raisins and white sugar frosting, sometimes with cinnamon sprinkled on top. (From 1940s)

bear grass
■ n See **sacahuista.**

Bear Revolution
■ n Reference to a movement that flourished in 1846 in California, in which insurgents rebelled against Mexican authorities and proclaimed "The California Republic" (a designation still used semi-facetiously by habitués of Berkeley and the university there). The insurgents called themselves "bear men" and the flag they designed had a single star (influenced perhaps by the Texas flag) and a grizzly bear (then numerous in the territory and reputed to be the most ferocious of all bears). The bear re-

mains on the California state flag. See also **California battalion.**

bearweed

■ n See **yerba santa.**

Beaver State

■ n A nickname for the state of **Oregon.** Also **Hard-Case State, Webfoot State.**

beavertail cactus

■ n A common succulent found in the Southwest, *Opuntia basilaris.* The flattish pads of the cactus are up to one-half-inch thick and up to ten inches across. They have fine needles and produce masses of lavender-red blossoms. (From 1940s) See **barrel cactus** for list of succulents that share these features.

bed

■ n In logging, a soft spot on which large trees can fall without breaking. Especially used for cutting down redwoods. A bed is created by cutting smaller pine and fir trees and filling in low spots to be a cushion for the giant, which may be more than two to three hundred feet tall. (From 1930s)

bed

■ v In logging, to level a path in which a tree is to fall. Although the term did not originate in the Northwest, it became most frequently used there and in the redwood country, given the massiveness of the trees that grow there. (From 1790s, but western since 1900)

bedding ground

■ n An area for settling a herd of cattle or a flock of sheep for the night, especially when driving the animals from one feeding ground to another. (From 1870s)

bed wagon

■ n In ranching, a wagon on which all the bedrolls are loaded for men who will be out working cattle or sheep for several days. (From 1860s)

beehive cactus

■ n A squat, round succulent with sharp spines, here *Echinocactus johnsonii.* Common to the Southwest. (From 1940s) See **barrel cactus** for entire list of succulents that share these features.

Beehive State

■ n A nickname for **Utah,** whose state flag features a beehive, symbolizing the industrious nature of the citizens. Also **Basin State, Great Basin State.** (From 1930s) See also **Deseret.**

belly pad

■ n A jocular reference to a hotcake, pancake. (From 1950s)

bellyboard

■ n In surfing, a small surfboard used often in body surfing.

bellyboarding

■ n The act of body surfing while holding a small kickboard or planing board in front of the body.

bellyflower

■ n Desert bloom so small that the observer must lie down on the ground to see the pinhead-sized blossom. (From 1970s)

below

■ adv Also called **down below.** In Alaska, a reference to the lower contiguous forty-eight states, as in "He went *below* to Seattle, but remained *below* for less than a year." (From 1900)

below

■ postnoun modifier Also **below discovery.** In the Yukon and Alaska, designating a strike claim on a stream other than the first one. The first strike on a stream is the **discovery claim,** the next strike downstream is called "number one below," or "number one below discovery." (From 1900) Compare **above.**

beluga

■ n Also spelled *belukha.* The small white whale of the northern waters, about the size of a dolphin. *Delphinapterus leucas* has visible teeth, and is no relation to the large white sturgeon of the Black and Caspian seas that produces the inordinately expensive caviar. (From 1860s, Russian *belyi* 'white')

beneficiate

■ v To reduce ores in a mining operation, especially in preparation for smelting. (From 1870s, Spanish *beneficiar*) The term also gave rise to the noun form "beneficiation" in the 1880s.

benitoite

■ /buh NEE toh ite/ n A greenish blue crystal (titanosilicate) found in San Benito County, California. Valued as a gem mineral. (From 1910s)

bentonite

■ n A soft clay, absorptive and colloidal, containing mainly silica, alumina, and water. It was first discovered in Wyoming in a stratum named for nearby Fort Benton, Montana. It is used in oil filters and as a filler in paper and drugs. (From 1900)

Bering time

■ n The time zone that includes part of western Alaska and the Aleutian Islands; the eleventh zone west of Greenwich Mean Time. (From 1960s)

berm pile

■ n See **burn pile.**

berrendo

■ n Also called **antelope.** The pronghorn antelope of the American West. (From 1840s, Spanish)

bidar

■ n A large, skin-covered boat used in the Aleutian Islands. The boat can be up to thirty feet long, and is used to transport numbers of men or large amounts of cargo. (1880s, Russian *baidara*) See also **bidarka, umiaq.**

bidarka

■ n Also spelled *bidarki*. Also called **kayak.** A light, covered boat used in the Aleutian Islands and other parts of Alaska. The light wooden or bone frame is covered with seal skin or canvas with a hole in the top for the occupant, who is thus covered from the waist down. Sometimes two or even three holes in the top accommodate hunters or oarsmen. (From 1860s, Russian *baidar* + diminutive suffix *ka*) See also **umiaq.**

bidarki

■ n Also spelled *bidarka, bidarky.* Also called **gumboot.** A mollusk of the type chiton that is three to five inches long. It has a pod or "foot" on the bottom that allows it to cling to rocks and to move about. The *Katharina tunicata* somewhat resembles an overturned **bidarka,** which may account for the name. (From 1870s, Russian)

Big Bend

■ n 1. A region adjacent to the Columbia River in northern Oregon and southern Washington, created by a large bow in the river course (from 1850s). 2. A region adjacent to the Rio Grande in southwestern Texas, created by a large bow in the river course (from 1930s).

big-cone(d)

■ attributive Referring to any of several western trees noted for having very large cones, such as those of the Coulter pine, which grow to fourteen inches long and can weigh up to six pounds; *big-cone(d) fir, big-coned pine, big-cone spruce.*

Big Dan

■ n See **Danite.**

Bigfoot

■ n Also called **Sasquatch.** A large and hairy human- or bear-like creature reportedly seen living in the forests and mountains of northern California. The creature is said to stand nine feet tall and to leave a seventeen-inch-long footprint. (From 1950s)

big hole

■ n In railroading, an emergency stop, made when the brake valve allows a sudden, large volume of air to be applied to the air-brake mechanism. By extension among tramps and others familiar with railroading, it has come to mean any sudden cessation of activity. (From 1930s)

big hole

■ v To suddenly stop a train by applying full pressure on the air brakes; by extension, to suddenly cease any activity. (From 1930s)

big hook

■ n In railroading, the large crane mounted on a railway car used to hoist engines or derailed cars. (From 1930s)

bighorn sheep

■ n Also called **Rocky Mountain sheep.** The western wild sheep, *Ovis canadensis,* marked by large horns that grow nearly circular in shape and noted for the ability to move about quickly on very steep and rocky terrain. (From 1780s)

bight

■ n In logging, a slack portion or loop in a rope or cable. The area of a bight is extremely dangerous because a snap or sudden tension on the line caused by a rolling log has injured or killed loggers standing nearby. (From 1920s) "Don't let the bight take a bite out of you!"

big-leaf maple

■ n Also called **California maple, canyon maple, Oregon maple, white maple.** An indigenous maple, *Acer macrophyllum,* found mainly on the Pacific Coast and in the Sierra Nevada. (From 1900)

big tree

■ n The giant **sequoia** of the Sierra Nevada and northern California. (From 1850s) Even seeing a picture of twelve men linking hands to show the circumference of the giant tree does not prepare the tourist for meeting one face-to-face. See also **redwood.**

billiken

■ n A small, squat figurine of a human with a pointy head, big ears, slanting eyes, and wide grin. Such figurines have become associated with Eskimo carvers and are ubiquitous in souvenir shops in Alaska. In fact, the figurines originated in Kansas City in the early years of this century and enjoyed a brief popularity in the United States and Great Britain. But after a native carver was persuaded to make a copy of the figurine, the object quickly became associated with Eskimos, and instant traditions were invented, making the figurine a good-luck charm. (From 1910s)

Bing cherry

■ n A dark, fleshy, and large sweet cherry introduced by S. Lewelling in Oregon in 1875. The "Bing," as it is often called, is the favorite table cherry. Other cherries are more popular for canning and pie making.

biscuit

■ n 1. Cowboy slang for the saddle horn (from 1940s). Also **apple** (from 1930s). 2. In logging, the flat piece of wood from the undercut when a tree is felled by a power saw. The undercut determines the direction the tree will fall (from 1950s).

biscuit root

■ n See **camas.**

biscuit shooter

■ n The cook at a ranch who is also the camp cook when cowboys or sheepherders spend several nights on the range for branding, sheep dipping, and such. (From 1890s)

bisnaga

■ n Also spelled *bisagre, biznacha, visnada, visnaga.* One of several types of cactus having a cylindrical shape and spines like sharp toothpicks and growing to about five feet tall. Here, the reference is to *Echinocactus horizonthalonius, ~ wislizeni, ~ johnsonii, ~ polyancistrus, ~ acanthodes, Ferocactus wislizeni.* (From 1840s) See **barrel cactus** for a complete list of these plants.

bizzing

■ n Also called **skijogging, bumper-bumming.** The act of hanging on to the rear bumper of a moving vehicle on an icy or snow-slick street. Mainly used in central Utah. (From 1960s) See also **hookey bob.** Compare **skijor.**

blab

■ n A device for weaning a calf; a thin flat board, about six inches by four inches, that has a piece cut out of one of the long sides, shaped in such a fashion that the opening fits tightly over the membrane separating the nostrils of a calf, allowing it to graze but not to suckle. (From 1880s)

black

■ attributive A term used in the description of plants, fish, animals, or birds that are peculiar to the West, though other forms of the plants, fish, animals, or birds may be widespread. For example, the fish called "sea bass" is widespread, but the black sea bass is peculiar to the coastal waters of Alaska. There are specifically western plants: *blackberry, black brush, ~ chapparal, ~ sage, ~ seaweed, ~ willow;* western fish include *black bass, ~ cod, ~ sea bass;* western animals, birds, and reptiles include *black-billed magpie, ~ diamond snake, ~ duck, ~-footed ferret, ~ fox, ~-headed grosbeak, ~ racer, ~ snake, ~-tailed deer* (see **black-tailed deer**), *~ woodpecker.*

black ball flag

■ n A yellow flag with a circular black center that is flown on beaches in Southern California forbidding the use of surfboards.

blackie

■ n Also called **blue bear, cinnamon bear, Emmons bear, glacier bear.** A shortened form for the **black bear,** *Ursus americanus,* found along the coast of Alaska from Glacier Bay to Yakutat. (From 1950s)

black salmon

■ n Also **blackmouth salmon.** Another name for the **Chinook salmon,** so called because of the dark skin on the back and around the gills. See **salmon** n for a complete list of types and names.

bladderpod

■ n See **burro fat.**

blanket

■ n Now historical. A unit of value established by

the Hudson's Bay Company for trading with the Indians of the Pacific Northwest. The woolen blanket itself was a medium of exchange, and the company issued paper scrip called "blankets." (From 1870s to 1900)

blanket busted   ■ n Absolutely broke from gambling. (From 1940s) Army blankets were laid on the floor and used for dice gambling.

blanket stiff   ■ n Also called **blanket man.** An itinerant agricultural laborer who carries a bedroll from job to job. By the 1960s, the term referred to a hobo or tramp. (From 1870s)

blanket toss   ■ n Among the Indians of Alaska and the Yukon, a practice celebrated at festivals of tossing a person up and down repeatedly on a skin or blanket. The practice is called *Nalukataq* in the Inupiaq language. (From 1910s)

blind shot   ■ n A dynamite charge or other explosive device that fails to explode, usually in logging or mining operations. (From 1950s)

blocker   ■ n Also called **blocker loop.** A large loop formed in a rope to catch a cow by the front legs. Named for John Blocker, a Texas cowman who originated

blanket toss

the procedure. (From 1920s) See also **forefoot, mangana.**

blood alley

■ n A portion of Highway 101 in California, south of Gilroy, where a narrow portion of highway resulted in many accidents. Now generally applied to stretches of roads where freeways become two- or four-lane highways and where many accidents take place. (From 1960s)

blood drawing

■ n In the Pacific Northwest, the collection of voluntary blood donations; a blood drive. (From 1960s)

blossom rock

■ n In prospecting, a quartz flecked with metallic oxides indicating the presence of gold or silver ore. (From 1870s)

blow a stirrup

■ v phr In a **rodeo,** to lose control or footing in a stirrup while riding a bucking horse. It is grounds for disqualification. (From 1930s)

blueback salmon

■ n A **sockeye salmon,** *Onchorhyncus nerka,* found especially in the Columbia and Snake rivers. (From 1880s) See **salmon** n for a complete list of types and names.

blue bear

■ n Also called **blackie, glacier bear, Emmons bear.** A color phase of the black bear, *Ursus americanus.* The fur is blue to light gray. The habitat is the coast of Alaska from Glacier Bay to Yakutat. (From 1920s)

bluebell

■ n See **baby blue-eye.**

blue blizzard

■ n Also called **blue norther.** A strong wind from the north out of a blue-black sky that causes a sudden drop in temperature, sometimes thirty to forty degrees Fahrenheit. (From 1900)

blueblossom

■ n Also called **blue bush, blue myrtle, California lilac, deer brush.** A flower (*Ceanothus thyrsiflorus*) or a shrub (*Ceanothus integerrimus*) found along the Pacific Coast. The flower blossoms in panicles up to six inches long. The shrub is normally five to eight feet high, but can range up to fifteen feet in height. (From 1890s)

bluebonnet

■ n The lupine, state flower of **Texas,** *Lupinus texensis.* (From 1920s)

blue butt

■ n In logging, the base of a large pine, fir, or redwood that usually sinks when dropped into water. The top part of the log then floats above the water. (From 1950s)

blue fox

■ n A color phase of the Arctic fox, *Alopex lagopus,* sometimes also called **white fox.** The winter coat is bluish gray, which changes to slate gray or brownish gray in summer. The fox was transplanted to many islands in the Aleutians so it could freely propagate and be trapped for its winter pelt, a popular fur in the trade.

blue king crab

■ n Also called **brown, red, golden king crab.** A commercially harvested species of crab, *Paralithodes platypus,* that is one of many sold under the general designation of **king crab.** The name is often shortened to **blue crab** or **blue.** (From 1980s) See **Alaska king crab** for a complete listing.

blue norther

■ n Also called **blue Texas norther.** A cold wind blowing from the north or northwest, across Texas and into the Gulf of Mexico. Often it is a dry wind that can drop the temperature by thirty degrees Fahrenheit in a short time. (From 1870s)

boat puller

■ n A man on a two-man fishing boat in Alaskan waters who is responsible for pulling the net and fish aboard. The boat is pulled through the water as the net is brought aboard. (From 1890s)

bodyboard

■ n Also called **boogie board.** A flexible foam-filled thin raft used to ride waves, usually in areas shared with other swimmers where use of the hard surfboards is restricted. (From 1970s)

bog rider

■ n The cowboy who must go out on horseback in the spring as the snow melts and pull cows out of the mud, or "bog," when they get stuck. The job is still done on horseback, though four-wheel-drive vehicles with winches are also used if the location of the cow makes the task feasible. (From 1910s)

bolson

■ n A low area or desert basin, surrounded by hills. (From 1900, Spanish)

bolt

■ n In logging, especially in sawmills, a thin layer of wood split from a log, used to make shakes or shingles. (From 1950s)

bonanza

■ n High ore production in a mine; profitable mining; by extension, anything immensely profitable, lucky, or successful. (From 1840s, Spanish 'prosperity, success') Compare **borasca.**

book count

■ n An estimate of the amount of stock on a ranch by perusing ranch records. Such records are notoriously inaccurate in the springtime when cows are calving, horses foaling, and sheep lambing. (From 1920s)

boom

■ n A raft of loose logs floating in water, circled by a series of logs chained together to keep the loose logs together in a pack.

boomer

■ n 1. The mountain beaver, *Aplodontia ruffa,* found mainly in Oregon and Washington (from 1880s). 2. An itinerant worker, especially one who moves from town to town, following projects that require intensive amounts of labor for short periods of time (from 1920s). 3. A logger who is in charge of a **boom** (from 1940s).

boot hill

■ n A term associated with the West, referring to a cemetery where gunfighters were supposedly buried with their boots on. This usually jocular reference, while identified as western, may have been a literary coinage devised by a magazine writer, then freely adopted through the West by townspeople wishing to give their town a romantic flair. (From 1900)

bootie

■ n Also called **dog bootie, dog moccasin, moccasin.** A small bag made of leather, canvas, or fabric designed to cover the feet of sled dogs on icy trails in Alaska and the Yukon. (From 1980s)

borasca

■ n Also spelled *borrasca, borraska.* The lack of rich ore in a mine; a pocket of soil without value; by extension, ill luck, lack of prosperity. (From 1860s, Spanish *borrasca*) Compare **bonanza.**

borax lake

■ n A lake or dry lake bed that contains a high

concentration of borates from which borax can be prepared for commercial purposes; an alkaline lake or dry lake bed. (From 1870s)

borracho

■ n A person who is regularly drunk. (From 1840s, Spanish)

borrego

■ n 1. A sheep, especially one with a light, fleecy appearance. The term, from Spanish, is attested in English from the 1960s, though clearly it is much older in New Mexico, even appearing as a place-name. 2. By extension, fleecy white clouds (from 1960s).

borrow ditch, borrow pit

■ n See **barrow pit.**

bosal

■ n A rope halter around the nose of a horse. (From 1840s, Spanish *bozal*) See also **hackamore.**

bosque

■ /BOSS kee/ n A dense patch of woods and brush; a clump of trees. (From 1770s, Spanish)

boss dice

■ n Also called **bull dice.** A bar game in which each player shakes a cup with five dice a set number of times. The best hand wins. The game may require two wins out of three tries or three wins out of five. Rules vary from place to place. (From 1960s)

Boston

■ attributive A **Chinook** term, now historical, referring to things or people from the United States. The term referred to any white man or his clothes or goods. Anything of British origin, however, was referred to as **King George.** (From 1870s)

bota

■ n A fancy dress boot worn by ranchers, marked by intricately carved leather, often with silver ornaments. (From 1830s, Spanish *bota* 'boot')

bottle butt

■ n A log with a large diameter at the base and a small diameter at the upper end. (From 1950s)

box canyon

■ n A narrow canyon with steep sides, closed at one end by steep rocks. The canyon is thus accessible at only one end and makes either a fine shelter or a fine trap. (From 1970s) See also **cahon, 1.**

box rustler

■ n Also called **box hustler.** Now a Northwest historical term. A woman who entertained on the stages of saloons, then circled the room, visiting the boxed booths to encourage customers to buy drinks for her. (From 1880s)

bracero ■ /bruh SAIR oh/ n A Mexican allowed into the United States seasonally for agricultural labor; now any laborer of Mexican descent, whether a U.S. citizen or not. (From 1950s, Spanish *bracero* 'strong arm')

brand ■ n A collective term for bovine animals carrying a specific design burned into their hides. (From 1880s)

brand artist ■ n Also called **brand blotter, brand burner.** A person skilled at changing brands on stolen cattle. (From 1920s) See also **burnt brand, running iron.**

brand book ■ n A book or record of ranch brands, illustrating the brand and listing the owner. Although the term is three centuries old, it has come to be associated with the American West.

branding ■ attributive Used as the first element in combinations relative to ranch operations for placing a brand on livestock: *branding camp, ~ chute, ~ corral, ~ fire, ~ iron, ~ season.*

brand owner ■ n The person or corporation listed in a brand book as the owner of a particular design that is placed on ranch property, including cattle, horses, equipment, and buildings. (From 1930s)

brand reader ■ n A person skilled in interpreting brands and remembering the owners of specific brand designs. (From 1880s)

brasada ■ n A region covered densely by brush and thickets, common to West Texas; an area fit only for grazing hardy cattle. (From 1920s, Spanish *brazada* 'having many branches, arms, as of firewood')

brasero ■ n A container for lighted charcoal, originally used to keep the charcoal between the times required for cooking fires, now used more often for barbecues. (From 1890s, Spanish)

brasil

■ n In west Texas, a common chaparral plant used for limited grazing; *Condalia obovata*. (From 1890s, Spanish)

brea

■ n Pitch or tar. (From 1850s, Spanish) The most famous use of the word is in reference to the La Brea tar pits in Los Angeles County, site of an ancient water hole filled with the bones of extinct animals.

break

■ n A succession of sharp interruptions of the terrain. Usually plural. (From 1820s) Though the term was first used by explorers east of the Rocky Mountains, it has become associated with the West, even appearing in place-names, such as Cedar Breaks, Utah.

breakup

■ n Also called **break, icebreak.** In Alaska and the Yukon, an event in the spring of the year when the ice on rivers and lakes melts sufficiently to the point that the ice breaks up, often with a rumbling sound. Citizens consider the event an important transition and often have celebrations and lotteries based on the precise time of the ice breaking on a specific river or lake. (From 1870s) See **ice pool.** Compare **freeze-up.**

breakup boot

■ n In Alaska, rubber slip-on boots worn especially during breakup season, designed more to keep feet dry than to keep feet warm. (From 1970s) See also **bunny boot, vapor barrier boot.**

breed

■ n A derogatory term for a person of mixed parentage, especially the offspring of any Caucasian and any Indian. (From 1890s)

breeding

■ attributive Used as the first element in *breeding ranch, breeding range,* the place where livestock are taken to allow open range breeding. (From 1890s) Nowadays, artificial insemination programs are making the terms rare.

breedy

■ adj Descriptive of a horse exhibiting certain characteristics that are worth preserving by putting the animal into a breeding program. (From 1940s)

bridle

■ n In **dogsled** racing, the line and ring permanently affixed to the bottom of the sled. The **tow-line** from the dog harness is attached to the bridle. See also **gangline, neckline.** (From 1970s)

Brigham tea

■ n Also called **Mormon tea.** Either of two twiggy, rushlike plants used to brew a tonic or diuretic. *Ephedra verde* is found below eight thousand feet, *Ephedra nevadensis* is found at lower elevations. Named for early Mormon leader Brigham Young. (From 1910s) See also **canatillo, clapweed.**

bristlecone pine

■ n An ancient, hardy pine, *Pinus aristata,* found in the upper altitudes in the Southwest and Rocky Mountains. The tree grows to great age, though not to great height. (From 1890s)

British Columbia

■ n Canadian province. Settled in 1778 and made a colony in 1858. Entered confederation in 1871. Capital: Victoria. The intention was to name the province "New Caledonia" from the Romans' word for Scotland. The name was changed to British Columbia to avoid confusion with the French island of New Caledonia and as a tribute to Christopher Columbus.

brittlebrush

■ n See **yerba del vaso.**

brockle-faced

■ adj Descriptive of the splotchy color on the face of a cow, especially of a Hereford, indicating that the cow is not of pure blood stock. The term dates from an obsolete seventeenth-century dialect, but is now used chiefly in the West.

brodie

■ n A skidding turn by a vehicle of 360 degrees or of 180 degrees (sometimes called a "half brodie"). According to common usage, one does not "do" or "make" a brodie—one "flips" a brodie. (From 1960s, supposedly after a daredevil named Steve Brodie, who performed dangerous deeds, even claiming to have jumped from the Brooklyn Bridge in 1886.)

broken-mouthed

■ adj Descriptive of old ewes having lost teeth while grazing; a sign of aging in sheep. (From 1910s)

broken trail

■ n In Alaska, a dog-sledding trail on which snow

has been packed down and frozen hard, making for easier traveling. (From 1910s)

bronco

■ n Also shortened to **bronc.** 1. A small, wiry horse, sometimes half wild, noted for its willingness to toss riders from its back (from 1850s, Spanish). See also **fuzztail, broomtail, mustang.** Compare **outlaw.** 2. As the first element in activities relative to riding such an animal: *bronco breaker, ~ fighter, ~ peeler, ~ buster, ~ rider, ~ scratcher, ~ snapper, ~ squeezer, ~ twister.*

bronco

■ adj Also spelled *broncho.* Mean or rough; wild, whether applied to people or animals. (From 1860s, Spanish)

broomtail

■ n A wild range horse with a short, bushy tail. The term is mainly colloquial and refers mainly to mares. (From 1910s) See also **bronco, fuzztail, mustang.**

bronco

brow log

■ n In logging, a large log laid parallel to the railroad track or a road to serve as a buffer while other logs are being loaded or unloaded. (From 1950s)

brown bear

■ n Also called **brownie, Kodiak bear.** The large, dark bear of coastal areas in southern Alaska was thought to be a species (*Ursus middendorffi*) separate from the **grizzly bear,** but both are now known to belong to the species *Ursus arctos.* (From 1930s)

brown-capped rosy finch

■ n A finch that nests and breeds mainly above the timberline in the Colorado Rockies. (From 1910s)

brown king crab

■ n One of a variety of crabs often referred to as **king crab.** The *Lithodes aesquispina* is undergoing a face-lift by advertisers promoting its sales by calling it **golden king crab.** (From 1980s) See **Alaska king crab** for a complete listing.

brown trout

■ n See **speckled trout.**

brujo

■ n Also **bruja.** This borrowing from Spanish has been regularly used in English since the 1920s. In the Southwest, it refers to a witch or sorcerer. The man or woman so designated is said to use spells to cause drought, crop failure, impotent men, barren women, just about any disaster than one might want to blame on someone else.

brush

■ adj A term used in describing a number of cattle-related activities in higher Southwest altitudes where brittle trees and bushes snap easily when ridden through rapidly. Terms are applied to cowboys and horses experienced in this activity: *brush breaking, ~ buster, ~ busting, ~ hand, ~ horse, ~ popper, ~ popping, ~ rider, ~ thumper, ~ whacker.* (From 1920s)

brush bow

■ n In dog-sledding, a curved piece of hardwood fastened to the front of the sled to prevent trees and brush from getting under the runners. (From 1970s)

brushman

■ n See **woodsman.**

brush monkey

■ n In logging, particularly in California pine country, the person who performs menial tasks around the logging operation, especially those jobs requiring more muscle than brains. (From 1950s)

buck

■ n In **poker,** the marker (at one time a buck-handled knife) used to identify the next player to deal the cards, or alternatively, the next player to act on the wager. (From 1860s) The most famous use of the term was by President Harry S Truman, a noted poker player, who had a sign on his desk stating, "The buck stops here," which indicated he had the final authority and responsibility to act.

buck

■ v 1. Also **buckjump.** Of horses and bulls, to leap upwards suddenly and twist around, which, in case a rider or load is on the animal, may be thrown off (from 1860s). 2. In surfing, to fight through breaking waves with a surfboard to get to smoother outer water. 3. In card games, to gamble (and lose) money. The notion is that one cannot force Lady Luck. Hence, the term "buck the tiger," to gamble money in playing faro. (From 1850s)

buckaroo

■ n Also spelled *baccaro, bacquero, buckaree, buckeroo, buckhara, bukkarer, buccaroo.* In the Southwest, a working cowboy. The term was generalized during the last century to refer to ranch hands. (From 1820s, Spanish *vaquero*) See also **vaquero.**

bucker

■ n 1. A horse that bucks (from 1880s). 2. A gambler, especially at cards (from 1890s). 3. A logger who saws felled trees into logs of specific lengths (originally done with a bucksaw) (from 1900).

bucking season

■ n The season for breeding sheep, usually in late December for spring lambing. (From 1930s in the West) Though the term "bucking" in the sense of breeding any animal is much older, its most frequent use is western and relative only to sheep.

buckle bunny

■ n A female rodeo groupie. A woman who haunts rodeos to pick up cowboys who ride in the **rodeo.** So named because they are attracted by the large belt buckles that go with the championships of certain riding events. Their place in history has been immortalized in several country-western songs. (From 1970s)

= 48 =

buckwheat butterfly

■ n A desert butterfly, usually pale or white, *Apodemia deserti,* the larvae of which feed on buckwheat. (From 1940s)

bud sagebrush

■ n Also called **bud sage, bud brush.** A low, shrubby sage with conspicuous buttonlike clustered flower heads; *Artemisia spinescens.* (From 1920s)

bug

■ n A light source or lantern fabricated by making a hole in the side of a tin can and inserting a lighted candle. The low level of light resulting from the device resembles a lightning bug when carried outdoors at night. (From 1920s) See also **California lantern.**

bull

■ adj 1. In logging, a descriptor placed before a variety of words to indicate the biggest, strongest, or toughest of the type. Hence, *bull car, ~ chain, ~ hook, ~ of the woods* (the top man on the crew), ~ *bucker* (the man in charge of those who fell trees and those who saw the logs to length). 2. In logging, a descriptor placed before a variety of words to indicate work of a menial or repetitive nature, like the oxen once used in logging camps. Hence, ~ *cook* (chore boy who fed oxen, now cleans the bunkhouse), ~ *gang* (a labor crew). (From 1920s, but probably much earlier) McCulloch (*WW*), lists thirty-seven terms preceded by bull. Eighteen of the terms include the sense of "big" or "tough," while five terms carry the sense of "odd jobs" or "menial."

bullcorn

■ expletive In the Southwest, especially Texas, a euphemism expressing disbelief or disgust. (From 1960s)

bull dice

■ n See **boss dice.**

bulldog

■ v To grab a running steer by the horns and, by twisting its head by the horns, throw the animal to the ground; to grab a calf and hold it down for branding. (From 1900)

bulldogger

■ n A cowboy who catches calves and holds them down while they are branded. (From 1900)

bullhead	■ n Also called **Irish lord, devilfish.** Any of a variety of large-headed fish called sculpins found in Alaskan waters. Sculpins are spiny fish prized neither for looks or eating. (From 1950s)
bull ledge	■ n Also called **bull quartz.** In mining, a streak, usually of quartz, running underground or along the face of an escarpment. (From 1890s)
bull pen	■ n In the Rocky Mountains, a level area or meadow at a high elevation, surrounded by higher mountains. (From 1820s)
bull pine	■ n Any of several varieties of pine in the West, but especially the yellow pine, *Pinus ponderosa.* (From 1880s) *DARE* lists a number of western pines that fall into this generic category: *bishop pine, Coulter ~, Digger ~, Jeffrey ~, limber ~, lodgepole ~, ponderosa ~, Monterey ~.*
bull-puncher	■ n A cowboy who rides herd on steers that are being fattened for market. (From 1880s)
bull ranch	■ n A set of fields and corrals at low elevation where the bulls of a cattle herd are wintered. (From 1930s)
bull snake	■ n See **gopher snake.**
bull-whacker	■ n Originally, the driver of a train of oxen or steers (from 1850s). By extension, the political functionary who keeps party members in line (from 1870s). The term gave rise to adjectival use because of the long whip used to make a loud cracking noise above the heads of the lead oxen and to the figurative sense of the verb: to keep political party members in line with party policy (from 1890s).
bum	■ n Also called **bummer.** A lamb that has lost its mother or has been deserted and must be fed by hand. (From 1930s)
bummer	■ n 1. An unpleasant hallucinatory experience while taking drugs. 2. Any unpleasant experience. In the 1960s the sense originated in the Haight-Ashbury district of San Francisco, and was general-

ized from drug use by young people across the country.

bumper-bumming

■ n See **bizzing.**

bunch

■ v Since the 1860s, this verb has meant to collect a herd of cattle or horses into a compact group. By the 1880s, the meaning had been extended and the distribution was national. The expanded meaning: to form a cluster or group of anything from flowers to baseball hits.

bunchgrass

■ n Any of a variety of western grasses that grow in tufts or clumps. The grass is good for grazing even when dry. (From 1830s)

bungo

■ n Historical. A dugout boat or canoe used on rivers in the Southwest. (From 1780s, Spanish, probably from an African language)

bunkhouse

■ n A building (occasionally a railroad car) used as sleeping and living quarters for railroad crews, ranch hands, itinerant laborers, loggers, or other such work crews. (From 1870s)

bunkmate

■ n Shortened to **bunkie.** A person who shares one's living quarters. (From 1850s)

bunny boot

■ n Also called **vapor barrier boot.** A white, rubber insulated boot developed by the U.S. military for cold weather use and sold in surplus stores in Alaska. The rubberized version replaced an earlier form of uninsulated white boot made of felt. (From 1950s) See also **breakup boot.**

burn

■ v Also in the form **burn down.** To sink a shaft in the frozen ground in the Yukon or Alaska by making a fire atop cleared ground, then removing the fire and the portion of ground melted under the fire. The process is then repeated. (From 1890s) See also **freeze down.**

Burney Bay oyster

■ n A particularly large and succulent oyster found in Burney Bay, on the west coast of Vancouver Island. The oysters are reputed to be edible year around.

burn pile

■ n Often called **berm pile.** In Alaska, long, low

ridges of trees and brush bulldozed into rows during the clearing of land. The debris is burned. Perhaps the term developed on analogy with "berm," a bulldozed ridge running alongside a road. (From 1950s)

burnt brand

■ n Historical. A changed or defaced brand on a cow or horse. (From 1890s) Compare **counterbrand, cross-brand, road brand.** See also **running iron.**

burrito

■ n A **tortilla,** usually made of flour rather than *masa,* about twelve inches in diameter, wrapped around meat, cheese, beans, or other fillings. Sometimes the burrito is deep fried or heated and covered with **salsa.** (From 1960s, Spanish 'little donkey') See also **chimichanga.**

burro

■ n A donkey. (From 1840s, Spanish) Jocularly called by a variety of descriptive, if not poetic, names: **Arizona nightingale, Colorado mockingbird, desert canary, Washoe canary, western nightingale.**

burro deer

■ n Also called **desert mule deer.** A pale, large deer, *Odocoileus hemionus eremicus,* found in western deserts. The deer has heavy horns and ranges to 130 pounds in weight. (From 1910s)

burro fat

■ n Also called **bladderpod.** A common Southwest

shrub with long stalks topped by an inflated pod; the *Isomeris arborea.* (From 1920s)

burroweed

■ n Any of a variety of small western shrubs, but especially *Allenrolfea occidentalis,* marked by having few leaves and succulent branches and growing in alkaline areas. Supposedly a grazing staple of wild **burros.** (From 1910s)

burrowing

■ adj As the first element in *burrowing owl, Speotyto cunicularia hypuogaea,* which lives in the burrows left by other animals, such as prairie dogs. Also as the first element in *burrowing squirrel,* any of the western ground squirrels of the genus *Citellus.* (From 1810s)

bush

■ n 1. The first element in *bush pilot* and *bush plane,* referring to people who deliver mail and goods by small plane to settlers in remote areas of Alaska and the Yukon. 2. Often capitalized. The large open spaces of interior Alaska, scarcely populated, and then mainly by native tribal people. The term has been generalized to refer to any out-of-the-way place. (From 1930s) See also **tule.**

busheler

■ n Historical. In logging, the collective name given to fallers and those who man bucksaws on a piecework basis, figuratively, "by the bushel." (From 1940s)

bushy

■ adj Also **bushed.** Describing a person who has lived in isolation in the wilderness, especially the Northwest, for an extended period of time and who has become eccentric from the experience. (From 1890s) See also **cabin fever, desert rat.**

bust

■ v To break a horse for riding or to harness for pulling; to make a horse tractable. (From 1890s)

buster

■ n A ranch hand who specializes in or is especially good at breaking horses. (From 1890s)

butte

■ n Though this term is found in isolated instances as early as the seventeenth century, the first complete description was given in 1842: "The French word *butte* . . . is naturalized in the region of the Rocky mountains; and, even if desirable to render it in English, I know of no word which would be its precise equivalent. It is applied to the detached hills and ridges which rise abruptly and reach too high to be called hills or ridges, and not high enough to be called mountains." —John C. Frémont, *Expedition to the Rocky Mountains.* See also **cerro.**

butter clam

■ n Also called **Washington clam** or **money shell.** A common, edible clam, *Saxidomus nutalli,* found along the coast of the Pacific Northwest. (From 1940s) See also **gaper.**

butt thong

■ n Also called **butt floss.** The bottom part of a G-string bikini. The rear strap is very thin. (From 1980s)

button

■ n A beginner who is setting out to learn the skills of a cowboy. (From 1910s) Hence, the term, "fresh as a button," meaning "unworn, inexperienced." More generally, any child.

butte

caballada

■ /kab uh YAH duh, KAV uh yah duh/ n Also spelled *cavayard, caballado, cavalyard,* and by folk etymology, *cavalry yard* and *calf yard.* Also called **cavvy.** A herd of horses or mules kept by a ranch as working stock. (From 1820s, Spanish) See also **remuda.** Compare **manada, mulada.**

caballero

■ /kah bah YER oh/ n 1. A horseman; a gentleman (from 1820s, Spanish). 2. A cowboy, especially one of Mexican descent or one who dresses himself and his horse in finery (from 1950s, Spanish).

caballo

■ /kuh BYE yo/ n Also spelled *cavallo* /kuh VAL low/. A horse. (From 1840s, Spanish) Used especially in southwest Texas, southern Arizona, and southern California.

cabana

■ /kuh BAN uh/ n A cabin or a small bathhouse, often of canvas, on a beach. (From 1890s, Spanish *cabaña* 'hut, cabin')

cabaret

■ /KAB uh ray/ n Originally, a small liquor shop in the Southwest, now an establishment serving liquor, often with entertainment. (From 1830s, French)

cabestro

■ /kuh BES troh/ n Also spelled *cabresto* /kah BRES toh/ A halter or tether rope made of hair. (From 1840s, Spanish, though the same sense is found earlier with *cabras, caboris, cabris*)

cabeza

■ /kuh BAY zuh/ n A jocular term for the head. (From 1850s, Spanish)

cabin fever

■ n A state of nervousness or depression caused by confinement to close quarters or isolation from society, especially in wintertime in the Northwest. (From 1920s) See also **bushy.**

cabrito

■ /kuh BREE toh/ n A young goat, usually male, barbecued. (From 1940s, Spanish)

cabrón

■ /kuh BROHN/ n A fool; derogatory in the Southwest. (From 1930s, Spanish, literally, 'big goat,' but in Spanish slang means 'cuckold')

= 55 =

cache

■ /KASH/ n A small storage building, often raised on poles, found in wilderness areas of the Northwest. (From 1860s, French 'secret hiding place'; the sense of the earlier use in 1800 was replaced in the Northwest)

cachimilla

■ n A shrub, *Pluchea sericea,* used in making arrows. It is found from west Texas to California and northern Mexico. (From 1900s, Spanish) See also **arrow bush.**

cack

■ n Also spelled *kack, kak.* An old, worn-out, ill-fitting saddle. (From 1930s, perhaps from a shortened form of "cactus")

cacomistle

■ /KAK uh missle/ n A small, raccoonlike animal, the size of a house cat, with a long furry tail marked with black and white rings. Found in the Southwest and northern Mexico. (From 1860s, Nahuatl via Spanish)

cactus

■ n As a first element in a number of self-explanatory words relating to animals and birds residing in and around cacti: *cactus mouse,* ~ *quail,* ~ *rat,* ~ *thrush,* ~ *woodpecker,* ~ *wren.* See **barrel cactus** for a complete listing of this succulent.

cactus candy

■ n A sweet made by boiling the pulp of certain cacti, especially **bisnaga,** with sugar. (From 1850s)

cactus forest

■ n Any close growth of tall cacti or other succulents such as yucca or **saguaro,** found in the Mojave or Sonoran Deserts. (From 1910s)

cahon

■ /kuh HONE/ n 1. A **box canyon;** a small basin of land nearly surrounded by steep sides. 2. A squarish or boxlike building constructed of **adobe** (from 1860s, Spanish *cajón* 'box'). The word is prominent in many place-names in the Southwest.

calaboose

■ n A jocular name for a local jail. (From 1860s, Spanish *calabozo* 'dungeon') Compare **carcel.**

caliche

■ /kuh LEE chee/ n A hard deposit of calcium carbonate that forms near the surface of the soil in arid regions in the Southwest. The deposits can be up to thirty feet deep and create enough difficulty in excavation that homeowners can buy "caliche insurance" when building a swimming pool. (From 1880s, Spanish)

calico salmon

■ n Often shortened to **calico.** Also called **chum, dog salmon.** One of a variety of salmon, the *Oncorhynchus keta.* It received the calico appellation because of the mottled appearance of red and green splotches at spawning season. (From 1900s) See **salmon** n for a complete listing of all the western forms.

California

■ n 1. Thirty-first state of the Union. Settled in 1769. Seceding from Mexico, it became an independent republic in 1846, joining the Union in 1850. Capital: Sacramento. Spanish explorers named it *Alta California* 'Upper California' because they had named the lower peninsula *Baja California* 'Lower California'. Americans later dropped the adjective. The name first appears in *Las Sergas de Esplandián,* a sixteenth-century Spanish text, in reference to an island rich in gold and precious gems, an island the explorers believed they had found when they sailed to the Baja peninsula (from 1530s). 2. Called **El Dorado State** (from 1900s). 3. Called **Eureka State** (from 1860s). 4. Called **Golden Bear State** (from 1940s). 5. Called **Golden State** (from 1840s).

California

■ An attributive or adjective used with variations of fauna and flora found in the state that are slightly different from those found in other states. With animals: *California black sea bass, ~ condor, ~ goose, ~ gray whale* (see **gray whale**), *~ hare, ~ horse, ~ jay, ~ lion, ~ mustang, ~ nuthatch, ~ quail* (compare **valley quail**), *~ sardine, ~ sticklebill, ~ stingray, ~ trout, ~ vulture* (see **vulture**), *~ widgeon, ~ woodpecker, ~ yellowtail;* with plants: *California bay, ~ bayos, ~ bee plant, ~ bluebell* (see **baby blue-eye**), *~ blue oak, ~ buckeye, ~ buckthorn, ~ bulrush, ~ coffeeberry, ~ fan palm, ~ grass, ~ grape, ~ holly, ~ laurel, ~ lilac* (see **blueblossom**), *~ live oak, ~ maple* (see **big-leaf maple**), *~ nutmeg, ~ olive, ~ pine, ~ pitcher plant, ~ poplar,*

~ poppy, ~ redwood (see **sequoia**), *~ rose bay, ~ strawberry, ~ sunflower, ~ walnut, ~ white pine.*

California battalion

■ n Historical. The group of Americans living in California who, in 1846, began a series of protests aimed at Mexican authorities. See also **Bear Revolution.**

California bet

■ n In the dice game of bank craps in a casino, a simultaneous place bet on the numbers 4, 5, 6, 8, 9, 10. When one of the numbers wins, the player takes the winnings and leaves the original wager. Considered a foolish bet among serious dice-players. (From 1950s)

California bible

■ n Also called **California prayer book.** A deck of playing cards. (From 1850s)

California blackjack

■ n In the casino game of twenty-one, an ace and a nine, which totals twenty. Used facetiously when a player doubles the wager and asks for one card when the dealer has a ten up on the table. The player turns a sure push or win into a likely loss. (From 1970s)

California C-note

■ n A jocular term for a ten-dollar bill. A C-note is a one-hundred-dollar bill. (From 1970s)

California fourteens

■ n Misspotted dice, on which one die has two facets with five pips, the other die has two facets with two pips. The combination of pips is a sum of fourteen. (From 1960s)

California lantern

■ n A makeshift light created by breaking the bottom off a clear glass bottle and inserting a lighted candle through the neck of the bottle. The flame is protected from a breeze. (From 1940s) See also **bug.**

California pants

■ n Heavy wool pants with a double weave and striped or checked design. Supposedly very good for riding horses for long periods. (From 1920s, though claimed to be in existence since 1870s)

California peacock

■ n Also called **Arizona peacock.** A jocular name for a **roadrunner.** (From 1950s)

California salmon

■ n Another name for **Chinook salmon.** See also **salmon** n for a complete listing.

California sight

■ n A rear sight on a rifle that features a series of notches to raise and lower the sight for shooting various distances. (From 1880s)

California toothpick

■ n A large knife, similar in appearance to the bowie knife and to the knife called the "Arkansas toothpick." (From 1850s)

californicate

■ v To pass legislation encouraging people and businesses to move to states near California; to adopt Californialike attitudes toward people, relationships, and environmental concerns. The term is used semifacetiously by people in Oregon, Washington, Nevada, and Utah who resent residents from California moving to their states, increasing property rates and population density, and bringing to them what they consider problems created by Californians. (From 1970s, blend of *Califor* + for*nicate*)

californite

■ n An ornamental stone, olive-green to grass-green in color, resembling jade, and found in California. (From 1900s)

calliope hummingbird

■ n A hummingbird found in the Southwest, the *Stellula calliope.* (From 1870s)

calochortus

■ n Herb of the lily family found in the western United States. (From 1860s, Greek *kalo* + *chortus* 'beautiful grass, fodder')

camai

■ excl A greeting in Alaska, developed by Alaskan tourist promoters from a native language, in the hopes of creating a greeting similar to the *aloha* used in Hawaii. (From 1900s, Alutiiq and Central Yupik *chamai* 'hi, hello')

camas

■ n Also spelled *camass, camus, kamas, quamash.* Also called **biscuit root, swamp sego, wild hyacinth, Indian potato, Indian squill, indigo squill, railroad hyacinth, soaproot.** A plant of the Pacific Northwest, whose bulb was an important part of the diet for the natives and white settlers living there. So important was *Camassia esculenta* that

Indian tribes were known by their neighbors as "the camas eaters," and early settlers in Oregon referred to themselves jocularly as "camas eaters." It is still a sought-after root. (From 1800s, Nootka *chamas* 'sweet' via Chinook Jargon)

camino real

■ /kuh MEE no ree AL/ n A highway, especially a broad and smooth highway. The term is now mainly historical and found primarily in place-names in the Southwest. (From 1840s, Spanish 'royal highway')

camisa

■ /kah MEE sah, KA mee sah/ n A loose, blousy shirt or chemise. (From 1830s, Spanish)

camp jack

■ n Also called **camp jerker, camp mover, camp tender, camp rustler.** In sheepherding, the person responsible for fetching supplies from town or ranch, moving the sheepherders' wagons from place to place, and assisting the herders when needed. (From 1910s)

campoody

■ n A hut or group of huts, originally inhabited by Indians, but later occupied by weekend hunters at higher elevations in the Southwest. (From 1850s, Piute via Spanish *campo* 'camp')

campo santo

■ n In the Southwest, a cemetery, especially one with elaborate and decorated grave markers. (From 1850s, Spanish)

camp robber

■ n Also called **Canada jay, Rocky Mountain jay.** Any of a variety of jays that frequent campsites. (From 1890s) Compare **Alaska jay.**

can

■ n An outhouse or outdoor toilet; any room with a toilet. (1900, but became chiefly more western from 1940 on)

canal

■ n In earlier times, a large irrigation ditch in arid areas of the Southwest; more recently, any concrete-lined waterway for carrying large amounts of water for commercial and residential use to large cities. (From 1850s)

canatillo

■ /kan uh TILL oh/ n Also called **Mormon tea.** A form of the plant species *Ephedra* known for its diuretic properties when boiled with water. (From 1910s, Spanish *cañatillo, cañatilla*) See also **Brigham tea, clapweed.**

candlefish

■ n A fish found in the Pacific Northwest, *Anoplopoma fimbria,* that is rich in oil and used by Indians for food and formerly for light. When dried, the fish could have a rush or twig pushed length-wise through the body and be used as a torch. (From 1880s, loan translation from Chinook Jargon *ulâkân* 'candle') See also **eulachon, Columbia River smelt.**

candlewood

■ n Also called **ocatillo** (q.v. for a complete list-ing). A succulent of the Southwestern deserts, *Fouquieria splendens,* said to burn with a steady, deep yellow flame. (From 1890s)

candy side

■ n In a logging operation, the crew or unit that has the best equipment and most efficient workers. (From 1940s) Compare **haywire side.**

candy wagon

■ In the Pacific Northwest, a light truck, station wagon, or small bus or van that is used to haul crews to road, logging, or construction sites. Or the vehicle is used to transport food and supplies to a work site. (From 1940s)

cane cactus

■ n Also called **cane cholla.** Any of a variety of cacti that feature long, straight stems that can be dried and made into walking canes. The varieties include *Opuntia arborescens, O. arbuscula, O. spinosior, O. imbricata.*

cantina

■ n A barroom; a small tavern in the Southwest. (From 1890s, Spanish)

canyon

■ n A deep valley, gorge, or ravine with steep sides. Water may be flowing through it. (From 1830s, Spanish)

canyon maple

■ n See **big-leaf maple** for a complete listing. (From 1970s)

canyon oak

■ n See **Valparaiso oak.**

caporal

■ /kap per AL/ n The manager of a ranch, espe-cially a sheep operation; the subforeman who directs the workers, but who does not pay them. (From 1890s, Spanish)

capper ■ n A shill or decoy, originally for a faro game, but later as a phony bidder at auctions; a paid, enthusiastic customer for a snake-oil salesman. (From 1850s)

cap rock ■ n 1. In mining, the barren waste that lies above the ore (from 1860s). 2. Also shortened to **cap.** A rock covering, resistant to erosion by wind and rain, that overlies many **buttes** and mesas. One such geological layer is the limestone cap over Aztec sandstone at Redrock, in Nevada. (From 1910s)

carajo ■ /kuh RAH ho/ 1. excl A shout of disgust; a mean or base fellow (from 1840s, Spanish 'penis'). 2. n The tall, upright stem of a maguey or similar bush, used as a goad or long walking stick (from 1880s).

caramba ■ /kuh RUM buh/ excl A declaration of vexation or admiration; a mild expletive. (From 1830s, Spanish)

carcel ■ /KAR sell/ n A jail. Not so frequent in usage or widespread as **calaboose.** (From 1840s, Spanish)

carne asada ■ /KAR nee uh SAH duh/ n Beef or pork cooked over a fire, then usually shredded for use in **tacos, burritos,** and such. (From 1970s, Spanish)

carne seco ■ n Also spelled *carne seca.* A form of beef, preserved by being cut into long strips, then dried. (From 1890s, Spanish) See also **jerky.**

Carnegiea ■ n The giant **saguaro** (q.v. for a complete listing), state flower of **Arizona;** *Carnegiea gigantea.* (From 1900s, named for Andrew Carnegie)

carreta ■ /kuh RET tuh/ n A crude cart or wagon with two solid wooden wheels. (From 1840s, Spanish)

carrot eater ■ n Also called **carrot snapper.** A derogatory term for a Utahn, especially a Mormon. The reference is to the heavy use of carrots by Mormon pioneers. (From 1960s) The term is used frequently in Idaho, often as a response to being called "spud head, spud eater." Compare **cricket stomper.**

casa

■ n A house, a dwelling place, especially one constructed with walls of **adobe** and a tiled roof. Often used in the naming of one's house. (From 1840s, Spanish)

casa grande

■ n 1. An extensive pueblo in the Southwest (from 1840s, Spanish). 2. The dwelling of the owner of a ranch, the largest habitation on a ranch (from 1910s, Spanish).

cascara sagrada

■ /kass KARE uh suh GRAH duh/ n Also shortened to **cascara.** The bark of the bearberry buckthorn, *Rhammus purshiana,* found along the Pacific Coast; also, the mild laxative made from the bark. (From 1900s, Spanish 'sacred bark')

cascaron

■ n An eggshell whose contents have been removed by means of a small hole in each end and then filled with confetti. Used at carnivals and parties. In days gone by, the eggshells might be filled with scented water. (From 1880s, Spanish 'cracked eggshell')

cat's claw

■ n Also called **angry acacia.** Any of a number of thorny bushes which catch clothing. On some, the leaves curl and give off an offensive odor. The various plants include the genera *Acacia, Mimosa, Pithecellobium, Schrankia.* (From 1850s)

cattle

■ n The first element in a number of western words dating from the middle of the nineteenth century having to do with raising, owning, and tending cows and bulls: *cattle baron, ~ broker, ~ buyer, ~ car, ~ corral, ~ country, ~ czar, ~ drive, ~ feeder, ~ fever, ~ herder, ~ hunt, ~ king, ~ queen, ~man, ~ puncher* (see **puncher**), *~ ranch* (see **ranch),** *~ rancher, ~ range* (see **range**), *~ rustler* (see **rustler**), *~ thief, ~ town, ~ trade, ~ trail, ~ train.*

cattle guard

■ n A parallel series of bars placed over a shallow ditch across a road to keep cattle from moving out of a fenced section of land. The guard is often a series of white stripes painted on the blacktop of a road and serves the same function. The cattle perceive the painted stripes as a series of narrow ditches and will not walk on them. Since the guard crosses the road from fence post to fence post, a gate is not required. (From 1830s)

cavvy

■ n Also called **caballada.** A shortened form of **cavayard,** which in turn is a folk etymology for **caballard.** A small herd of horses used as working stock on a ranch. In some rural areas, it seems also to be referring to stray cows on the basis of a folk etymology of "cavvy" being related somehow to "calfie." (From 1930s, Spanish 'group of horses') See also **remuda.** Compare **manada, mulada.**

cayuse

■ n Originally, a smallish horse or "Indian pony" bred by the Indian tribe of the same name in what is now Washington and Oregon; now, any horse of doubtful lineage or stubborn behavior. (From 1870s)

Centennial State

■ n A nickname for **Colorado,** which was admitted to the Union in 1876. (From 1870s)

center fire

■ n A saddle with a single cinch. (From 1900s, transferred sense from the shell of a bullet, the base of which must be struck in the center by the gun's hammer) compare **double cinch.**

cerro

■ /SEH roh/ n A hill or **butte.** The term occurs frequently in place-names. (From 1830s, Spanish)

ceviche

■ /suh VEE chay, suh BEE chay/ n A fish dish prepared by using lime and lemon juice and peppers as a marinade for raw fish. The juice "cooks" the fish. (From 1960s, Spanish)

chalupa

■ n A small, oblong corncake, made in the shape of a boat with an indentation for placing fillings of beans, meat, and vegetables. (From 1890s, Spanish 'little boat')

chamise-lily

■ n Also called **Adam-and-Eve, chaparral lily.** A plant that is lilylike, *Lilium rebescens,* that has edible bulbs. It is found mainly in northern California. (From 1910s)

chaparral

■ /shap uh RELL/ n 1. An expanse of ground covered with tangled thickets of brush, shrubs, vines, and stunted trees, found mainly in Southwestern arid regions. 2. Any of a variety of thicket-forming shrubbery, including *Acacia, Ceanothus, Condalia, Foresteira, Quercus.* 3. As the first element in a number of plants found in chaparral areas: *chaparral lily* (see **chamise-lily**), *~ pea, ~ shrub, ~ tea.* (From 1850s, Spanish)

chaparral berry

■ n Also called **barberry** (q.v. for a complete listing). The **agarita,** used in jellies and preserves. The plant is *Berberis trifoliolata.* (From 1890s)

chaparral cock

■ n Also called **chaparral bird.** Another name for the **roadrunner** (q.v. for further information). (From 1850s) See also **paisano,** 2.

chapo

■ n Short and stubby, or stocky; fubsy. Said of a man or horse. (From 1850s, Spanish)

chaps

■ /SHAPS, CHAPS/ n Shortened from **chaparreras,** which is spelled in various ways: *chaparros, chaparajos,* etc. Leather leggings worn by cowboys

cowboy wearing chaps

when riding through brushy country. Often a slit leather apron tied at the waist, then fastened with thongs around the legs (**armitas**). The simplest styles are functional and utilitarian, but as a costume item may be made very fancy, with silver studs and animal hair left on the outside (**angoras, chivarras, hair pants**). (From 1880s, Spanish) See also **bat wings, Cheyenne cut.**

charco

■ n A watering hole, pond, pool, puddle. Usually the reference is to standing water after a rain, but may sometimes be to a spring. (From 1890s, Spanish 'puddle')

Charlie's dead

■ excl A warning to a woman that her slip is showing. Used especially in California and Nevada, now somewhat old-fashioned. (From 1940s)

Charlie Taylor

■ n Old-fashioned. A butter substitute made by campers and herders from sorghum or molasses or syrup and bacon or ham grease. (From 1930s)

charreada

■ n Also **charreria.** The precurser of the modern **rodeo,** but still an active event in many states, from California to Maine. Mexican **vaqueros,** or cowboys of Mexican descent, meet regularly to indulge in many of the same events that are part of every rodeo. Some additional events include breathless wild riding tricks by women and **horse-tripping.** (From 1890s, Spanish)

charro

■ n 1. The fancy full-dress Mexican costume worn in parades by horsemen in the Southwest. The large **sombrero,** with rolled edges, is decorated with silver or gold embroidery and the short, tight-fitting jacket and tight trousers, which flare at the bottom, are fully embroidered, trimmed in buttons and braid. The suit is often made of soft leather. The horse's trappings are equally elaborate in decor (from 1890s, Spanish). 2. A churl; a coarse, ill-bred person (from 1930s).

cheechako

■ n A newcomer; a **tenderfoot.** Used in Alaska and the Northwest. (From 1890s, Chinook Jargon) See also **Arbuckle.**

cheese block ■ n In logging, a wedge-shaped steel block used to keep a log from rolling off a truck or railroad flat-car. (From 1900s, the shape of the wedge looks like a piece of cheese cut from a cheese wheel)

chesterfield ■ n A piece of furniture that seats two people and has upholstered arms and back. The term dates from 1900 and is known in England and used in Canada, but is especially common in recent years in the Pacific Northwest.

Cheyenne cut ■ n Also called **Cheyenne leg.** A type of **chaps** (q.v. for complete listing) with the inside leg cut narrowly below the knee, and without straps or snaps below the knee. (From 1940s, after Cheyenne, Wyoming, where they were popularized) Compare **bat wings.**

chica ■ n A girl; a sweetheart; term of endearment; reference to any female under the age of twenty. (From 1900s, Spanish)

chicharron ■ n Fried bacon or pork rind; crackling. (From 1850s, Spanish)

chicken-fried steak ■ n Also **chicken-fry steak.** A cut of beef, usually a cube steak, breaded and fried. (From 1960s)

chicken halibut ■ n A Pacific halibut or a California halibut (*Paralichthys californicus*) that weighs between ten and thirty pounds. (From 1890s)

chicken ranch ■ n 1. A very large chicken farm (from 1870s). 2. A whorehouse; a brothel (from 1950s).

chilaquiles ■ /chill uh KEE luz/ n pl A mixture of red peppers used for seasoning vegetables and **tortillas.** (From 1890s, Nahuatl *chilli* 'pepper' + *quilitl* 'edible herb' via Spanish)

chili ■ n Also spelled *chile, chilli.* Any of a wide variety of peppers, or *Capsicum.* (From 1830s, Nahuatl *chilli* 'pepper' via Spanish)

chili bean ■ n A dark red bean, usually a kidney bean, used in making **chili con carne.** (From 1900)

chili colorado ■ n A red pepper sauce used in beef dishes. (From

1870s, Nahuatl *chilli* 'pepper' + Spanish *colorado* 'red') Compare **chili verde.**

chili con carne

■ n Also shortened to chili. A dish made with peppers, tomatoes, shredded beef, kidney beans, and spices. (From 1850s, Spanish 'pepper with meat')

chili con queso

■ n A dish prepared with tortilla chips or fried **tortillas** covered with cheese and peppers. (From 1960s, Spanish 'pepper with cheese')

chilipitin

■ n Also **chiltecpin, chilipequin, chitipequin.** Shortened to **pepino, pequin.** A small, often wild, red pepper. The *Capsicum baccatum* used in its entirety in making spicy hot dishes in Thai, Szechuan, and Spanish cookery. (From 1820s, Spanish *chiltipiquin*)

chili relleno

■ /~ ray YAY no/ n A dish made with a roasted green pepper filled with cheese. (From 1890s, Nahuatl *chilli* + Spanish *relleno* 'refilled, filled or stuffed')

chili sauce

■ n Any of a variety of mixtures made with hot peppers and vinegar. Sometimes tomatoes, onions, garlic, and other spices are added. (From 1880s) Compare **salsa.**

chili verde

■ A green pepper sauce used in pork dishes. (From 1890s, Nahuatl *chilli* 'pepper' + Spanish *verde* 'green') Compare **chili colorado.**

chimichanga

■ /chim ee CHONG guh/ n A flour **tortilla** filled with vegetables and beef, pork, or chicken, then rolled and deep fried. Served with sour cream and **salsa.** (From 1960s Spanish 'trifle, small delight') See also **burrito.**

Chinese lottery

■ n See **keno.**

Chinese parsley

■ n See **cilantro.**

chinook

■ /shuh NOOK, chuh NOOK/ n 1. See **Chinook Jargon.** 2. A warm winter wind blowing from the southwest that can melt snow and temporarily raise outdoor temperatures (from 1850s).

Chinook Jargon

■ n Also called **Chinook.** A trade language used

widely in the Pacific Northwest well into this century. The language is comprised of elements from Chinook, Nootka, French, English, Spanish, Kwakiutl, and other languages. A number of individual vocabulary items from the jargon are still used in the Northwest, but the trade language itself is a historical artifact. (From 1830s)

Chinook salmon

■ n Often shortened to **Chinook.** A large, red-fleshed fish (*Oncorhynchus tshawytscha*) that attains an average weight of twenty pounds. Also called **black salmon, California ~, Columbia River ~, fall ~, king ~, quinnat ~, Sacramento ~, sawkwey, spring ~, tschawytscha, tyee ~, winter ~.** (From 1850s) See also **chum, coho, pink salmon,** and **sockeye salmon.** See **salmon** n for a full listing.

Chinook State

■ n A nickname for the state of **Washington.** (From 1890s) Also **Evergreen State.**

chip

■ n Short for **poker chip.** A round token representing a specific denomination of money, used as a betting device in gambling games. (From 1870s)

chip board

■ n See **Malibu board.**

chiquita

■ n The diminutive form of chica; little girl; a term of endearment. (From 1860s, Spanish)

chivarras

■ n A type of **chaps** (q.v. for a complete listing) made of goatskin. The hair is worn on the outside. (From 1890s, Spanish, perhaps from *chiva* 'goat'?) See also **angoras, hair pants.**

chocho

■ n Also spelled *choch.* A boy. Used in Oregon, Nevada, and Idaho in areas influenced by the Basque language. (From 1960s, Basque)

choker

■ n In logging, a cable with a loop in one end and a hook on the other. Used for encircling a log, then pulling it into place. (From 1900s)

cholla

■ /CHOH yuh/ n Also spelled *choya.* Also called **jumping cholla, staghorn cholla, tree cholla.** Any of a variety of spiny cacti that have easily breakable joints; especially *Opuntia cholla.* (From 1850s, Spanish)

cholo

■ /CHO loh/ n 1. A Mexican-American man, usually young, perhaps with Spanish-Indian blood. Often a member of a group known loosely as **pachucos** or **lowriders.** The term is often a term of address or reference among such young people, but a derogatory term when used by outsiders. (From 1880s, Spanish) A female in such a group is usually called **chola.**

chongo

■ n A woman's hair worn in a bun or topknot. (From 1960s, Spanish)

chopper gun

■ n A special spray gun used in laying down predetermined lengths of fiberglass and resin on a surfboard blank to build the shape of the board. (From 1970s)

chopping horse

■ n Also called a **cutting horse.** A horse especially trained by its rider to separate a specific cow from a bunch. (From 1910s)

chorizo

■ /choh REE soh/ n A type of sausage made with pork and peppers that has a reddish color due to the particular red peppers and cumin in the mix. (From 1960s, Spanish)

chouse

■ v Originally, to handle cattle roughly, as on a drive; now, to be rude or rough in behavior. (From 1900s)

chow

■ n Food; a meal. (From 1850s, perhaps from a pidgin word influenced by a Chinese language, first around Sacramento, which had a large Chinese population)

chowchow

■ n A relish made of chopped pickles and vinegar and spices. (From 1850s, Chinese/English pidgin in California)

chubasco

■ n 1. A strong wind or squall from the south, off the coast of Mexico (from 1940s, Spanish). 2. Among surfers, a large swell or wave that comes in from the south, driven by a storm off the Baja Peninsula (from 1970s).

chuck

■ n 1. Food carried for cowhands or sheepherders who are to be away from the ranch overnight (from

1900s). 2. Also called **salt chuck, skookum chuck.** In the Northwest, a body of water, often saltwater, that floods into or out of a tidal basin. (From 1890s, Chinook Jargon)

chuck box

■ n Also called **chuck block.** A large box that is fitted on the back of a wagon that has numerous compartments filled with cooking utensils and food bins. Used by sheepmen and cattlemen when men will be working away from the ranch buildings overnight. (From 1900s)

chuck house

■ n A cookshack on a ranch where meals are prepared for large numbers of workers. Often a separate building that is used during labor-intensive periods like roundup or harvesttime. By extension, a boardinghouse for itinerant workers. (From 1900s)

chuck wagon

■ n 1. The wagon that carries the **chuck box** (from 1890s). 2. Also called **chuck wagon buffet.** A dining area featuring a large number of dishes, including beans and barbecued chicken and beef. Often the restaurant decorates the room in a western motif. The patron pays at the door and is allowed to eat as much as desired. (From 1950s)

chuckwalla

■ n Also spelled *chuckawalla.* A lizard native to the Southwest that is eight- to twelve-inches long and up to seven inches in circumference; the *Sauromalus obesus.* (From 1890s)

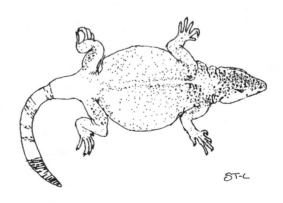

ST-L

chum

■ n Short for **chum salmon.** Also called **calico salmon, dog salmon.** A salmon found up many rivers of the Pacific Northwest, British Columbia, and Alaska. The mature fish is splotchy or mottled in appearance, weighs eight to ten pounds and has a pale, though tasty flesh. The fish is *Oncorhynchus keta*. (From 1900s, Chinook Jargon 'mottled, spotted') See **salmon** n for a complete listing.

Church of Jesus Christ of Latter-day Saints

■ n Official name of the Mormon church founded in 1830 by Joseph Smith.

chy

■ n In Alaska, a reference to tea by the cup or in reference to the meal or snack that accompanies tea. The custom of having tea and a snack was adopted early from Russian settlers and is similar to English "teatime." (From 1860s, Russian *chay*)

cienega

■ /SIN nih guh/ n A marshy tract of land, usually an acre or less in size, created by water seeping from underground on the side of a slightly slanting hillside. The term occurs in many western place-names. (From 1840s, Spanish *ciénaga* 'marsh, swamp')

cilantro

■ /sih LON troh/ n Also called **Chinese parsley.** A Southwestern name for coriander. Much used in **salsa** and Southwestern cookery. (From 1960s, Spanish)

cinch

■ n The bellyband or strap used to hold a saddle or pack on a mule or horse. (From 1860s, Spanish *cincha*)

cinch

■ v To tighten the bellyband or strap of a saddle on a mule or horse. (From 1870s)

cinnamon bear

■ n A color phase of the black bear, called by different writers *Ursus americanus* or *Euarctos americanus*. (From 1820s) See also **blackie.**

cioppino

■ /chuh PEE noh/ n A stew made with clams, mussels, shrimp, and other shellfish, along with fish, tomatoes, and spices. (From 1950s, Italian, developed in the many Italian seafood restaurants in the San Francisco area)

circle

■ n The area circumscribed by a group of cowboys when gathering cattle into a herd. (From 1880s)

circle horse

■ n A horse selected for stamina and endurance, rather than training, to participate in the initial stages of a cattle **roundup.** (From 1940s)

circus beetle

■ n Also called **pinacate bug.** A beetle found in the Southwest, about an inch long, that stands almost vertically when disturbed; the *Eleodes armata.* (From 1950s)

City, The

■ n A nickname for San Francisco. In northern California, especially, but throughout most of the West, San Francisco has been "The City" since the 1850s. That the term is also applied to the commercial section of London does not bother Californians. Natives in the Bay Area claim to be scandalized when confronted with the dreaded nickname, **Frisco.**

civet cat

■ n Also spelled *civic cat, civvy cat.* A term most frequently used in the West, though recognized elsewhere, for a skunk or a polecat. (From 1950s) The word is a term for an Old World animal, but was adopted in the West for a different creature.

claim

■ n A piece of land taken by a miner or prospector for the mineral rights under the surface, in accordance with mining law. (From 1850s) See also **above, below** postnoun modifier.

claim jumper

■ n A person who takes by force another's piece of property for the mineral rights on it. By extension, any person or animal that encroaches on another's territory. (From 1840s)

clam gun

■ n Along the Northwest coast, a facetious name for a shovel. (From 1920s)

clapweed

■ n Also called **Mormon tea.** A western shrub, *Ephedra antisyphilitica,* supposedly useful in the treatment of venereal disease when boiled with water and taken internally. (From 1930s, *clap* 'gonorrhea') See also **Brigham tea, canatillo.**

Clark's

■ poss As the first element in certain western species of birds first described in the journals of

William A. Clark in his expeditions or named after him: *Clark's crow, ~ grebe, ~ nutcracker.* (From 1810s)

cleanup

■ n 1. In a mining operation, the process of extracting the valuable mineral from the debris, gravel, and mud in sluices or at the stamping mill (from 1860s). 2. The mineral, usually gold, extracted from the process (from 1930s).

cliff dweller

■ n Historical. The people who once lived in the elaborately carved-out and constructed houses found high up on cliff sides in the Southwest. The descendants of these people are the modern Pueblo Indians. (From 1880s)

close-herd

■ v Originally, to keep a group of cattle in a compact bunch. Compare **loose-herd.** Now extended to mean keeping any small group tightly together: students, dancers, prisoners, audience, etc. (From 1870s in original sense; 1880s in extended sense)

closeout

■ n In surfing, a wave that breaks along its entire length at one time. (From 1970s)

coachwhip

■ n Short for **coachwhip cactus.** Another name for the **ocatillo** (q.v. for a complete listing). (From 1910s)

coachwhip snake

■ n See **whipsnake.**

coarse gold

■ n Grains or small nuggets of gold, distinct from gold dust. (From 1840s) Compare **fine gold, flour gold.**

Coast, the

■ n A reference to the West Coast, but more specifically, to the Los Angeles/Hollywood area or to San Francisco. (From 1950s, when more regular and faster travel, especially from the East, became available to business executives and people in the movie industry)

cohab

■ n Short for *cohab*itant. A person who lives in a polygamous marriage. Formerly applied to any Mormon found guilty of polygamy, now used in reference to polygamists in Utah, along the Utah/Arizona border, and near the U.S./Mexico border. (From 1880s)

coho

■ n Short for **coho salmon.** Also called **Arctic trout, hookbill, hooknose, hoopid salmon, quisutch, silver salmon, skowitz.** A light-red-fleshed fish (*Oncorhynchus kisutch*) that attains an average weight of seven pounds. It is elongated, with metallic blue back and silver color on the sides and underneath. (From 1880s, Musquam) See also **jack salmon.** See **salmon** n for a complete listing.

coho clam

■ n See **horse clam.**

cojones

■ /kuh HO nees/ n Courage, often of a reckless and daring nature. (From 1960s, Spanish 'testicles')

colcha

■ n A bedspread or coverlet, often with an intricate design reminiscent of Southwestern pottery. (From 1930s, Spanish)

colchon

■ n A thin mattress, often narrow enough to serve as a pad for a straight-backed chair or rocking chair. (From 1850s, Spanish)

cold deck

■ n A specially prepared pack of cards introduced into a card game for purposes of cheating. Used also as a verb. (From 1850s)

cold-jawed

■ adj Descriptive of a horse, referring to an insensitive mouth, thus making the horse difficult to control with a bit, or referring to a horse getting the bit between the teeth and not responding to the rider's pulling on the reins. Also **cold jaw** used as a noun and **cold-jaw** as a verb. (From 1930s)

cold shut

■ n A link in a metal chain that can be closed by hammering and perhaps inserting a pin through the two ends of the link. (From 1870s, referring to the fact that the link of chain is closed without heat, the normal fashion for closing a link of chain)

colear

■ /koh lee AR/ v Also spelled *colea, colliar*. Originally, to throw a bull to the gound by grabbing its tail; now, to grab a bull, calf, or goat by the tail as part of a chasing game on a ranch. (From 1840s)

colemanite

■ n The most common source of borax and boracic acid is this hydrous borate of calcium, found in Death Valley. (From 1915, after W. T. Coleman, leader of a San Francisco vigilance committee)

Colorado

■ n Also called **Centennial State.** Thirty-eighth state of the Union. Settled in 1858, it became a territory in 1861, and a state in 1876. Capital: Denver. From the Colorado River, named by Spanish explorers for the color of its water. The sonorous name of the distant river was proposed, among many alternatives, because the river's source was in the territory, even though the branch upriver of the junction with the Green River was known as the Grand River at the time. The upper branch was renamed in 1921 to conform with the name of the state. (From 1859; Spanish, "reddish brown") See also **Jefferson Territory.**

Colorado

■ n 1. Used as the first element in names of birds with special varieties found in the state: *Colorado raven, ~ turkey.* A *Colorado mockingbird* is a jocular name for a **burro** (q.v. for a list of other names). 2. Used as the first element in names of insects with special varieties found in the state: *Colorado beetle, ~ bug, ~ potato beetle, ~ potato bug.* 3. Used as the first element in names of plants with special varieties found in the state: *Colorado bee plant, ~ blue grass, ~ blue spruce, ~ blue stem, ~ bottom grass, ~ fir, ~ grass, ~ hemp, ~ white fir.*

Columbia

■ n As the first element in the names of creatures with varieties found in the Columbia River Basin: *Columbia ground squirrel, ~ jay, ~ owl, ~ sharp-tailed grouse.*

Columbia River salmon

■ n Another name for the **Chinook salmon.** (From 1880s) See **salmon** n for a complete listing.

Columbia River smelt

■ n The **eulachon,** or **candlefish.** A food fish that grows to about twelve inches long and is caught in

February and early March in the Columbia River system. (From 1920s)

comadre ■ /koh MAH dray/ n A godmother; a sponsor at baptism; less formally, a mother's best friend and "aunt" to her best friend's children. (From 1830s, Spanish)

comal ■ n A slightly concave griddle, formerly of stone or earthenware, but now usually metal, used for cooking **tortillas.** (From 1840s, Nahuatl, via Spanish)

compadre ■ n Originally, a godfather; now a close male friend or companion. (From 1830s, Spanish)

compañero ■ /kohm pan YAY roh/ n A companion; a close male friend; a male partner. (From 1840s) The less-frequently used **compañera** means specifically a female friend, a mistress to a male)

compass cactus ■ n A form of **barrel cactus** (q.v. for a complete listing) that leans southwest toward the afternoon sun. (From 1960s)

compie ■ n Shortened from *comp*osition. Also spelled *comp.* A marble made of porcelain or of clay that is glazed. (From 1950s)

Comstock ■ n The region around Virginia City, Nevada, named for Henry Tompkins Paige Comstock, who located the site of a large silver and gold field in 1859, but who sold his portion for a pittance. Hence, **Comstock lode, Comstocker.**

concha ■ n Also **choncho.** A silver ornament, originally shell-shaped, attached to fancy cowboy dress: hat, belt, **chaps,** and horse tack. (From 1880s, Spanish 'shell')

coney

■ n Also called **starved rat.** A small animal about the size of a guinea pig found mainly in Colorado; a pika. (From 1870s)

cony

■ n Also spelled *coney, coony.* Frequently called **shee.** A sport fish found in fresh water in Alaska and Siberia that weighs thirty to sixty pounds. (From 1930s, shortened from French *poisson inconnu* 'fish unknown')

coppery whipsnake

■ n See **whipsnake.**

cordillera

■ /kor dee YEH ruh/ n A range of mountains or mountain systems; specifically applied to the **Rocky Mountains** of the United States and Canada. (From 1800s, Spanish) Also as adjective, **cordilleran.**

cork

■ v In Northwest ocean-fishing, to obstruct the seines of another boat by letting out a seine uptide from it, cutting off the fish that would have drifted into its nets. (From 1900s)

corral

■ n A pen or enclosure made of boards, logs, timber, or wire for horses, cows, sheep, and other livestock. (From 1820s, Spanish) Also used as a verb.

corral snake

■ n Another name for a **king snake.** A brown and yellow nonpoisonous snake found around corrals where rodents often find refuge. (From 1960s)

corrugate

■ n A small irrigation ditch or furrow leading off from a large **irrigation ditch** bordering a field. Used mainly in Idaho and Colorado. (From 1960s) See also **primary ditch.** Also used as a verb.

cottontop cactus

■ n A short, round cactus, *Echinocactus polycephalus,* marked by white tufts around the base and on the fruit. (From 1940s) See **barrel cactus** for a complete listing.

cougar

■ n Also called **mountain lion, puma.** The large, wild feline that grows thirty to forty inches high, weighs up to sixty pounds, is tawny yellow in color, and is carnivorous. (From 1800s)

Coulter pine

■ n The large-cone pine of southern California. The cones grow up to fourteen inches and weigh ten pounds or more. (From 1880s, after Thomas Coulter)

counterbrand

■ n An identifying mark put next to the original brand on cattle that have been sold. The new mark was originally made with a branding iron, but now may be made with paint or a dye. (From 1850s) See also **cross-brand, road brand.** Compare **burnt brand.**

cow

■ n As the first element in a number of compounds related to cattle raising: *cow boss, ~ brand, ~ call, ~ camp, ~ country, ~girl, ~hand, ~ horse, ~ hunt, ~ hunter, ~man, ~ outfit, ~ people, ~poke, ~ pony, ~ prod, ~ prodder, ~puncher* (see **puncher**)*, ~ ranch, ~ range, ~ saddle, ~ stable, ~ thief, ~ town, ~ trail, ~ waddy* (see **waddy**)*, ~ work.*

cowboy

■ n As the first element in a number of compounds relative to ranch work or people who dress like the movie version of ranch hands: *cowboy boots, ~ hat, ~ land, ~ levis, ~ movie, ~ pen, ~ poet, ~ reunion, ~ saddle, ~ song, ~ suit.*

cowichan sweater

■ n A bulky sweater knitted by natives of western British Columbia. The sweaters have a very high lanolin content and are often worn in rainy and misty weather with no other covering. (From 1950s)

cow parsnip

■ n See **wild celery.**

coyote

■ /KYE oat, kye OH tee/ n 1. A small wolf, *Canis latrans,* found throughout the West; a carnivore that preys on small animals, snakes, birds and their eggs, and sometimes on lambs or small sheep. The animal is very important to the culture of most western Native American groups (from 1820s, Nahuatl *coyotl* via Spanish). 2. In mining, a shallow excavation or short tunnel dug into a hillside (from 1850s). Also used as a verb in the mining sense. 3. A slang term for a smuggler or guide who leads illegal immigrants across the southwestern border of the United States (from 1980s). 4. As the first element in a number of compounds that have a metaphoric extension of characteristics of the animal: *coyote berry,* a type of wild currant found in arid areas of eastern Oregon and Washington (from 1960s); ~ *bush,* ~ *brush,* an evergreen shrub, *Baccharis pilularis,* found mainly in arid regions in California (from 1920s); ~ *cactus,* another name for **prickly pear,** *Opuntia leptocaulis* (from 1930s); ~ *dog,* a dog related to or exhibiting characteristics of the coyote (from 1860s); ~ *farming,* drilling wheat into marginally productive soil, then depending on regular rainfall to produce some crop (from 1960s); ~ *gold,* very fine gold dust taken from near the surface of a shallow dig (from 1850s); ~ *hole,* ~ *diggings,* in mining, small drift tunnels that run horizontally in several directions from the bottom of a shaft excavated to a depth of twenty or so feet (from 1850s); ~ *house,* a dugout house or excavated cellar covered with boards (from 1870s); ~ *melon,* another name for the calabacilla desert gourd (from 1900s); ~ *thistle,* another name for the weed, button snakeroot, found in arid California and Oregon areas (from 1920s); ~ *tobacco,* a wild tobacco, *Nicotiana trigonophylla* (from 1910s); ~ *well,* a desert spring, usually small and hard to find (from 1930s); ~ *willow,* another name for the sandbar willow found along dry washes in arid regions of the West (from 1960s).

crazy weed

■ n See **white loco.**

creek poacher

■ n In the Northwest, a person who illegally sets nets at the mouth of a stream to capture salmon returning to their spawning grounds. (From 1950s)

creek robber

■ n Another name for **creek poacher.** (From 1980s) Hence, the activity, **creek robbing.**

creek seining

■ n The activity of a **creek poacher.** (From 1950s)

creosote bush

■ n Another name for **greasewood.** Also called **creosote brush.** Often shortened to **creosote.** A resinous shrub found in arid regions of the Southwest, outside of alkaline areas. The bush has dark wood, small and shiny bright green leaves, and small yellow flowers. The strong chemical smell recalls the phenolic compounds distilled from beech-wood tar called "creosote," and this may be why it is so called. Different forms of the shrub are *Larrea tridentata* and *L. divaricata.* The resinous bark and stem are sometimes boiled into a tea for folk medicines. (From 1840s, Greek *kreas* 'flesh' + *sōtēr* 'preserve') See also **hediondilla, toroso.**

cricket stomper

■ n A derogatory term for a Mormon. Used mainly in Idaho. (From 1950s) Compare **carrot eater.**

cross-brand

■ v To place a brand over or next to a brand already on a cow, indicating that the cow has been sold. Sometimes done illegally. (From 1870s) See also **counterbrand, road brand.** Compare **burnt brand.**

cross fox

■ n In Alaska, a color phase of the red fox, *Vulpes vulpes,* in which a dark band of fur runs down the back and is crossed by another dark band of fur across the shoulders. (From 1870s)

crossroader

■ n A cheater who moves from one gambling establishment to another, looking for opportunities to cheat. Mainly used in Nevada and Southern California. (From 1950s)

cuidado

■ /kwee THOU/ excl A warning; literally, "watch out, look out, beware." (From 1840s, Spanish)

cui-ui

■ /KWEE wee/ n A round-bodied, slender sucker-fish that is found in northern Nevada and used as a subsistence food by Indians in the region. *Chasmistes cujus* is black-skinned when found in Pyramid Lake, gray-skinned in Lake Winnemucca. Both varieties grow to about twenty inches long. (From 1870s, Northern Piute *kuyui*)

cuitan

■ n In the Pacific Northwest, an Indian pony. (From 1920s, Chinook Jargon)

culinary water

■ n In Utah, potable water, as distinct from untreated water used only for **irrigation.** (From 1980s, though the term may have been used as early as the 1880s)

cultus

■ adj Also spelled *kultus.* Worthless, bad, useless. (From 1840s, Chinook Jargon)

cultus cod

■ n A ling cod, *Ophiodon elongatus,* found along the Pacific coast from Santa Barbara to Alaska. Though the name means "worthless" in Chinook Jargon, it is an important food fish. (From 1880s)

currant

■ n Any of a variety of wild berry bushes, but especially *Berberis trifoliata,* found in marshy areas in Texas. (From 1910s) See **barberry** for a complete listing.

cutter

■ n Also called **cutter-out.** The cowboy who separates cattle from the herd, one by one. (From 1910s)

cutthroat trout

■ n Also called **mountain trout.** *Salmon clarkii* is distinguished by a red mark under the jaw, near the gills. Found especially at higher elevations and in colder streams and lakes, it has firm flesh and a delicate taste. See also **rainbow trout, speckled trout, Yellowstone trout.**

cutting horse

■ n Also called **chopping horse.** A horse trained to cut cattle from a herd, a maneuver requiring a well-trained animal. (From 1880s)

D

dab

■ v To throw the loop of a **lariat** or **lasso** and catch the target. (From 1920s)

dago red

■ n Originally, wine made at home for domestic consumption. As the term spread eastward, it picked up the connotation of cheap red wine. (From 1900s, *dago* 'Italian or Spaniard,' usually considered derogatory)

dalea

■ n A plant of the pea family with usually purplish blooms, found in arid regions of the West. (From 1890s, after Samuel Dale, English botanist and pharmacologist, 1659–1739)

Dall sheep

■ n Also **Dall's sheep.** A white mountain sheep found mainly in Alaska and the Yukon Territory. *Ovis dalli* is considered a prized gaming trophy by hunters. (From 1880s, after William H. Dall, 1845––1927)

dally

■ n Also called a **dally welta, dally welter.** A looping of rope around a saddle horn or a post to act as a brake. The earlier method of using a **lariat** was to tie the end of the rope to the saddle horn or post before lassoing the animal. Hence, by extension, to move or go slowly, as if a brake had been applied (from 1910s, Spanish *dale vuelta* 'give a turn!'). Also used as a verb (from 1920s). As an adj: **dally man, dally roper** is a cowboy who uses the method to slow a lassoed animal (from 1930s).

damp

■ adj Referring to the condition in some towns in Alaska in which alcoholic beverages may be possessed by citizens, or imported by them, but not resold. A condition between "wet," in which alcoholic beverages are retailed, and "dry," in which those beverages are not allowed at all. (From 1980s)

dancing devil

■ n In the Southwest, a small whirlwind or **dust devil** that blows across a dusty land surface, raising a dust funnel up to fifty feet high. (From 1930s) See also **sand spout.**

Danite

■ n Also called **Big Dan, Daughters of Zion, Danite Band, Danite Society.** A member of a secret society supposedly organized within the Mormon church to silence dissenters. Now believed historical. (From 1830s, allusion to Genesis xlix:17 "Dan shall be serpent by the way, an adder in the path") See also **avenging angel, Destroying Angel.**

datil

■ n Also called **banana yucca, Spanish bayonet.** A desert succulent that produces a fruit similar to a date. The plant is *Yucca baccata.* (From 1880s, Spanish *dátil* 'date')

Daughters of Zion

■ n See **Danite.**

daveno

■ n In the Northwest, especially in Washington and Idaho, a piece of furniture on which two or three people can sit; a davenport; a couch with arms. (From 1950s)

day herd

■ n A group of cattle separated from a main herd for a special reason, for shipping, branding, etc. (From 1880s) Also used as a verb, **day-herd.**

dead man's hand

■ n In **poker,** a hand with a pair of aces and a pair of eights. So called because it was the hand held by Wild Bill Hickok when he was shot by Jack McCall in the Mann-Lewis saloon in Deadwood, South Dakota on August 2, 1876.

death camas

■ n Also called **wild onion.** A poisonous root, *Zygadenus venenosus,* common to the West. Resembles camas root, or **wild hyacinth,** much sought as a food staple. (From 1880s)

deerbrush　■ n See **blueblossom.**

Denali　■ n The official state name of former Mount McKinley in **Alaska,** the tallest mountain in North America, at 20,320 feet. Opposition to the name change in federal documents has been by a representative in the Ohio congressional delegation, who argues that, although McKinley had nothing to do with the mountain or with Alaska, McKinley was from the representative's hometown of Canton. (From 1960s, Koyukon *Deenaalee* 'the high one')

Denver mud　■ n A patent medicine found mainly in the Rocky Mountains, consisting of a treated mud used as a poultice in a cloth wrapping placed on the chest to break up congestion. (From 1950s)

Denver omelet　■ n An omelet made with eggs, chopped onions, green peppers, ham, and sometimes tomatoes. Often cooked solid and served as a sandwich. (From 1920s)

deseret　■ n 1. A honeybee (from 1830s, Book of Mormon). 2. Capitalized: Utah Territory, especially the Salt Lake Valley (from 1840s). 3. As "State of Deseret," originally proposed as the name for the state of **Utah** (from 1850s). See also **Beehive State.**

Deseret alphabet　■ n A symbol system of forty-one characters based on the sounds of English as spoken in the Salt Lake Valley in the 1850s. Offered as an alphabet to supplant the standard English alphabet, the Deseret alphabet is now a historical artifact. (From 1850s) Apparently invented by George D. Watt, an Englishman and Mormon convert.

desert　■ n 1. As the first element in the names of birds and animals found in arid western regions: *desert ant,* ~ *blackthroat sparrow,* ~ *brush rat,* ~ *deer mouse,* ~ *gray fox,* ~ *mule deer* (see **burro deer, mule deer**), ~ *pocket rat,* ~ *quail,* ~ *song sparrow,* ~ *sparrow,* ~ *sparrow hawk,* ~ *tortoise,* ~ *woodrat.* 2. As the first element in plants found in arid western regions: *desert almond,* ~ *bush,* ~ *catalpa,* ~ *cedar,* ~ *flowering willow,* ~ *holly,* ~ *juniper,* ~ *lily,* ~

mistletoe, ~ oak, ~ peach, ~ saltbush, ~ tea, ~ trumpet, ~ weed, ~ willow.

desert canary

■ n Also called **desert canary bird.** A jocular reference to a **burro** (q.v. for a listing of other names), especially a wild burro found throughout the Southwest. The harsh bray of the wild burro invites a comparison to the sweet song of birds. (From 1920s)

desert rat

■ Originally a prospector or miner who lived in the desert, now anyone who lives in the desert away from population centers or who frequents the desert and spends long periods of time alone in the desert. (From 1900s) Compare **bushy.**

desert varnish

■ n Also called **desert pavement, desert polish.** A polished and hardened film, blackish brown in color, that covers the surface and rocks in desert regions, thought to be the result of a chemical, or chemico-microbiological formation. (From 1900s)

desk-top publishing

■ n A process by which a standard office computer can be used to set material for brochures, magazines, and books without resorting to typographers and printing concerns. (From 1970s, coined by Paul Brainerd, president of Aldus Corporation of Seattle)

Destroying Angel

■ n Also called **Destroying Band.** Another of the alleged secret militant organizations among Mormons. Now referred to only historically. (From 1830s) See also **avenging angel, Danite.**

devilfish

■ n One of a variety of sculpins found in Alaskan waters. (From 1900s) See also **bullhead, Irish lord.**

devil's head

■ n A variety of cactus that is round and squat, especially *Echinocactus horizonthalonius.* (From 1930s) See **barrel cactus** for a complete listing.

devil snow

■ n Same thing as **diamond dust.** Fine ice crystals that are formed when a layer of cold air settles above a layer of warm air, freezing moisture in the warmer air, which precipitates out. Often the sky is cloudless when this meteorological phenomenon occurs. (From 1970s)

devil's pincushion ■ n A short, round cactus; specifically, *Echinocactus polycephalus*. (From 1900s) See **barrel cactus** for a complete listing.

dewberry ■ n See **nagoonberry.**

dewlap ■ n A strip of skin under the neck of cattle that was cut and allowed to hang as an identifying mark on range cattle. The term has been in English since the 1400s, but the system of marking cattle seems to have begun in the American West in the 1880s. See also **jinglebob.**

diamondback ■ n A rattlesnake with a diamond pattern on the back, usually growing to five feet in length; *Crotalus adamanteus.* (From 1890s)

diamond dust ■ n Same thing as **devil snow.** (From 1970s)

dicho ■ n A saying or proverb. (From 1890s, Spanish)

dime, get off the ■ phrase A command or order to get busy, to move, to do something; mainly California use. (From 1920s)

dinero ■ n Money. Considered slang or colloquial. (From 1850s, Spanish)

dingleberry ■ n Also **dangleberry.** A slightly derogatory term for a person who is incompetent or difficult to deal with. (From 1950s) Apparently from reference to the clots of dung hanging from hairs near the anus of sheep, implying incompetence at self-cleaning.

dingy ■ /DING ee/ adj Foolish or silly; a bit unbalanced or eccentric. (From 1910s)

discovery claim ■ n Also shortened to **discovery.** Originally in the Yukon, now general to the Northwest, the first claim made on a stream or creek when gold is found. (From 1890s) See also **above, below** post-noun modifier.

ditch rider ■ n A person who watches over an **irrigation** system, keeps channels clear and open, and measures water allotted to users. (From 1900s)

dobe ■ /DOH bee/ n Also spelled *dobie, doby.* Shortened form of **adobe.** 1. Building block made of mixed straw and clay and dried in the sun (from 1830s, Spanish). 2. A building or structure made from such building blocks (from 1860s). 3. A Mexican dollar or peso. Now historical (from 1910s). 4. A clay marble (from 1920s).

dog bootie ■ n Also called **bootie, dog moccasin, moccasin.** In Alaska and the Yukon Territory, leather coverings put on the feet of **sled dogs** to prevent sores on rough trails. (From 1900s as dog moccasin; from 1980s as dog bootie)

dog box ■ n A large plywood box mounted on a pickup truck, with individual compartments for transporting a **dog team.** (From 1970s)

dog derby ■ n A **dogsled** race. (From 1930s) See also **Iditarod.**

dog driver ■ n Same as **dog musher.** A person who keeps a dog team and travels over snow and ice on a **dogsled.** (From 1910s, though **dog driving** is from 1880s)

dogfish ■ n Also called **dog salmon, calico salmon, chum.** A subsistence fish that grows to eight to ten pounds; *Oncorhynchus keta.* Because of its general availability, it was used extensively as dog food. (From 1910s) See **salmon** n for a complete listing.

dogie ■ n 1. A calf, especially one without a mother (from 1880s). 2. By extension, a lamb without a mother (from 1920s).

dog moccasin ■ n See **dog bootie.**

dog driver,
dog musher

dog musher
■ n Same as **dog driver.** (From 1910s; **dog mushing** dates from 1920s) See also **musher.**

dog salmon
■ n Also called **dogfish, calico salmon, chum.** A common salmon often caught for dog food before salmon became a general delicacy and was renamed officially the chum salmon. (From 1860s) See **salmon** n for a complete listing.

dogsled
■ n Also spelled *dog sled, dog sledge.* A small snow vehicle with runners designed to be pulled by a team of dogs. (From 1800s)

dog team
■ n A group of dogs trained to pull a sled through snow and ice. (From 1850s)

dog tooth salmon
■ n Any of a variety of salmon that are close to spawning. So called from the distinctive hook that grows on the snout of a spawning salmon. (From 1850s) See **salmon** n for a complete listing.

Dolly Varden
■ n A spotted trout of the Rocky Mountain country and the Pacific Northwest, marked by scarlet dots near the gills and similar in appearance to the **cut-throat trout.** (From 1870s, in reference to a brightly dressed character of that name in Charles Dickens's *Barnaby Rudge*)

doney
■ n In Colorado mainly, a round and smooth stone fit for throwing. (From 1940s, perhaps influenced by "dornick")

double cinch
■ n Also called **double-barreled saddle, double-rigged saddle.** The straps at the front and the rear of a western saddle. (From 1900s) See also **flank girth.** Compare **center fire.**

double jack
■ n In mining, a sledgehammer wielded with two hands. (From 1940s) As a verb, **double-jack,** to work in a team, with one person holding a drill, the other wielding a sledgehammer with both hands. (From 1920s)

dough gut
■ n A calf that has lost its mother and is fed with the cattle. The change in diet causes the body to swell, giving rise to the notion that **dogie** comes from this term. (From 1880s)

Douglas
■ n As the first element in *Douglas fir* (also known as **yellow fir**), ~ *pine,* ~ *spruce,* ~ *spirea,* and ~ *squirrel,* all varieties named for David Douglas, 1798–1834, a Scottish botanical explorer of the Northwest.

dout
■ v Mainly in Utah and Wyoming, to extinguish or put out a fire. (From 1930s, though the term, from *do + out,* has been in English since the 1520s)

down below
■ adv Also shortened to **below.** In Alaska, a reference to the lower forty-eight states. (From 1900s)

downwinder
■ n A person who lived in central or southern Utah during the 1950s and 1960s when above-ground testing of nuclear weapons was frequent at the Nevada Test Site. Radioactive contamination of grassland resulted in cows passing radioactive milk on to human consumers. Many citizens absorbed much higher levels of radiation than nor-

Downwinder.
Above-ground nuclear test at
Frenchman Flats, Nevada
Test Site, 1957

mal, allegedly resulting in increased incidences of leukemia and other cancers. (From 1960s)

drag

■ n 1. The rear section of a herd of cattle or a flock of sheep. 2. A weak or lame cow or sheep that trailed behind the rest of the herd or flock in a drive. (From 1900s)

drag rider

■ n Also **drag driver.** The cowboy who rides at the rear section of a herd of cattle that is being moved. The rider must range back and forth in the dusty trail, forcing the cattle that lag behind because of weakness, illness, or exhaustion to keep up with the rest of the herd. (From 1880s) See also **swing rider.**

drift

■ n 1. Movement of a herd of cattle, especially during a constant wind or a storm. The herd tends to shift downwind and away from the home range (from 1900s). 2. A conglomerate of material which is tunneled into and followed in a mining operation.

drift

■ v 1. To drive cattle slowly (from 1890s). 2. To make a mine tunnel (from 1850s).

drift diggings

■ n In gold mining, placer works used in conjunction with tunnels dug off the main shaft, following conglomerates of material, or **drift.** (From 1900s)

drift fence

■ n A lightweight fence designed to keep cattle from moving off their range during storms or during winter. (From 1900s)

= 91 =

drift log

■ n A dead tree or a log that has come to shore along a stream or river. Mainly used for firewood. (From 1910s)

drill parka

■ n In the Yukon Territory and Alaska, a lightweight, hooded cloth garment, usually white to allow the wearer to blend into the snow background while stalking or hunting. (From 1940s)

drive

■ n The collecting of cattle together in a herd and moving it to another location. (From 1840s)

driver

■ n A cowboy who rounds up cattle and moves them in a herd from one place to another. (From 1880s)

drop band

■ n The group of pregnant ewes and ewes with newborn lambs in a sheep herd. (From 1930s, so called because the pregnant sheep "drop" lambs, and a "band" is smaller than a "herd")

drum ice

■ n Also called **shell ice.** In the Yukon Territory and Alaska, ice forms on a river or lake. Then, if the water recedes under the ice, leaving an air space between the ice and the surface of the water, the result is a sheet of ice that resonates and may shatter under the weight of a man or animal. (From 1930s)

dry

■ n As the first element in *dry farm, ~ farmer, ~ farming.* The process of growing crops and plants with little or no rainwater, using only meager amounts of irrigation water. Initiated by Mormon pioneers and practiced in semiarid regions of the West. (From 1870s)

dry camp

■ n A stopping place in a journey where drinking water must be carried in. Frequently used by Boy Scouts and other campers in western arid regions. (From 1890s)

dryfish

■ n Salmon strips that have been cured by drying in open air or by being smoked. Used for dog food as well as human consumption. (From 1860s)

dry gulch

■ n A twisting ravine with steep sides up to thirty feet high through which rainwater runs after a storm. No natural stream runs in such a place. (From 1870s) See also **arroyo, wash.**

dry-gulch

■ v To be ambushed or shot by someone lying in wait, originally in an area, such as a **wash,** where one's movements are restricted.

dry lander

■ n A farmer who grows crops that are wholly dependent on irrigation water. (From 1920s)

dry meat

■ n Strips of venison cured by drying in the sun during colder months or in an enclosed building. Unlike **jerky,** which is sun-dried at high altitudes, dry meat is cured at any altitude. In the spring or summer, the strips are hung from high rafters or poles inside an enclosure, with enough smoke introduced to keep away insects. (From 1960s)

dry placer machine

■ n Also called **dry washing machine.** In mining, a device used to hold material dug from a mine while air is blown through it to remove the lighter dust, dirt, and debris. The remaining small amount of material can then be transported to a water supply where rocks and gravel can be removed, leaving only the heavier gold or silver. (From 1850s)

duck

■ n One or two stones set atop a larger one to mark a trail for those coming after. Used by hikers, climbers, and Boy Scouts. (From 1920s, from the fact that two smaller rocks atop a larger one often resemble a duck)

duckfoot

■ n A farming implement with flanged disks resembling a splayed duck foot. Used for cultivating ground. (From 1880s)

dude

■ n An Easterner, usually a fancy dresser, who vacations on a ranch in the West. (From 1880s) The original term may have given rise to a variety of words relating to highly dressed individuals who are newcomers or naive: **dudedom, dudeness, dudery, dudess, dudie, dudine, dudish, dudism,** all from 1880s.

dude ranch

■ n A ranch, sometimes a working ranch, that takes in boarders as paying guests and provides entertainment in horseback riding, cowpunching, and camping out in nice weather. (From 1920s) See also **guest ranch.**

dude wrangler

■ n A cowboy who works on a **dude ranch,** caring for the horses used by guests, leading rides, performing ranch chores. The term plays off the concept of cow **wrangler** (one who wrangles cows). A dude wrangler is one who wrangles **dudes.**

dueno

■ /DWAY noh/ n A proprietor or owner, especially of a general store, restaurant, or other small business. (From 1910s, Spanish *dueño*)

dugout

■ n A shelter scraped from the side of a hill, often with a door frame and door attached to the front. Often used for storing potatoes and root vegetables. (From 1860s)

dugway

■ n A sloping road or path cut from a steep bank, perpendicular to a river or stream that has high sides. (From 1880s, used also as a place-name in Utah)

dulce

■ /DULL see/ n 1. A piece of candy or other sweet refreshment (from 1840s, Spanish 'sweet'). 2. By extension, a sweetheart or girl friend (from 1910s).

Dungeness crab

■ n A commercially important crab of the Pacific Northwest waters. The *Cancer magister.* (From 1920s, after a town on Juan de Fuca Strait in northwest Washington State)

dust

■ n Shortened form of **gold dust.** (From 1840s)

dust devil

■ n Also called **dancing devil.** A small whirlwind of dust, sometimes reaching one hundred feet high that moves across an arid landscape during hot periods. (From 1880s) See also **sand spout.**

eagle bill

■ n An ornamented tapadero that hoods the front of a stirrup on a western show saddle. The leather hood was originally designed to keep the stirrup from catching in brush, but for highly decorated saddles used in parades the hood, resembling the beak of an eagle, is decorated with silver and hangs nearly to the ground. (From 1950s) In Mexico, the **vaqueros'** term is **tapadera.**

eagle claws

■ n pl A cactus that often carries hooked or curved needles that catch at clothing; *Echinocactus horizonthalonius.* (From 1970s) See **barrel cactus** for a complete listing.

Eagles

■ n pl A fraternal organization founded in Seattle in 1898. Full name: Fraternal Order of Eagles.

ear

■ v 1. To keep a horse under control by holding and twisting its ears. 2. By extension, to get any person's attention; literally, "to catch one's ear." (From 1920s)

earthquake weather

■ n Hot, quiet, humid, and usually overcast weather thought to precede or predict an earthquake, especially in California. (From 1860s)

ear weight contest

■ n Also called **ear pull.** An Eskimo game in which contestants hang up to seventeen pounds in weights on their ears by means of looped string, then see how far they can walk. The record is more than a thousand feet. A spectator sport in Alaska.

Easter daisy

■ n A low-growing plant with a daisylike flower. Typically, *Townsendia exscapus.* The flower is one of the earliest blooms on western slopes and is always out for Easter. (From 1950)

Eastern Slope

■ n Originally, the eastern side of the Sierra Nevada running into Nevada, that drains into the **Great Basin.** Now the eastern side of the **Rocky Mountains**. (From 1860s)

eating fish

■ n In Alaska and the Yukon Territory, fish that is cured and smoked and destined for human consumption, as opposed to fish preserved for dog food. (From 1960s)

Echinocactus

■ n A genus of round or cylindrical cactus with prominent spines. (From 1850s) See **barrel cactus** for a complete listing.

E Clampus Vitus

■ n A mock fraternal organization that was popular in the California mining camps in the 1850s and revived in the 1930s. Any man may be a member, and all members carry card number one. The initiation involves buying drinks for all other members present.

eight-up

■ n A team of eight draft animals for pulling a wagon or stagecoach or the like, often in parades. The most common form; if fewer animals are used, the team may be called "six-up" or even "four-up." (From 1920s)

elder

■ n Among Mormons, a member of the **Melchizedek priesthood.** Generally regarded as a prestigious religious leader in the church hierarchy. (From 1840s)

El Dorado

■ n 1. **El Dorado State,** a nickname for **California** (from 1900s). Also **Eureka State, Golden Bear State, Golden State.** 2. The West, or a place in the West, especially where gold is discovered or thought to be. (From 1830s)

elf owl

■ n A small owl, hardly bigger than a sparrow, found in Arizona and California. *Micropallas whitneyi* feeds on grasshoppers and lizards. (From 1880s)

elk-horn cactus

■ n A many-branched cactus that grows to four feet in height and features branches up to two inches in diameter. The branches appear to be covered with light tan velvet or a furry surface, but are actually stiff spines clustered together that easily penetrate the flesh of a person or animal; *Opuntia acanthocarpa.*

elm fork

■ n A saddle. So called because of the wooden frame used under the western saddle. "Stay in the elm fork" became an admonition or shout of encouragement in any endeavor, not just in bronc riding. (From 1930s)

embarcadero
■ n A landing place for ships, usually a wharf or port, often on a river. Used as a site location in California cities with ports. (From 1880s, Spanish)

emigrant
■ n 1. A person who migrates, especially from the eastern United States to the West or Southwest (from 1780s, but especially from 1840s on). 2. As the first element in a number of terms relative to moving westward: *emigrant road, ~ route, ~ train, ~ wagon.* Also *emigration road* or *train.* (From 1840s) See also **immigration.**

Emmons bear
■ n Another, less frequent, name for the black bear, *Ursus americanus.* (From 1930s) See also **blackie.**

enchilada
■ /en chill ODD duh/ n A **tortilla** rolled up around meat or cheese and chilies, baked in a pan and served with a sauce of tomatoes, chilies, and usually cheese over the top. (From 1890s, Spanish)

encino
■ /en SEE noh/ n Also spelled *encina, encinal.* Any of a variety of **evergreen oaks** or live oak. Also used in place-names in the Southwest. (From 1850s, Spanish)

endowment
■ n In the Mormon church, a course of instruction relative to ordinances and dispensations. (From 1840s)

endowment house
■ n The place or building in which endowment rites take place. (From 1850s)

endowment robe
■ n A special undergarment bestowed on a Mormon during certain church rites, especially marriage, nowadays. (From 1870s) See also **garments.**

Ephraim
■ n Used jocularly as a nickname for a **grizzly bear.** Now historical. (From 1850s)

Equality State
■ n Nickname for **Wyoming.** First state to enfranchise women.

escapement
■ n The salmon that return to the stream of their birth. Used collectively in this sense. (From 1920s)

escusada

■ /ess koo SAH duh/ n A jocular euphemism for a toilet. (From 1960s, Spanish *escusado* 'washroom, toilet')

Eskimo candy

■ n A narrow strip of salmon, cut lengthwise, that has been salted, dried, and smoked. (From 1950s) See **squaw candy** for a complete listing.

Eskimo dog

■ n Any of a variety of double-coated dogs used to pull sleds in snow and ice in the Yukon Territory and Alaska. (From 1860s) See **Alaskan husky** for a complete listing.

Eskimo doughnut

■ n A bread or biscuit fried in seal oil. The precursor of this food was the Inupiaq *muqpauraq*, first made around the turn of the century, when flour was introduced to Alaskan and Yukon natives. (From 1940s) See also **aladik, fry bread.**

Eskimo ice cream

■ n A dish made with tallow or fat, mixed with berries, snow, and sugar, and whipped to the consistency of soft ice cream. The native term is *akutaq*. (From 1910s)

Eskimo potato

■ n Any of a variety of plants that produce edible tubers or roots dug by natives in Alaska and the Yukon Territory and by hunters, campers, and fishermen. The *Hedysarum alpinum* is also known as **Indian potato** and **masu** or **masru.** (From 1950s)

Eskimo yo-yo

■ n A toy consisting of two leather or fur balls attached to strings about sixteen inches long. The object of the game is to make the two balls twirl in opposite directions. (From 1950s)

estafiata

■ /uh STAH fee ah tuh, STAFF ee ah duh/ n A **sagebrush** used as a grazing plant by Southwestern and Mexican sheepherders, especially the *Artemisia frigida*. (From 1910s, Nahuatl *yztauhiatl* via Spanish *estafiate*)

estero

■ /ess TAIR oh/ n The inlet of a river, especially when part of a marshy delta or swamp. (From 1910s)

eulachon

■ /YOO luh kun/ n Also called **candlefish, Columbia River smelt.** A smeltlike food fish that is very

= 98 =

oily and can be burned like a candle. (From 1800s, Chinook Jargon *ulâkân*)

Eureka State

■ n A nickname for **California,** in reference to the motto "Eureka" (I have found it) on the state shield. (From 1860s) Also **El Dorado State, Golden Bear State, Golden State.**

evergreen oak

■ n The live oak found along the central California coast; *Quercus agrifolia.* (From 1840s)

Evergreen State

■ n A nickname for the state of **Washington** in reference to the abundance of evergreen trees in the state. (From 1900s) Also **Chinook State.**

faded midget

■ n A subspecies of the prairie rattlesnake found in eastern Utah, western Colorado, and southwestern Wyoming. *Crotalus viridus concolor* is dusty colored and grows to two feet long. Its bite is poisonous, but not usually fatal. (From 1960s)

fag

■ v Also **fag along.** To ride fast; to leave in a hurry. (From 1920s)

fairground

■ v In a **rodeo,** to rope a calf, throw it to the ground, and tie its feet together. (From 1920s)

falda

■ n Also spelled *valda.* An alluvial fan at the mouth of a canyon, produced by erosion and runoff. The fan spreads out like a cloak across the floor of the valley. (From 1850s, Spanish 'cape')

fall chum

■ n Salmon that enter the Yukon River for spawning in late July and August. (From 1980s) See also **summer chum.** See **salmon** n for a complete listing.

fall salmon

■ n Salmon that are moving back upstream to spawn; usually **chum** or **Chinook salmon.** (From 1850s) See **salmon** n for a complete listing.

falltime

■ n In Alaska, another term for "autumn." (From 1960s, on analogy with *springtime, summertime, wintertime*)

false bedrock

■ n In **gold panning,** a layer of impervious clay that underlies gravels which in turn may contain gold particles. (From 1900s)

false garlic

■ n One of a variety of spring plants found in the Southwest that has a small bulb and a faint odor of onion or garlic when freshly dug. (From 1900s) See also **ajo.**

fan

■ v 1. To hit the flanks of a horse with a hat while riding it. The colorful practice is no longer allowed in **rodeos** (from 1910s). 2. To spin a pistol around the finger several times (from 1900s). 3. To hit the hammer on a revolver repeatedly, causing it to fire rapidly (from 1900s).

fan leaf palm ■ n A western palm tree, *Washingtonia filifera,* that has leaves shaped like the semicircular wedges of a handheld fan. (From 1880s)

fan plant ■ n A variety of the palmetto, found in the Southwest, that grows fan-shaped leaves. (From 1840s)

fandango ■ n 1. A rapid Spanish or Spanish-American dancing style, often accompanied by castanets (from 1800s, Spanish). 2. The rapid music itself, in triple time, for dancing with the castanets (from 1840s). 3. A social gathering, especially in the area of New Mexico, at which dancing was the primary activity; by extension, a rowdy gathering or even a free-for-all brawl. Now historical (from 1840s).

feeder king ■ n Also called **feeder, feeder king salmon.** An immature **king salmon,** one ranging from ten to twenty-five pounds and available to beach fishermen year-round. (From 1980s) See also **salmon** n for a complete listing.

fence cutter ■ n During the range wars of the Southwest in the 1880s, a person who cut the wire fences that surrounded grazing lands. By extension, the term came to refer to a generally law-abiding citizen who resented and broke specific laws "on principle," such as laws concerning grazing rights, water rights, prohibition, and so on. (From 1880s)

fence rider ■ n A person who rides a horse or jeep along the wire fences erected to contain range cattle. The fencer's job is to repair broken wires, replace toppled posts, close gates, and ensure the security of the cattle. (From 1880s) See also **line rider, outrider.**

fernhopper ■ n A jocular name for a logger on the Pacific Northwest coast. The damp forests feature much ground vegetation such as ferns. (From 1950s)

fiador ■ n Also spelled *theodore* by folk etymology. The length of doubled cord or braided horsehair that is attached to the **hackamore** on a horse's head and is tied below the neck. (From 1930s, Spanish) See also **bosal.**

fiesta

■ n A festival or holiday, originally celebrated on a saint's feast day, but now the celebration of any occasion, sometimes lasting for several days. (From 1840s, Spanish)

fifty-four-forty

■ n The degree and second of the parallel marking the boundary between United States and British possessions, from the Rocky Mountains to Puget Sound. The boundary was in dispute and the degree and second became a rallying cry of the Democratic Party during the presidential campaign of 1844. Polk used the slogan, "Fifty-four-forty or Fight," in his successful bid to become president. Historical.

fifty-niner

■ n A participant in the Pike's Peak gold rush in Colorado in 1859. The term was derived from the earlier sobriquet for the **forty-niner** gold miner. Historical.

fine gold

■ n Extremely small particles of gold, found mainly washed down from higher elevations to the flat plains or broader, slowly moving streams. As opposed to **coarse gold** or gold nuggets, whose greater weight keeps them at higher elevations. (From 1840s) See also **flour gold.**

finner

■ n Among salmon fishermen, a salmon that swims close to the surface. Such a fish signals two things: a fish considered good for eating, and one marking a group of salmon just under the surface of the water. (From 1950s)

fire assay

■ n A process for subjecting ore to high heat in order to determine the percentage of gold, silver, and base metals in the mass. (From 1869)

fish burner

■ n Also spelled *fish-burner.* In Alaska, a **sled dog,** especially one used in competitive sled racing. (From 1960s, on analogy with "hayburner," a jocular term for a horse)

fish camp

■ n In Alaska and the Yukon Territory, a seasonal site along a river or shore used by Indians for catching, curing, and storing fish. The camps are used year after year by the same family and have a semi-permanent status. (From 1900s)

fishhawk cactus

■ n A type of cactus with hooked spines; specifically, *Echinocactus wislizeni*. (From 1890s, perhaps a respelling of **fishhook cactus**) See **barrel cactus** for a complete listing.

fishhook cactus

■ n Any of a variety of cactus plants with a bent or hooked spine. Some of the genera of such cacti include *Ancistrocactus, Echinocactus, Ferocactus, Mammillaria*. (From 1870s) See **barrel cactus** for a complete listing.

fish pirate

■ n Also called **salmon pirate, trap pirate.** In Alaska, one who steals salmon from traps placed on streams. Until statehood, large commercial corrals on streams trapped fish until they could be harvested. The fish corrals were guarded by watchmen. More recently, fish corrals are smaller and unguarded. (From 1930s) The term is gradually being replaced by **trap robber.**

fish poisoning

■ n In the Northwest, an infection introduced through cuts on the hands while handling the viscera of fish in the cleaning process. Fishermen and cannery workers often have open cuts that will not heal because the hands are constantly immersed in saltwater. (From 1960s)

fish camp

fish strips

■ n In Alaska and the Northwest, pieces of skinned salmon that have been sliced lengthwise, salted, smoked, and dried. Usually sold commercially. (From 1980s) See **squaw candy** for a full listing.

fish wheel

■ n In Alaska, a large floating device with two baskets mounted on a wheel driven by river current. Salmon are caught up in the baskets and dropped onto a slide leading to a wooden box built on the raft. Farther south (Oregon, California), the device is known as a **salmon wheel.** (From 1900s)

flank girth

■ n The rear cinch on a **double-cinch** saddle. Used especially in **rodeos** on bucking horses to make them buck harder. (From 1920s)

floathouse

■ n In British Columbia and Alaska, a house built on a raft. The dwelling can be moved from place to place until it is finally moved onto land. A careful distinction is made by local people between floathouse and "houseboat." The latter is designed to be much more mobile and is usually not made of wood. (From 1940s)

flour gold

■ n Extremely fine flakes of gold dust. (From 1900s) See also **fine gold.** Compare **coarse gold.**

flunky

■ n Originally in a logging camp, a menial worker who assisted the cook, swept the **bunkhouse,** and performed chores. The term soon came to refer to anyone performing menial labor. (From 1900s)

fly honeysuckle

■ n Any of various types of honeysuckle, but especially *Lonicera canadensis.* (From 1940s) See **bearberry honeysuckle** n for a complete listing.

flying brand

■ n A cattle brand that has a wavy flourish added to it. Usually a letter of the alphabet is given a wavy appearance. (From 1880s)

fofarraw

■ /FOO fuh rah/ Also spelled *foofaraw*. 1. n The trinkets, baubles, and excessive makeup on a woman who acts haughty and vain. Hence, a term of contempt for a "fancy woman" (from 1850s, Spanish *fanfarrón* 'braggart,' perhaps French *fanfaron* 'blusterer'). 2. As an adjective: gaudy;

tawdry; a descriptor of bawdiness, as a **fofarraw house** 'bawdy house, whorehouse' (from 1940s).

fog

■ v 1. To rush, especially to ride a horse rapidly or chase cattle quickly (from 1890s). 2. To fire a gun rapidly, to draw quickly and fire (from 1910s).

fold up

■ v Of a bucking horse in a **rodeo,** to buck repeatedly. (From 1930s)

Folsom point

■ n A flint point from a spear or javelin, originally described from a find in northeastern New Mexico. Found primarily in the High Plains areas of Wyoming, Montana, Texas, and Colorado. The users of the tool are dated to 8,000 B.C. (From 1930s)

fool hen

■ n Any of a variety of easily caught birds, especially the grouse or young quail. (From 1870s)

fool quail

■ n Also called **fool hen, fool bird.** An easily captured Southwestern quail, the *Cyrtonyx montezumae.* The bird has a black and white "clownish" face, but gets its nickname from being easy to snare. (From 1890s)

foot

■ n In mining, twelve inches of an ore vein, regardless of width or depth. Such an amount of ore can be very large if the vein is wide and deep. (From 1860s)

foot burner

■ n Also called **foot warmer.** An old-fashioned, shallow, walking plow. Now replaced by a tractor-drawn plow. (From 1940s)

forefoot

■ v To catch an animal, especially a horse, by throwing the loop of a rope in such a fashion as to catch both front feet. If only one foot is caught, the animal may suffer a broken leg. (From 1920s) See also **blocker, mangana.**

forty-niner

■ n A prospector or miner who participated in the California gold rush in 1849. (From 1850s) See also **fifty-niner.**

fossil ivory

■ n Also called **old ivory.** Mammoth, walrus, and mastodon tusks that have been buried for a long time and stained by earth and water. This material is highly prized by carvers in the northwestern region of North America. (1890s) Compare **green ivory, new ivory.**

four-five-six

■ n A dice game often played in bars and saloons. Normally, five dice are rolled, and three of a kind wins, as does the combination of four, five, and six on three of the dice. (From 1950s)

free gold

■ n Gold that occurs naturally, not bound in ore. Normally, such gold has been freed by erosion of the matrix which held it. (From 1880s)

free range

■ n Also called **free grass.** Unfenced land that belongs to the federal government on which cattle or sheep are allowed to roam, given certain restrictions by the Bureau of Land Management. (From 1910s)

freeze down

■ v In Alaska and the Yukon Territory, to sink a mine shaft in the wintertime. The process involves burning a fire to melt the permafrost, then scooping out the dirt to get to the water table, which is then allowed to freeze before building another fire in the hole. (From 1920s) See also **burn.**

freeze-up

■ n In Alaska and the Yukon Territory, the closing up of rivers and lakes with ice at the beginning of winter. (From 1900s) Compare **breakup.**

freight wagon

■ n A sturdy wagon with large wheels designed to carry heavy loads in the early West. Several oxen were required in each team to draw the wagons. Old wagons are highly prized by modern decorators who want to give a western flavor to the exterior design of buildings and shopping malls. (From 1850s)

Fremont

■ n The first element in the names of several plants and animals named for or discovered by John C. Frémont (1813–1890), early western explorer: *Fremont cottonwood, ~ mahonia, ~ phacelia;* as an adjective: *Fremont's chickaree, ~ nut pine, ~ squirrel;* also *Fremontia.*

French frog

■ n A large frog, especially those considered edible. (From 1960s, perhaps from the belief that frog legs are a French delicacy)

freno

■ /FRAY noh/ n A bit for a horse's mouth; sometime the bridle and the bit together. (From 1930s, Spanish)

fresno

■ n Any of a variety of ash trees of the genus *Fraxinus.* Also used in place-names in the West and Southwest. (From 1910s, Spanish 'ash tree')

frijole

■ /free HO lee/ n In the Southwest, a kidney or pinto bean (from 1830s, Spanish). Used in the plural, the term usually refers to beans cooked into a paste with lard, then reheated for serving with tortillas (from 1950s).

Frisco

■ n A nickname for San Francisco. Derided as a nickname by many inhabitants of that city, who believe it to be a contraction of *San Francisco.* (From 1850s) Perhaps originally a term used by sailors for a place of refreshment. See also **City, The.**

fruit ranch

■ n A large fruit farm, especially in the Southwest; large orchards often owned by a consortium or corporation. (From 1890s)

fruit tramp

■ n An itinerant or migrant worker who moves from place to place in the West, following the harvests. (From 1910s)

fry bread

■ n Also spelled *fried bread.* In the Southwest, a bread prepared by Hopis, Navajos, and others; pieces of dough fried in oil or sauteed or deep fried, sometimes made with baking powder (from 1830s). In Alaska and the Yukon Territory, a bread prepared by native peoples who share the skill with hunters and campers (from 1970s). See also **aladik, Eskimo doughnut.**

fuzztail ■ n Also called a **broomtail.** A range horse; a cowboy's horse. (From 1920s) See also **bronco, mustang.**

Gadsden Purchase ■ n The southern parts of New Mexico and Arizona purchased from Mexico in 1853. The purchase established the northern boundary of Mexico and helped define the boundary of Arizona Territory. (From 1850s) After James Gadsden, 1788–1858, U.S. minister to Mexico.

gaffer ■ n This term has been in English since the fourteenth century, but took on special meaning in the North American West. The **gaff** was a pole with an iron or steel hook used by loggers to snare and maneuver logs in the water and by fisherman to snare large fish and pull them in. The gaffer was the person in charge of the gaff users. Soon the term came to mean foreman or boss of a shift in logging, mining, or fishing operations. Because of the occupations, the term became more frequently used in the West. In the fledgling motion-picture industry in southern California, the gaffer served a similar function as foreman of an operation on a movie set. By the 1920s, the gaffer was an important part of making movies.

gallito ■ n A wildflower in the temperate areas of Califor-

Gadsden Purchase

nia; a violet with a long spur (from 1900s, Spanish 'little rooster'). In Texas, the term is used for a form of prairie coneflower (from 1930s).

galloping goose　　■ n An elongated passenger car or vehicle designed to run on railroad tracks; a dilapidated or shaky piece of rolling stock modified for passenger use on railroad tracks; a rickety trolley car; the term covers any number of steam-, gasoline-, or diesel-driven rail conveyances used in logging and mining country. (From 1940s)

Gambel　　■ n Used as the first element or in possessive form for plants, animals, and especially birds found in the West: *Gambel oak, Gambel's finch, ~ goose, ~ partridge, ~ quail, ~ sparrow, ~ woodmouse.* (From 1850s) After William Gambel, American ornithologist, 1821–1849.

gancho　　■ n A shepherd's crook, used to catch a specific ewe or lamb by hooking it around the neck. (From 1890s, Spanish)

gangline　　■ n Also called **towline.** In **dogsledding,** the main line connected from the front of the sled toward the dog team. This central line is connected to the **bridle** under the front of the sled at the one end, and runs the length of the harnesses for the dogs. (From 1970s) See also **neckline.**

gaper　　■ n Also called **horse clam, Washington clam.** A clam found along the Pacific Northwest coast that is flat, with a rounded and broad back end and with a large gap for siphons. Various clams of the *Tresus* genus are called gapers, and are used both for food and for fish bait. (From 1870s)

garbanzo　　■ n Also called **gabanzo bean.** The chick pea. (From 1840s, Spanish)

garments　　■ n Plural in form, but singular in occurrence. Also called **endowment robe.** A body covering worn under the outer clothing of Mormon faithful who have participated in certain temple ceremonies. The garments feature specific symbols. The wearer is admonished to never be without them, changing into a clean set while still touching the first set. (From 1880s)

gazook

■ n An awkward, clumsy person. The term seems to have moved from the Rocky Mountain area (Wyoming, Utah) in the 1910s eastward. In the 1960s it was found in New York State as well as Utah.

gee pole

■ n A pole six to eight feet long attached to the right side of a dogsled in order to facilitate steering a heavily loaded sled. The dogsled driver moves along the trail, riding in the front of the sled and steering it by means of the pole. (From 1900s) See also **ouija board.**

Gem State

■ n A nickname for **Idaho,** supposedly in reference to the Indian word signifying "Gem of the Mountains." (From 1880s)

gentile

■ n Among the Mormons, one who is not a Mormon. In 1947, *Time* magazine reported that "Salt Lake City is probably the only city in the world where a Jew is a Gentile too." (From 1830s)

geoduck

■ /GWEE duck/ n Also spelled *gooeyduck, gweduck.* Also called **giant clam.** A large clam found along the Pacific coast from Washington to Alaska. *Panope generosa* grows to six or seven inches in diameter, weighs eight or nine pounds, and has a neck four to five feet long. Restaurants serve it as a delicacy (from 1880s, Chinook Jargon). From the 1940s, **geoducking** has been a pastime in which **geoduckers,** armed with shovels, patrol the mud flats, digging for the huge clam.

ghost dance

■ n Originally a ceremonial religious dance among Indians of the **Great Basin,** influenced by the Messiah doctrine. In the 1880s, the performance of the dance and the dancers were associated with notions of insurrection and rebellion. By the 1890s, the dances were thought to be opportunities for gathering together Indians who had nefarious plans for their neighbors' livestock. Into the 1930s, **ghost dancers** were talked about as members of a secret society with its own agenda. In recent years, Indians in the Great Basin area keep their own counsel about **ghost dancing,** and rarely speak to outsiders about the phenomenon.

ghostflower

■ n A form of desert snapdragon with a large, flowing corolla, making it unusual among desert flowers, which normally have small blossoms and petals. The *Mohavea confertiflora* is found in Baja California, Arizona, and Nevada and throughout the Colorado and Mojave Deserts. (From 1940s)

ghost town

■ n An abandoned mining camp or village; a deserted habitation. As gold or silver mines were depleted and abandoned, the towns and encampments were deserted. Often several houses and buildings, some constructed of stone and brick, were left to mark the boom and bust of a mining region. Most such towns were built between 1860 and 1900 and abandoned before 1930. Terms for such towns included **ghost mining camp, ghost city, ghost mining town.** By 1930 the current term, "ghost town," was being used.

giant cactus

■ n Another name for the **saguaro** (q.v. for a complete listing) that grows in the Sonoran Desert of southern Arizona and southeast California. (From 1860s)

giant cedar

■ n Also called **redwood, giant redwood.** The giant arborvita, *Thuja plicata.* The tree attains a height of two hundred feet and a diameter of eighteen feet. Lumber from the tree is desired for fencing because it is durable in any weather. (From 1850s) See also **sequoia.**

giant clam

■ n Another name for **geoduck.** (From 1880s)

Gila

■ n As the first element in a number of place-

= 112 =

names and plants and animals in desert regions of the Southwest: *Gila bat, ~ chipmunk, ~ grass, ~ trout, ~ woodpecker* (see **saguaro woodpecker**). (From 1860s, Yuman 'salty water' via Spanish)

Gila monster

■ n A large poisonous lizard (*Heloderma suspectum*) of the desert area of the Southwest. It grows to two feet long and is stubby in appearance, with its thick tail. It has colorful rings of scales circling its body like shining beads, alternating black with bright orange, yellow, or pink. (From 1870s)

glacier

■ This term has a specialized meaning in Alaska and the Yukon Territory. As a noun and verb, and in the noun form **glaciation,** the term carries the notion of annual forming of layers of ice, one upon the other, until the ice becomes quite thick. The important aspect of this is that the ice melts annually. In the more traditional meaning of glacier, the ice sheet is semipermanent and centuries old. (From 1900s)

glacier bear

■ n A color phase of the **black bear**. Sometimes called **blue bear.** The bear is bluish gray to light gray in color. This form of *Ursus americanus* is found in the Alaska Range. (From 1920s) See also **blackie.**

globe cactus

■ n A large cylindrical spiny cactus, *Echinocactus horizonthalonius,* found in the Southwest. The cactus grows to about three feet high, and two to three feet in diameter. (From 1850s) See **barrel cactus** for a complete listing.

glory hole

■ n 1. An open pit caused by surface mining. The hole, 150 to 200 feet deep and several hundred feet across at the top, sloped downward in a funnel shape. 2. A pocket or hole in a mine with a rich concentration of valuable ore. Removing the ore leaves a roomlike hole. 3. A deserted stope in a mine; the hole or room left by removing a rich pocket of ore (from 1910s). The verb was formed within ten years of the meaning of the noun: to mine ore by means of a **glory hole** (from 1920s).

glossy snake

■ n See **gopher snake.**

= 113 =

goat

■ n Also called **goat antelope.** The pronghorn of the Mountain West. The *Antilocapra americana* is not a true **antelope** (q.v. for further information) because it sheds its horns. Furthermore, each horn has a short prong sticking up from the side, near the base. (From 1870s)

gofer match

■ n The paper match, manufactured in books of twenty or so. So called because paper matches blow out more quickly in the out-of-doors than wooden matches or stick matches, making the user "go for" another. (From 1960s)

gold

■ n The first element in many terms related to the collecting, mining, and processing of gold: *gold (-mining) dredge,* ~ *camp,* ~ *claim,* ~ *country,* ~ *creek,* ~ *digger,* ~ *dirt,* ~ *discovery,* ~ *district,* ~ *dust* (also known as **yellow**), ~ *fever,* ~*field,* ~ *gulch,* ~ *hunt(er),* ~ *land,* ~ *ledge,* ~ *mania,* ~ *nugget* (also known as **yellow**), ~ *pan(ning)* (see **batea, pan, washbowl**), ~ *placer,* ~ *quartz,* ~ *range,* ~ *region,* ~ *rock(er),* ~ *rush,* ~ *seeker,* ~ *separator,* ~ *sluice,* ~ *strike,* ~ *washer,* ~ *weight.* (From 1850s)

Golden Bear State

■ n A nickname for **California.** (From 1940s) Also **El Dorado State, Eureka State, Golden State.**

golden finned trout

■ n Also called **golden fin, golden trout.** A trout of the **Dolly Varden** variety found in the Kenai peninsula and interior of Alaska, or a variety of **cutthroat trout** found in California. It grows to twelve inches in length and is highly colored, iridescent golden. (From 1880s)

Golden Gate

■ n 1. The strait at the entrance of San Francisco Bay, California (from 1840s). 2. Shortened name for the **Golden Gate Bridge** (from 1940s).

golden king crab

■ n A large ocean crab, up to fifteen pounds in weight, found in deep Alaskan waters. The term is apparently being used to replace **brown king crab.** (From 1980s) See **Alaska king crab** for a complete listing.

golden spike

■ n A special railroad spike used in the ceremonies connecting the eastward-moving Central

Pacific Railroad with the westward-moving Union Pacific Railroad. The ceremony marking the meeting of the two lines was held at Promontory, Utah, on May 10, 1869.

Golden State
■ n A nickname for **California.** (From 1840s) Also **El Dorado State, Eureka State, Golden Bear State.**

gooeyduck
■ n A pronunciation spelling for **geoduck.**

goosepen
■ n The stump of a large **redwood,** hollowed out by fire, then scraped and used for storage. Such stumps are often twelve to twenty feet in diameter. (From 1900s)

gopher
■ v Also **gopher around.** To prospect or dig in several areas on a claim in a haphazard fashion. Such digging was done without thought toward permanent development, and the holes were not reinforced or braced. In more recent years, the term has been used in reference to prospecting in one's free time with simply a rock hammer and shovel, without using explosives or water sluices. (From 1880s)

gopher hole
■ n A shallow opening dug in the ground by a prospector for checking the possibilities of ore or by a logger for placing blasting compound under a log or stump. (From 1880s)

gopher snake
■ n Also called **bull snake, glossy snake.** Any of a variety of common, nonpoisonous snakes of the West and Southwest. The genus *Pituophis* grows to five feet long, is brownish or yellow, sometimes bright yellow and brown, and feeds on rodents. (From 1900s)

gospel sharp
■ n A preacher or a sanctimonious person. The term was first recorded by Mark Twain in the 1870s, when he traveled west. The term now has an old-fashioned flavor, but was still being used in the 1940s and 1950s in the West.

gotch
■ adj Drooping or bent, as an ear on a horse, donkey, rabbit. Or the effect of the eyes being crossed, or one eye looking askew. Animals that have had

an ear clipped for identification purposes are **gotch-eared.** (From 1900s, Spanish *gacho* 'bent over')

go under

■ v phr To die. The term originated in the Southwest, influenced by the figurative language of Indians in the region. Gradually the term spread north and east, where it is still found. (From 1840s)

grab the apple

■ v phr To hold the horn on a western saddle. Considered the action of a novice or greenhorn rider. Cowboys and rodeo riders disdain the ability of anyone who touches the saddle horn, especially a cowboy who touches the horn while on a bucking bronco. (From 1930s) See also **apple, biscuit, leather, to pull.**

gracias

■ excl 'Thank you'. The term, often preceded by *mucho* or *muchas,* is widely used in the Southwest and extensively in the West generally. Since the 1960s, the term has been *de rigueur* when dining in a Mexican or Spanish restaurant, regardless of whether or not the servers speak Spanish. (From 1950s, Spanish) Compare **quyana.**

grain ranch

■ n An extensive plot of land given to the growing of grain. Used almost exclusively in valleys of California and Nevada. The **grain rancher** of these states would be a large-operation farmer in other states. (From 1880s)

grama grass

■ n Also spelled *gramma grass.* Any of a variety of low-growing grasses of the genus *Bouteloua* of western flatlands. The term is from Spanish *grama* 'grass', so the tautology is probably the result of a folk etymology. (From 1820s)

grape stake

■ n A roughhewn split stake, five to six feet long, usually split from **redwood.** Originally used to support grapevines, the grape stake has often been used for fencing. Normally such a fence is constructed by placing these stakes close together, vertically. (From 1940s)

grasser

■ n A beef animal fattened on grass only. The sleek animal resulting from such a diet is worth somewhat less than a cow or steer with a varied diet. (From 1880s)

graveyard shift

■ n A work shift or time period that includes several hours after midnight. Originally, the time period referred to late-night card games and the time that professional gamblers plied their trade. As time went by, the time period was described as beginning at different times from ten P.M. to midnight and ending at six, seven, or eight A.M. The name was soon picked up by shift workers such as miners, policemen, and in the 1940s by defense-plant workers. (From 1900s)

gray whale

■ n Also called the **California gray whale.** A whale that inhabits the Pacific waters off the coast of California, known as *Rhacheanectus glaucus.* The whale grows forty to fifty feet in length and weighs up to twenty tons. (From 1880s)

greaser

■ n A derogatory nickname for a person of Mexican descent. As an offensive term, it has had an extremely long and active use. (From 1830s)

greasewood

■ n Also called **greaseweed, greasebush, greaseroot.** Any of a variety of resinous plants found in the arid West. The small spindly branches are dark in color, and the plant grows small, shiny bright green leaves after a rainfall. Blossoms are small and shiny bright yellow. The wood burns with a great deal of resinous black smoke and soot. In some areas of the Southwest, greasewood is more common than **sagebrush.** (From 1830s) See also **creosote bush, hediondilla, toroso, white sage.**

greasy sack

■ adj Descriptive of a ranch operation or chore of several days in which cowboys are forced to carry food on a pack mule. That is, the ranch does not have a properly equipped **chuck wagon,** so the implication is that the operation is a cheap one or the outfit is second rate. (From 1940s, perhaps from "greasy spoon," a second-rate cafe)

Great Basin

■ n A geographic region that has no river drainage to an ocean. The streams evaporate in the sands or flow into alkaline dry lakes and evaporate. The basin includes most of Nevada and Utah and parts of Idaho, Oregon, and California, and is bounded on the north by the Snake River, on the east by the Wasatch Range, on the south by the Colorado River, and on the west by the Sierra Nevada. The altitude ranges from plains at four thousand feet to mountains at more than twelve thousand feet. (From 1840s) See also **Basin State.**

Great Basin State ■ n See **Utah.**

Great Land, The ■ n A nickname for **Alaska,** used especially in promotional literature by tourist organizations. The sobriquet dates back to the time the Russian settlers characterized the land as such. But a misconception of the meaning of the word "Alaska" led early promoters to think the term a translation. It is not.

green fish ■ n In Alaska, fish that are caught as cold weather sets in and allowed to freeze rather than be dried or smoked. These are subsistence fish, thawed and eaten by humans and dogs alike during the cold months. (From 1930s)

green ivory ■ n Walrus tusks from freshly killed animals, used for carving purposes. The ivory is not green, but very white in color, so called because it is "fresh."

The ivory tusks become cream colored and then yellowed with age, and go through coloring stages referred to as "new," then "fossiled." (From 1930s) See also **new ivory.** Compare **fossil ivory, old ivory.**

Greenland tea

■ n See **Alaska tea.**

gringo

■ n A term for a person of the United States who is not of Mexican extraction. The term was originally used in contempt, but U.S. citizens have taken the term as a humorous badge of identity, in the same fashion as they turned the originally offensive term "Yankee" to their own favor. A folk etymology has the term coming from the refrain of a song, "Green Grow the Rushes, Ho." But that is not the case. (From 1840s)

grizzly bear

■ n Also spelled *grisly bear.* A large, ferocious bear, *Ursus arctos horribilis,* inhabiting the **Rocky Mountains** all the way through Canada and into Alaska. The grizzly, meaning "gray," is a color stage of the **brown bear.** But the name was early associated with the sense of "grisly, horrible." Standing on its hind legs, the bear can be more than ten feet tall. (From 1850s regularly, though attested as early as the 1790s) See also **Ephraim.**

ground cuckoo

■ n A nickname for the **roadrunner** or **chaparral cock.** The term comes from the fact that the roadrunner does not fly more than a few feet off the ground and never very far. (From 1930s) See also **Arizona peacock; California peacock; paisano,** 2.

grub box

■ n In the Northwest Territories, and later in Alaska, the storage chest used for storing provisions while moving overland by **dogsled,** boat, or packhorse. (From 1910s)

grub liner

■ n Originally an out-of-work cowboy who rode from ranch to ranch, looking for a job and taking advantage of the rancher's hospitality in providing meals. Now used especially among young men whose friends drop by for a handout or a beer or two. (From 1910s)

grub pile

■ n A store of provisions at a special job away

from the ranch or at a mine. Also, the time for eating or a call to eat. (From 1860s)

grubstake

■ n The food, tools, and transportation needed by a prospector, supplied by investors or a patron who shares in the profits. Originally, in the 1860s, the grubstake was purchased for a flat rate of exchange in gold dust. But as time went on and more prospectors required minimal furnishings, the ventures became speculative on the part of townspeople who hoped to share in a large find. Such a patron became known as a **grubstaker** by the 1880s. And the verb, **to grubstake,** was in use in the 1870s.

grub wages

■ n pl Originally subsistence pay for working in mines or on the railroad. Such payments were sneered at for two reasons: they meant that a person received the same wage as a Chinese laborer and that a person could not work for himself but must be in the employ of someone else. Both reasons were considered demeaning and to be avoided at all costs. Now used to denote menial labor for minimum wage. (From 1880s)

grub wagon

■ n The wagon in a ranching, construction, mining, or logging outfit that carries food and supplies for the operation. Such a wagon is larger and more greatly stocked than the **chuck wagon,** which carried mainly food and cooking utensils and little or no equipment. (From 1890s)

grueso

■ n In mining, especially quicksilver mines in California, bulky and coarse pieces of rich ore, several inches in diameter. This first-class ore is easy to mill and highly prized for ease of extraction. (From 1870s, Spanish 'coarse, bulky')

grulla

■ /GROO yuh, GROO luh, GROO yer, GROOL yer/ adj Also spelled *grullo, gruya, gruller.* The color shade of a horse, sometimes a mule, that ranges from dirty gray to brownish black. (From Spanish, 1860s)

grunion

■ n A small smelt found along the coast of Southern California; *Leuresthes tenuis.* The ten-inch fish is well known for its habit of coming onto the sandy beaches for the purpose of spawning. These events, called **grunion runs,** are predictable and announced in local newspapers. **Grunion running** takes place at night. Amateur fishermen go to the beaches with flashlights and catch the fish by hand when they ride the waves to shore. The fish, also called **silversides,** are very shiny and sparkle when the flashlights are turned on them. (From 1917, Spanish *gruñon* 'grumbler')

guaco

■ /GWA koh/ n An extract from the Rocky Mountain bee plant that is used as a standard black pigment for design elements in Pueblo pottery. The juice of the plant is put on the pottery, which is then fired. The pigment turns to a powdery ash. When the ash is brushed away, the bright black color remains. (From 1840s, Spanish for the plant itself)

guayule

■ /GWA yool/ n A latex-producing shrub found in the desert Southwest from California to New Mexico. During World War I and again during World War II, the *Parthenian argentatum* was considered a potential source for rubber, and intense research was devoted to the possibilities before alternate sources of rubberlike material were found. (From 1900s, Nahuatl via Spanish)

guest ranch

■ n A euphemistic alternative for **dude ranch.** During the 1930s, some developers and travel agents felt the term "dude" indicated a greenhorn without native intelligence, which didn't account for the fact that, more and more, the clients of such ranches were candidates for divorce or wealthy patrons looking for a few weeks of "roughing it." Consequently, the term came into use in advertising and, gradually, into general usage.

gulch

■ n A ravine, especially one with steep sides, created by running water during storms, but otherwise dry. The term did not originate in the West, but through the years has become closely associated with the West to the extent that the word serves as the first part in compounds having to do with mining: *gulch claim, ~ diggings, ~ gold, ~ man, ~ miner, ~ mining, ~ washing.* (From 1830s) The word also occurs as the second element in compounds: *dry-gulch,* to kill somebody, often from ambush; *Glitter Gulch,* nickname since the 1950s for the brightly lighted casino center in downtown Las Vegas.

gumboot
■ n A chiton, with a shell of overlapping plates. In Alaska, the large mollusk has a large base, or "foot," with which it moves or clings tightly to a rock. The resemblance of the mollusk to the high rubber boots worn by Alaskans results in the name. (From 1910s) See also **bidarki.**

gussuk
■ n A term used by Alaska Natives for a foreigner, white man, Russian. (From 1870s, Russian *kazak* 'cossack')

gut wrapper
■ n In logging, a chain or cable used within a load of logs on a truck or flat car to hold down a single tier of logs. The cable or chain is wrapped around the middle of several logs to keep them in place so that more may be loaded atop them. (From 1950s)

gyp
■ n Also called **gypwater.** Water that is alkaline or brackish because of the presence of gypsum. The adjective **gyppy** refers to the condition of such water. Drinking such water can cause severe, even life-threatening, diarrhea in humans or animals. (From 1900s, shortened from *gypsum*)

gyppo
■ n Originally, piecework done for a logging outfit. If a man thought he could make more doing work by the piece rather than by wages, he would work as a gyppo. As time passed, the term came to refer to any small outfit doing contract work for a larger outfit. The original sense of "gyp" ('to cheat') disappeared as the term came to be applied more and more to entrepreneurs who contract for specialty jobs or tasks requiring special equipment or skills. (From 1920s, probably from "gypsy" in the sense of an itinerant laborer)

hacendado
■ /hah send DAH doh/ n The owner of a ranch, especially a large ranch. The use in English was established in New Mexico and spread slowly through the Southwest. As large landholdings diminish, the word is becoming used more in a historical sense. (From 1840s, Spanish)

hacienda
■ /hah see END dah/ n 1. The main house on a **ranch,** often sprawling large enough to house the extended family of a wealthy rancher. The structure usually features a curved tile roof, red or reddish brown in color, and thick white stucco walls (from 1800s). 2. A large ranch or estate, especially in New Mexico and southwest Texas (from 1820s, Spanish). 3. Any large or opulent house featuring white stuccoed walls, a red tiled roof, and many guest rooms (from 1960s).

hackamore
■ n A rope halter with reins or a lead rope, used to control horses still in the process of being broken to riders or packs. Browband flaps can cover the eyes, and knots in the rope over the nose can place pressure on the nostrils. (From 1850s, Spanish *jáquima* 'headstall') See also **bosal, fiador.**

hair pants
■ n pl **Chaps** (q.v. for a complete listing) or leggings used by working cowboys from which the fleece or hair has not been removed. The fleece or hair side is worn outward to repel rain and snow. The term distinguishes this style from other chaps worn with smooth leather to the outside, which are designed for moving through brush and thorns. (From 1900s) See also **angoras, chivarras.**

handcart
■ n In western usage, reference to the carts that Mormon pioneers drew by hand over the Plains to Salt Lake City between 1856 and 1860. (From 1855)

Hangtown fry
■ n A dish popularized in northern California mining camps, consisting of scrambled eggs and oysters, traditionally the two most expensive items on

the menu. (From 1940s, after "Hangtown," an early name for Placerville, California)

Hard-Case State

■ n A nickname, originally for the Oregon Territory, later for the state of **Oregon.** So called because of the number of ruffians who migrated to that area. (From 1840s) Also **Beaver State, Webfoot State.**

hard-rock

■ adj Descriptive of a miner qualified to mine ore from granite or large igneous or metamorphic formations. Because such a miner is considered expert and special, the term came to connote a man of quality, one whose character "rings like steel when struck by an eight-pound hammer." (From 1920s)

Harvey

■ adj Reference to the chain of hotels and restaurants constructed in the West and Southwest beginning in the 1870s, and especially to the women who worked in them. Fred Harvey (b. 1835) established restaurants along well-traveled roads and hired young women of marriageable age and impeccable character as waitresses. The "Harvey girl" made the Harvey House an institution that lasted well into the 1940s. (From 1890s)

hasher

■ n A waitress, sometimes a waiter, at a lunch counter or truck stop, especially in the Northwest. (From 1910s, derived from earlier "hash house," a cheap eatery)

hassayampa

■ n Originally an old-timer from Arizona; a **desert rat** or prospector or lone miner. The river of that name, according to legend, makes liars of anyone who drinks from it. Consequently, the word came to mean one who exaggerates, tells whopping lies, or is incapable of telling the truth. (From 1900s, after the Hassayampa River)

haul road

■ n In Alaska, a rough road used to carry freight to an interior development or logs out to a terminus. Sometimes a temporary road similar to a logging road in timber country. (From 1970s)

hay corral

■ n An enclosure made of wire fencing or poles to

keep stock away from the stacks of baled hay. (From 1850s)

haywire side

■ n The unit of a logging operation that handles the bulk of wire or has the less desirable equipment or working conditions. (From 1950s) Compare **candy side.**

haze

■ v To direct the movements of horses or mules originally. Now, to control the movements of any herding animals, such as cattle, sheep, or wild horses. (From 1890s)

header

■ n In California wheat fields, a reaper that cuts the tips off the wheat stems, leaving the straw in the field. The wheat is delivered directly into a **header wagon,** or a **header barge,** that moves alongside the reaper. (From 1860s)

hedge cactus

■ n Also called **hedgehog cactus.** Any of a variety of cactus plants that can be used as a hedge along the border of a garden. Often the *Echinocactus texensis* of the southwest Texas and southern Arizona borders. (From 1870s) See **barrel cactus** for a complete listing.

hediondilla

■ /hay dee own DEE ya/ n A **creosote bush** found in the desert Southwest that gives off a strong and offensive odor when crushed or after a rain. (From 1840s, diminutive of Spanish *hediondo* 'stinking') See also **greasewood, toroso.**

heeled

■ adj 1. Descriptive of a person being armed; to be furnished with a weapon, usually a handgun kept out of sight (from 1860s). 2. Descriptive of a person who has plenty of money. The meaning derived from the first sense, in that a person who is **heeled** (now, usually "well heeled") is prepared for any eventuality, from defending oneself to buying one's way out of difficulty (from 1880s).

heel fly

■ n Also called **bot fly, warble fly.** A fly found around cattle early in the springtime. Supposedly the pesky fly (*Hypodermatis bovis*) stings cows on the tender part of the heel, just above the hoof, causing stampedes and general mischief. The term has been extended to refer to persons who act obstreperously or who otherwise disrupt orderly society. (From 1870s)

hen-skin

■ n A comforter or quilt stuffed with feathers. Sometimes two thin blankets would be sewn together, feathers put between the blankets, then tied in several places with short lengths of string to keep the feathers from shifting too much. The term is old-fashioned, though the article is still found on many western ranches. (From 1900s)

herd

■ combinatory Used as the first or last term in a variety of compounds and expressions stemming from the term for a collection of cattle. Nearly all the terms have extended meanings to refer to groups of animals or people: *to ride herd on,* to control; *herd boss,* group leader; *herd broke,* descriptive of one willing to become a member of a group; *herd guard,* the person in charge; *herd law,* originally the law for range grazing, now the will of the group; **close-herd** (compare **loose-herd**), to gather together; **day herd,** group brought together for a specific time or job.

hermit warbler

■ n The most distinctly recognizable bird in the Sierra Nevada. The small bird has a yellow head, black neck, white breast and belly. The warbling song is so loud and distinct that nearly every nature movie featuring a western meadow scene has the bird's song on the soundtrack, whether the bird can be found in that region or not. The bird, *Dendroica occidentalis,* is actually a denizen of the forest. (From 1830s)

high-climber

■ n Also called **high rigger.** In a logging outfit, the person who tops trees, removes the higher limbs, and sometimes rigs the spar tree for cable logging. Such a logger regularly works above two hundred feet up a tree. (From 1920s)

high fog

■ n A high overcast generally found specifically over the central California Coast. The cold water along that portion of the coast causes condensation that creates a fog that hangs two or three hundred feet above the surface of the ground and gradually dissipates as the sun warms the air mass later in the day. (From 1930s) Compare **pogonip fog,** 2; **tule fog.**

high-grade
■ adj Descriptive of ore from a mine that is particularly rich. (From 1870s)

high-grade
■ v 1. To steal metal-rich ore from a mine or mining operation (from 1900s). 2. To **salt** a mine by placing high-grade or rich ore in a mine, then showing the mine and its "riches" to a prospective buyer (from 1930s). 3. By extension, to select the best parts or pieces from a communal dish at a dinner or buffet; to pick through a dish and discard less desirable vegetables or edibles. (From 1960s)

high kick
■ n Also called **Alaskan high kick, two-foot high kick, one-foot high kick.** A traditional contest in Alaska where Eskimo-influenced games are played. The contestant stands in one spot, jumps up, and touches both feet simultaneously to a ball suspended from the ceiling. (From 1930s)

high lead
■ /hi LEED/ n Also called **highline.** In logging, a cable suspended from a crane or tower, to which a log is attached to be dragged to a work area. (From 1930s) See also **arch.**

high-muck-a-muck
■ n A person of importance or self-importance; a pompous person. (From 1850s, Chinook Jargon *hiu muckamuck* 'plenty to eat and drink')

high roller
■ n A gambler who places large bets often and has a reputation as a free-spending player. Especially used in Nevada, more recently in Atlantic City, New Jersey. (From 1960s)

hightail
■ v To run at full speed. Originally from the propensity of stampeding cattle or frightened animals to run with tails raised. (From 1920s)

hike
■ imperative A command used by **dog mushers** in Alaska and the Yukon to make the dogs begin pulling the sled. The command "Mush!" from earlier in the century is no longer used. (From 1910s;

origin obscure, but may be related to Chinook Jargon *hyak* 'hurry, quick')

hogan

■ /HO gun, ho GAN/ n A lodging built of earthen walls or sod held in place with timbers, sticks, or branches. The structure looks like an earthen igloo. (From 1870s, Navajo *qoghan* 'house')

hog dollar

■ n In northern California, a nickname for a silver dollar. The term is in decline as there are fewer silver dollars available for daily commerce. (From 1960s, recalled from oral tradition)

hogging game

■ n A card or shell game run or dealt by a cheater, especially a fairly obvious cheater. (From 1860s)

hogleg

■ n Originally, a single-action army Colt "six-gun," which was a formidable pistol. Later, the term was extended to any six-gun, and finally, across the country, to a sawed-off shotgun, whose shape resembles the haunch of a hog. (From 1920s)

hog ranch

■ n A brothel, especially in the Old West. The term is still used, though usually in historical contexts or somewhat facetiously. (From 1880s)

hog-tie

■ v To render an animal or person helpless, originally by tying together all four feet or the hands and feet together. (From 1900s)

hole

■ n A deep or narrow valley between high mountains, a feature of Rocky Mountain Cascade Range valleys. The term is frequently found in place-names in mountainous areas. (From 1830s)

holia

■ n Another name for **humpback salmon.** The *Onchorhynchus gorbuscha* grows to three to five pounds and was favored as dog food until salmon grew generally more scarce. (From 1880s) See **salmon** n for a complete listing.

hollygrape

■ n Any of several types of **barberry** (q.v. for a complete listing), a hollylike shrub that grows between eight thousand and ten thousand feet in altitude. The plant has yellow flowers, usually soft and fragrant, and blue berries. (From 1930s)

hombre

■ /OM bray/ n Originally a man of Mexican descent, but now any man. The word is used in much the same way as "fellow," somewhat casually and colloquially. Often used with an adjective: *big hombre, tough hombre, good hombre, bad hombre.* (From 1840s, Spanish 'man')

hombre viejo

■ n A name used in New Mexico and Arizona for **old man cactus** (q.v. for a complete listing). (From 1890s Spanish 'old man')

home evening

■ n Among Mormons, a specific evening during the week in which the family gathers together for spiritual study or some type of group activity. (From 1950s)

honda

■ n Also spelled *hondo.* The eyelet at the end of a **lariat,** used to slip the other end of the rope through when making a loop for lassoing something. Sometimes the eye is made of leather or metal, then fastened to the end of the lariat. (From 1880s, Spanish *hondón* 'eyelet' or 'eye of a needle')

hoodoo

honey wagon ■ n A wagon or cart used to haul human excretions or animal manure, usually in rural areas or places, such as Alaska and the Yukon, where sewage facilities are rare or nonexistent. (From 1920s)

hooch ■ n Shortened from **hoochinoo.** An alcoholic liquor, especially illicitly made and of poor quality. The term is unquestionably Alaska's most famous contribution to English, as the term spread immediately across North America. (From 1870s, Tlingit *xoóts* 'grizzly bear' + *noow* 'fort,' where the famous brew was first made from molasses and sold to natives)

hoodoo ■ n A spire or sharp pinnacle of rock or sandstone carved into a strange shape by wind and water erosion, especially in the vicinity of Yellowstone Park and the Grand Canyon. (From 1870s)

hookbill ■ n Also called **hooknose.** Another name for the **coho.** (From 1970s) See **salmon** n for a full listing.

hookey bob ■ v Also **hooky bobbing.** Crouching and holding onto the back bumper of a car or truck moving over snow-covered streets or roads and sliding along on the soles of the boots. (From 1960s) See also **bizzing.** Compare **skijor.**

hoopid salmon ■ n An alternative name for the **coho.** (From 1880s) See **salmon** n for a complete listing.

hoosegow ■ n Also spelled *hoozegow.* A jail. Normally used in reference to a small city or county jail, rather than a prison. Often used semifacetiously. (From 1910s, Spanish *juzgado* 'tribunal, court')

horned toad ■ n Also **horned frog, horn toad, horny toad, horned lizard.** A small, flat lizard found in the Southwest. *Phrynosoma cornutum* features small horns on its head and back. (From 1880s)

horned rattlesnake ■ n Also **horned snake.** A **sidewinder** with hornlike projections between its eyes, found on sandy slopes in the Southwest. *Crotalus cerastes* is especially common to the lower regions of the Sonoran Desert. The dusky-colored snake grows to about two feet long. (From 1870s)

horse clam

■ n Sometimes called **coho clam** or **Washington clam,** though it is found along the coast all the way to Alaska. A coarse clam of the Pacific Northwest, smaller than a **geoduck,** usually white and about ten inches long. Not considered particularly good for eating. (From 1920s) See also **gaper.**

horse crippler

■ n Also called **mule-crippler cactus.** A form of cactus that has downward pointing rigid spines; *Echinocactus texensis.* (From 1970s) See **barrel cactus** for a complete listing.

horse-tripping

■ n An event in the **charreada** in which the contestant lassos the legs of a horse, thereby causing the horse to stumble and fall. The event has come under criticism in recent years, and legislation has been passed or is pending outlawing the event in California, New Mexico, Nevada, Texas, Arizona, Colorado, Illinois, and Maine. (From 1900s, but frequent only in 1990s)

horse-wrangler

■ n See **wrangler.**

Hosteen

■ n Also uncapitalized. A term of respect similar to "mister." The word was applied to older, respected Navajos in New Mexico and Arizona, but is expanding. (From 1910s, Navajo *hastqín*)

hotdogger

■ n A surfer who performs antics and tricks on the board, sometimes endangering other surfers around. Normally boys who are showing off to girls on the beach, who are expected, in turn, to squeal with delight and buy **burritos** for such goings on. Hotdogging is frowned on by serious wave

horned toad

catchers, though sometimes enviously. See also **aerial.**

hot roll

■ n A bedroll and personal effects belonging to a cowboy. The roll had to be securely wrapped and tightly tied before being put into the wagon or truck with all the effects going onto the range. Now the usual hot roll is contained in a backpack or satchel, but still rides to the range camp in the back of the truck. (From 1930s)

hot shot

■ n An electrical charge given to a horse to make it buck. Used in **rodeo** chutes; electric cattle prod. (From 1930s)

huarache

■ n Usually plural, **huaraches.** A sandal made with thin strips of woven leather on the upper part and back heel. (From 1880s, Spanish)

Hudson Bay tea

■ n See **Alaska tea.**

huero

■ /WAY roh/ n A person with fair hair and light complexion. (From 1840s, Spanish *guero,* according to *DA. DARE* uses a later date, placing the earlier dates in brackets, indicating it was still Spanish until the 1920s)

humpback salmon

■ n Also called **humpback, humpy, holia, pink salmon.** A food fish found along the Pacific Coast from Washington to Alaska. The *Oncorhynchus gorbuscha* has the shortest life cycle of the Pacific salmon (two years), and grows to about four pounds. The male develops a pronounced hump on its back prior to spawning. It is a staple of the fishing industry. (From 1880s) See **salmon** n for a complete listing.

hurdy-gurdy house

■ n An establishment of ill report, featuring loud music, lewd dancing, prostitution, illegal gambling, and cheap liquor. Now somewhat old-fashioned. (From 1860s)

husky

■ n A nickname applied to almost any variety of **sled dog** used in Alaska and the Yukon. The term derived from "Husky dog," meaning a dog that belonged to a "Husky," in turn a pejorative term for an Eskimo. Consequently, the term is out of favor with **dog mushers** and those who know about the origin of the term. (From 1900s) See **Alaskan husky** for a complete listing.

hydrophobia skunk

■ n A skunk (*Spilogale putorius*) found in the Southwest that was thought to cause madness with its bite. The fact is that rabies is common to many pests and rodents in the region. (From 1910s)

I

ice anchor

■ n Also called **ice hook, snow hook.** A piece of curved metal on one end of a length of rope tied to a **dogsled.** The hook is pushed into snow or ice, or hooked to a tree, to keep the dogs from pulling a stationary sled while in harness. (From 1940s) Since the 1960s, **snow anchor** has been the preferred term.

icebreak

■ n See **breakup.**

ice bridge

■ n In Alaska and the Yukon Territory, a crossing over a frozen river in the wintertime, made by pumping water onto ice already formed to reinforce it and build a thicker layer. (From 1870s in Ohio, but used almost exclusively in the North since 1960s) See also **ice road.**

ice cellar

■ n A pit or room carved out of the frozen tundra in the Far North, used as a deep freeze. (From 1930s)

ice fog

■ n Water vapor frozen into ice crystals that float in the air when the outside temperature drops to -35 degrees Fahrenheit. The condition is so far peculiar to Fairbanks, Alaska, it being the only city of a size large enough to produce moisture from automotive exhaust, houses, and industrial production in sufficient quantities. Regular temperature inversions then keep the ice fog trapped near the ground. (From 1940s)

ice pool

■ n Also called **ice classic.** In Alaska and the Yukon Territory, a lottery based on the precise time in spring the ice will break on a river. A tripod is constructed in the middle of the river, and a line run to a clock on shore. When the ice moves a specific distance, the clock stops and a winner is declared. (From 1910s) See also **breakup.**

ice road

■ n A road constructed for hauling equipment across the frozen tundra of the north. Such a road is constructed by spraying water repeatedly on the surface and building up the road layer by frozen layer. (From 1880s, but almost exclusive to Alaska and the Yukon Territory since 1970s) See also **ice bridge.**

ice the runners

■ v phr In **dogsledding,** to wet the runners of the sled with water, allowing it to freeze, then repeating the process. The ice on the runners reduces friction and allows the sled to slip more easily across snow and ice. (From 1910s)

ice worm

■ n In Alaska and the Yukon Territory, a mythical creature, recorded from tales by **sourdoughs** by newspaper editors in Dawson and other towns. To the surprise of everyone, it was discovered many years later that an ice worm does exist and is found near the surface of glaciers. (From 1900s)

Idaho

■ n Forty-third state of the Union. Settled in 1842, it became a territory in 1863, and a state in 1890. Capital: Boise. Originally suggested as the name for Colorado, from the Kiowa-Apache name, *Idahi,* for the Comanche, both tribes being well known in the territory, and from the newly established village of Idaho Springs, Colorado. Congress, however, on learning that the name did not mean "Gem of the Mountains" as supposed, pushed through the name "Colorado" instead. The name "Idaho" got a second chance when the Senate chose it for the new state over James M. Ashley's suggestion of "Montana." It has also been suggested that the name is the Shoshone *Ed-dah-how* 'Good morning'. (From 1861) Also called the **Gem State.** Adjective: **Idahoan.**

igloo

■ n Also spelled *iglu*. A sod house or dwelling constructed of saplings or willows over a shallow pit dug into the ground. The saplings curve over the top of the shelter, and the entire is covered with soil and sod. A doorway and window are cut in the sides, and sometimes a wooden floor is installed. (From 1820s Inupiaq et al. *iglu* 'house')

Iditarod

■ n Shortened from **Iditarod race.** The most famous (in the lower forty-eight) of the dogsled races annually held in Alaska since 1972. The race commemorates the transportation of medicine in an

age when roads and bush planes were unavailable. In 1925 diphtheria serum was needed in Nome during an epidemic. Volunteers used **dogsleds** to transport the life-saving serum from Anchorage to Nome. Now the race lasts ten days, covers eleven hundred miles, and in 1993 carried a purse of $50,000 for the winner. See also **dog derby.**

immigration

■ n A body of immigrants, especially the group of Mormons who traveled westward under the influence of Brigham Young and settled initially in the Salt Lake Valley. (From 1850s)

incense cedar

■ n A light-colored cedar, sometimes called **light cedar** or **post cedar.** First described by John Muir, *Libocedrus decurrens* grows in the Sierra Nevada, with a girth of up to thirty feet. The fragrant wood of the tree is soft but durable in inclement weather. Thus, it was often used for storage boxes as well as for lining other boxes and closets. (From 1860s) See also **red cedar.**

Indian melon

■ n A small, roundish cactus found in the Southwest. See **barrel cactus** for a complete listing.

Indian potato, Indian squill, indigo squill

■ n See **camas.** For **Indian potato** see also **Eskimo potato.**

Indian tea

■ n See **Alaska tea.**

inkberry

■ n Another name for the **bearberry honeysuckle.**

Inland Empire ■ n A reference to the area around Spokane, Washington. (From 1880s)

inside ■ n Also **inside passage.** In southeastern Alaska and British Columbia, the waters between the mainland and the string of islands stretching northward from Puget Sound. (From 1870s)

Interior ■ n Often preceded by **The.** The part of Alaska away from the coast, but especially, in more recent years, the region around Fairbanks. (From 1890s)

ipanee ■ adj Traditional; old time. Used in reference to old-timers among Alaska Natives or to the traditional way of life before white men arrived. (From 1920s, Inupiag *aippaani* 'in ancient days')

Irish lord ■ n Also called **bullhead, devilfish.** Any of a variety of sculpins from the genus *Hemilepidotus*. The fish, large-headed and spiny in appearance, is found mainly in Alaskan waters. (1940s)

iron chink ■ n A fish-cleaning machine invented around the turn of the century and used in Alaskan canneries until about 1950. Edwin A. Smith invented the complex machine for the Alaskan salmon trade. The device could behead, split, eviscerate, cut tails and fins from salmon at the rate of one hundred a minute, leaving the firm flesh to be sent along the cannery belt. The name was overtly racist, referring to the Chinese labor it replaced. (From 1900s)

iron dog ■ n A jocular reference to a snowmobile in Alaska. The small, open, single-track machine has replaced the **sled dog** for many of the short-travel chores across the snow, such as going to a nearby store or picking up the mail. (From 1960s, on analogy with *iron horse*?)

irrigating ■ adj A modifier referring to the practice of watering fields in semiarid areas of the West. (From 1860s)

irrigation ■ n Used in combinations relating to watering fields in the West: *irrigation bill, ~ canal, ~ district, ~ ditch* (see **corrugate, primary ditch**), *~*

ivu

pump, ~ rancher, ~ valley. (From 1870s) See also **acequia, zanja.**

■ n The sudden movement of a pack of ice that is driven by offshore forces up over shoreline fast ice in Alaska. A sudden wall of ice can be pushed up on the shore, reaching over high bluffs and crushing down on everything hundreds of yards inland. People sleeping in houses close to the edge of a bluff have been crushed in this fashion. (From 1970s Inupiaq *ivu-* 'pressure ridge')

J

jackalope

■ n A fanciful creature supposed to have existed on the high plains of Wyoming and Utah. It is marked by having the body of a jackrabbit, surmounted with the horns of a small antelope. Stuffed specimens are available for purchase by tourists, and postcards featuring the animal are plentiful in roadside rest areas of the western high desert. (From 1950s)

jackhammer

■ n Originally, a small rock drill used in western hard-rock mining. It was soon replaced by a portable drill driven by compressed air and used to break up rock and concrete. (From 1930s)

Jack Mormon

■ n Originally, a non-Mormon who was friendly toward Mormons. More recently includes a former Mormon who has fallen away from the faith, usually practicing little, if any, religion. (From 1840s)

jackrabbit

■ n Any of several varieties of long-legged, long-eared hares found in the West and Southwest. (From 1860s)

jack salmon

■ n In salmon fishing in the Northwest, an early-

jackalope, a fanciful creature

maturing **king, coho,** or **red salmon** that returns to spawn a year or two early. The fish is usually a bit smaller than average. (From 1940s)

Japanese spider crab
■ n Also called **Alaska king crab** (q.v. for a complete listing), **spider crab.** The largest of the anomuran crabs found in the Pacific waters off the shores of Alaska. The crab can weigh up to forty pounds and have a reach of ten feet across with legs extended. (From 1920s)

javalina
■ /have uh LEE nuh, java LEE nuh/ n Also called **peccary.** A piglike animal found in the Southwest, hunted for food. (From 1820s, Spanish *jabalina* 'wild sow')

Jefferson Territory
■ n An old-fashioned name for the territory that later became the state of **Colorado.** Forty years later, the name was used for the area that became the state of **Montana.** (From 1850s)

jerky
■ n A thin strip of meat, usually beef, that has been dried in the sun. Originally this meat was prepared at high altitudes where the sun was strong, the air cool, and insects few. (From 1840s Nahuatl *charqui* via Spanish) See also **carne seco.**

jicama
■ /HICK uh muh/ n A large tuber prepared and eaten like a potato. The plant, *Pacyrhizus erosus,* is often eaten raw, alone and in salads. (From 1900s, Nahuatl *xicamatl* via Spanish)

jicara
■ /he CAH rah/ n A small, tightly woven basket or cup carved from the wood of a calabash tree. (From 1890s, Nahuatl via Spanish)

jinglebob
■ n Originally, an ear-cut on a cow that lets one ear flop down the side of the face, used for identification. Later the term came to refer to anything that dangled, from a metal piece on spurs to make them jangle, to earbobs worn by women. (From 1890s) See also **dewlap.**

jingler
■ n A loop of metal or leather strung with bells or bottle caps. The noisemaker is used to make **sled dogs** pull faster in Alaska and the Yukon. (From 1970s, perhaps related to **jinglebob**?)

Joshua tree   ■ n Also called **Joshua palm, Joshua yucca.** A succulent that grows with treelike branches in the Southwest. The *Yucca brevifolia* grows at an altitude of three to four thousand feet above sea level. It can attain a height of forty feet, though most specimens average twenty feet in height. (From 1870s)

jumping bean   ■ n Also called **Mexican jumping bean.** The seed of any of a variety of Southwestern plants containing the larva of a moth that causes the seed to move slightly and even turn over. (From 1880s)

jumping cholla   ■ /~ CHOY yuh/ n Also called **jumping cactus.** A cactus that grows in the Southwestern deserts. The spines of this jointed cactus attach so easily to anything that brushes against them that they seem to jump. (From 1940s) See also **cholla.**

jusgado   ■ /hoos GAH dho/ n Also spelled *juzgado.* A jail. Normally used in reference to a small city or county jail, rather than a prison. Often used semi-facetiously. (From 1910s, Spanish *juzgado* 'tribunal, court') Source of the word **hoosegow.**

K

kabluna

■ n In the Yukon Territory, a white person. This term found its way into Canadian English very early. Today it is nearly always used as a written term in stories about the early days. (From 1770s, Inuit 'person with big eyebrows')

kachina

■ /kuh CHEE nuh/ n A spirit or deification of the Hopi Indians, and, by extension, a dancer at Hopi ceremonies who wears a mask representing one of the spirits. (From 1890s, Hopi)

kachina doll

■ n A Hopi Indian doll carved and painted to represent one of the spirits. Often used as a household decoration or given to a child as a toy. The doll has become a popular collector's item. (From 1940s)

kalador

■ n Also spelled *calador, calidor, kalidor.* In Alaska, an entryway for a house, usually in the form of an enclosed porch or hallway, where heavy outdoor wear can be removed. (From 1910s, Russian *koridor,* 'corridor, hall' via Aleut *kaliduurax*)

kamik

■ n Also called **kameksak, kamesak.** In Canadian English, especially in British Columbia and the Yukon Territory, a type of boot made of animal skin and usually ankle-high. Similar to **mukluk.** (From 1890s, Inupiaq, Central Yupik) See also **luftak.**

kangaroo rat

■ n Also called **kangaroo mouse.** Any of the various rodents of the genus *Dipodomys* that burrow in sandy soil, have long hind legs which give them often a hopping motion, and sometimes have pouches. Found in most dry regions of the Southwest. (From 1850s)

kauk

■ /koak/ n In Alaska and the Yukon Territory, a food consisting of the skin of the walrus, with an attached layer of blubber. Usually served boiled. (From 1950s Inupiaq)

kayak

■ n See **bidarka, umiaq.**

kazunoko

■ n The eggs, still in the ovarian membrane, of female herring. The eggs are processed in the Alaskan fisheries for the Japanese market. But the delicacy is becoming popular in Alaska and along the West Coast of North America. (From 1980s, Japanese) See also **roe-on-kelp, sac roe, spawn-on-kelp.**

kelp fish

■ n One of the various names for the **Alaskan mackerel** (q.v. for a complete listing), or *Pleurogrammus monopterygius,* found along the whole of the Aleutian chain. It is a schooling fish and therefore of commercial interest to fish harvesters. (From 1880s)

keno

■ n /KEE no/ Also spelled *keeno, kino, quino.* Sometimes called **Chinese lottery** in California and Nevada. 1. A game played with eighty numbered balls. Players mark up to fifteen numbers on a ticket provided by the operator of the game. Twenty numbers are then randomly selected and payoffs made according to the number of spots the player has matched (adapted from French *quine* 'five' in the 1810s) Originally, the player had to match five numbers in order to win. The word was known along the Mississippi River, but became restricted almost exclusively to Nevada as various forms of gambling were outlawed in the rest of the country. 2. The exclamation made by a keno player who gets five winning numbers (1860s).

keno goose

■ n A sphere constructed of wood, plastic, or wire that holds the eighty balls used in a keno game. The sphere has a tube attached, resembling a gooseneck, through which one ball may pass at a time when the operator is drawing the numbers for the game. (From 1880s) See **rabbit ears.**

keno runner

■ n In the 1960s, large casinos in Nevada began a runner service to keno players who might be in dining rooms, at the gaming tables, or around the pool at large resorts. Scantily clad girls scurry through the public areas, calling for players to place their keno wagers and delivering the completed keno tickets, and occasionally the winnings, to the occupied customer.

keta

■ /KEE tuh/ n A type of **dog salmon,** the *Onchorhynchus keta* found along the Pacific Coast

old-fashioned keno goose

kiva

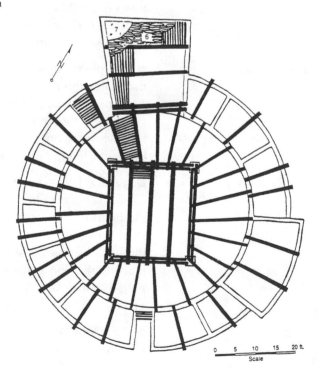

Scale
0   5   10   15   20 ft.

from San Francisco to Kamchatka. It is a small salmon that spawns near the saltwater and does not ascend a long way upstream. (From 1890s, Russian) See **salmon** n for a complete listing.

kicker

■ n Also called **kicker boat.** In Alaska and British Columbia, an outboard motor, or a small boat or rowboat outfitted with an outboard motor. The word has earlier use in sea slang, but came into frequent use in the Northwest. (From 1930s)

kickout

■ n Among surfers, a move on a surfboard to come out of a wave before reaching the shore; generalized to mean a move to leave any place or social situation that begins to get uncomfortable. (From 1980s)

king

■ n Short for **king salmon,** largest of the five types of Pacific salmon, or **Chinook salmon.** The *Oncorhynchus tshawytscha.* (From 1870s) See also **jack salmon.** See **salmon** n for a complete listing.

king crab

■ n Short for **Alaska king crab** (q.v. for a complete listing). Also called **brown king crab, blue king crab.** (From 1940s)

King George

■ attributive See **Boston.**

king snake

■ n See **corral snake**.

kiva

■ /KEE vuh/ n The assembly house of the Pueblo Indians for the observance of religious rites among the men. (From 1870s, Hopi 'old house', 'man house')

Klondike

■ n A region in the Yukon Territory that was the site of the gold rush of 1897. The name, from an Athapaskan dialect, was in reference to a stream, a tributary of the Yukon River. (From 1890s)

klootchman

■ n Also shortened to **klootch.** Also spelled *klooch, kloochman.* A woman native to the Northwest Territories, Alaska, or the Yukon Territory. The term was never used with a modicum of respect and is considered offensive today. (From 1860s, Chinook jargon 'female, woman')

kneeboarding

■ n Riding through the surf on a specially designed board, shorter than a surfboard. The rider is able to maneuver and perform certain tricks unavailable to the rider of the longer surfboard. (From 1960s)

Kodiak bear

■ n A form of the **brown bear** found in the Kodiak Island group. Sometimes considered a separate subspecies, *Ursus arctos middendorffi.* (From 1950s)

kokanee

■ n A freshwater or landlocked salmon found in southeastern Alaska and British Columbia. The small salmon grows to about a pound in size, and is a form of **sockeye salmon.** (From 1940s, Salish) See **salmon** n for a complete listing.

kooyah

■ n Also called **tobacco root.** A tuberous root found mainly on the western side of the Cascade Mountains. The black, sticky root does not have a pleasant smell, but is made into a pleasant-tasting bread by health-food enthusiasts, from recipes taken from Indians in the region. (From 1840s, Shoshonean)

kow-kow

■ n In Alaska, another word for food, similar to the function of other colloquialisms like "chow" (to which it seems related etymologically) and "grub." (From 1890s)

kulich

■ n A raised bread made with fruit and nuts. Originally made by the Russian Orthodox at Easter, the bread has become popular as a seasonal bread among many Alaskans. (From 1950s Russian)

kunzite

■ n A semiprecious stone, pink and purple or lilac in color, found near San Diego, California. The stones range from one to two hundred carats and are favorites of collectors, much like turquoise. (From 1900s, after George F. Kunz, a minerologist who died in 1932)

kyack

■ /KYE ack/ n A packsack, similar to a saddlebag, designed for mules and horses. (From 1900s, Spanish?)

L

Labrador tea ■ n See **Alaska tea.**

ladino ■ n Originally, a person who knew Latin. But in English, the term came to mean a crafty or wily person or animal, and was applied to unbroken horses by **vaqueros,** then by cowboys. (From 1890s, Spanish)

laftak, lavtak ■ n See **luftak.**

lagoonberry ■ n See **nagoonberry.**

Land of Enchantment ■ n See **New Mexico.**

lapball ■ n Also called **Lapp game.** A game similar to baseball in which the opposing pitcher throws the ball to a hitter. When the ball is hit, the batter runs back and forth to a specific goal (a stick or post) and scores as many points as possible before the person who caught the ball can tag the runner. The game may have been imported to Alaska Natives from Russia or Lapland before being taught to the children of settlers. (From 1950s)

lariat ■ n A rope made of hemp, horsehair, or rawhide used to catch range animals like calves and horses. The lariat has a small braided loop at one end, which allows the rope to slide through easily, making a larger loop that can be thrown over an animal's head, then tightened. (From 1830s, Spanish *la reata* 'the rope') See also **honda, lasso, riata.**

lasso ■ n A rope made of rawhide, hemp, or horsehair, used to catch range animals. The running loop at one end of the rope is thrown over the head of the animal to be caught. (From 1830s, Spanish *lazo*) Though lasso and lariat are interchangeable, the term **lariat** appears to be more frequently used in the Southwest and *lasso* more frequent throughout the rest of the West. See also **honda, riata.**

latigo ■ n Also called **latigo strap, larigo.** A strap used to connect the end of the **cinch** to the saddle. (From 1880s)

Latter-day Saint

■ n Also called **Latter-day Brethren.** Often shortened to LDS. A Mormon; a member of the **Church of Jesus Christ of Latter-day Saints.** (From 1830s) Members of this church are so prevalent in Utah, southern Idaho, and rural Nevada, that any reference to "the church" means specifically the Mormon church. See also **saint.**

lay

■ n A share in the profits of a gold-mining **claim** in the Yukon Territory and Alaska. Such a share can be set by buying into the claim or working the claim for a percentage of the gross or net profits. (From 1890s)

layman

■ n A person who works a mining **claim** in Alaska or the Yukon Territory for a share in the profits of the operation. (From 1900s)

lazy

■ adj Descriptive of the letters and figures found in a brand for a ranch in which the letter or figure is lying on the side or is flattened and elongated. For example, a lazy W is seen as a long wavy line, while a lazy 8 is seen as the figure 8 lying on its side. (From 1880s)

lead dog

■ n Also called **lead, leader.** On the **dog team** of a **musher** in the Far Northwest, the dog positioned at the front of a line of dogs pulling a sled. The dog is chosen for power, ability to follow commands, and dominance among the other dogs. (From 1860s) The term was adopted from terminology concerning teams of horses, but is used exclusively in the Northwest for **sled dogs.** See also **team dog, wheel dog.**

lean-to

■ n In Alaska, a wooden addition built and attached to the side of a trailer house or mobile home. Such an addition may be elaborate, with several rooms, full insulation, and sturdy roofing. The addition is built on skids, conforming to the notion (in theory at least), that the entire structure is portable. (From 1950s)

leather, to pull

■ v phr Originally, to grasp the saddle horn with both hands to keep from being thrown off a horse. But now generally means to hang on to any untenable position or notion. (From 1910s) See also **apple, biscuit, grab the apple.**

lechuguilla
■ /letch oo GHEE uh/ n Any of a variety of agave plants found in the Southwest, parts of which are used for making string and pulche or are roasted for eating. Agaves are popular in home landscapes in the Southwest. (From 1840s)

left limit
■ n The downstream, left side of a creek in a mining **claim** in Alaska and the Yukon Territory. (From 1900s) See also **right limit.**

leg wrestling
■ n An activity originally adopted from Eskimos, but now popular throughout the West, in which two contestants lie down on their backs, side by side and head to toe. At a signal, each contestant raises the inside leg, hooks the opponent's leg at the ankle, and tries to pull the opponent over. (1980s)

lemita
■ n Also called the **lemonade-and-sugar tree.** Any of a variety of sumacs found in the Southwest, whose berries are used to make an acidic drink similar to lemonade. (From 1900s, Spanish *limonita* 'little lemon, lime')

lemonade berry
■ n Another name for **lemita.** The berry of any of a variety of sumacs used to made an acidic drink. (From 1900s)

Levi's
■ /LEE vize/ n Trousers made of heavy blue denim, originally by Levi Strauss and Company. The earliest versions of the pants featured copper-rivet reinforcers at pockets and crotch. In later years, nearly any stylized preshrunk, prebleached denim pants have been called by the term. (From 1880s)

light artillery
■ n See **artillery,** 2.

light cedar
■ n See **incense cedar.**

line, the
■ n Also called **the row.** In Alaska, in areas featuring mining camps and boomtowns, the section of town in which prostitutes ply their trade, cheap whiskey is sold, and gambling is available. (From 1950s)

line cabin

■ n Also called **line camp, line house.** A temporary shelter for cowboys or trappers who ride along and check a trapline or fence line and must be out overnight. (From 1880s)

line rider

■ n A trapper or cowboy who is responsible for checking traps or keeping fences in repair. (From 1880s) See also **fence rider, outrider.**

llano

■ /YAH no/ n An extensive high plain without trees and generally arid. The most famous is the Llano Estacado, a high, arid plateau of forty thousand square miles, situated in Texas and New Mexico. (From 1840s)

lluva de oro

■ /YOO bah day OH roh/ n A name applied to various plants in the Southwest that have profusions of yellow blossoms after a wet springtime. The palo verde especially displays cascades of yellow blossoms in arid regions if by chance there has been rainfall in January or February. (From 1900s, Spanish 'shower of gold')

lobo

■ n Also called **lobo wolf.** The gray wolf; the timber wolf. (From 1850s, Spanish)

loco

■ adj Pertaining to a state of madness or marked by strange behavior. (From 1840s, Spanish 'crazy')

loco

■ n A distemper resembling madness exhibited by cattle that have eaten **locoweed.** Nervous symptoms are followed by paralysis and death. (From 1890s)

locoweed

■ n Also called **loco plant.** Any of a variety of alkaline-bearing plants of the genus *Astragalus*. Eating such weed causes livestock to stagger as if intoxicated, behave strangely, and sometimes to become paralyzed and die. (From 1870s)

locust

■ n The migratory Rocky Mountain grasshopper, which grows to about two inches in length, is pale green to brown and can fly considerable distances. (From 1820s)

lode claim

■ n A mining **claim** to an area that has minerals occurring in veins. (From 1870s)

lode mining

■ n Removing ore from veins, especially gold and silver, rather than using washing techniques or stripping topsoil. (From 1870s)

lodgepole

■ n A pole serving as the central support in the structures of various Indian tribes. (From 1800s)

lodgepole pine

■ n Any of various pines that grow tall and straight, but especially *Pinus murrayana,* that can be converted to structural poles with little trimming. (From 1850s)

loganberry

■ n A variety of red berry, said to have the shape of the blackberry, the color of a raspberry, and the taste of a combination of both. (From 1890s, after J. H. Logan, American jurist and horticulturalist, 1841–1928, who lived in Santa Cruz, California)

loma

■ n A small hillock or rise. Commonly used in place-names in the West and Southwest. (From 1840s, Spanish)

looloo

■ n Any of a variety of **poker** hands determined by local custom to beat anything on the table. Such a hand is usually invoked when a stranger or **tenderfoot** is in a game or when a visiting gambler seems to be unusually lucky. Said to have originated in Butte, Montana. (From 1890s)

loose-herd

■ v To turn the cattle of several ranches loose on a prairie. When **roundup** time comes, the cattle are separated by brand, then **close-herded** at night to keep the animals separate by owners. (From 1880s)

loose leader

■ n Also shortened to **loose lead.** Among **dog mushers** in Alaska and the Yukon, a dog allowed to run ahead of the dogs pulling the sled. The dog running in this fashion inspires the other dogs to strain harder to keep up. (From 1920s)

lowbush moose

■ n In Alaska, a jocular name for a rabbit. Perhaps it is so called because the rabbit vies with the moose for certain types of foliage. (From 1930s)

Lower 48, Lower Forty-eight

■ n Also **Lower 49, Lower States.** The part of the United States that is not Alaska. A point of pride for many Alaskans is that their state is isolated, is very large, and in relation to the rest of the states, on "top of the world." (From 1950s) See also **outside.**

lowrider

■ n 1. A highly customized car fitted with hydraulic jacks that allow the car to be lowered nearly to the ground or raised quickly at the front end so the front part of the car bounces off the pavement. 2. The person, usually of Mexican-American descent, who customizes and drives such a vehicle (see **cholo, pachuco**). The term denotes an entire life-style with its own clothing, jargon, and manners of behavior. (From 1970s)

luftak

■ n Also **laftak, lavtak.** A boot made from the hide of the bearded seal (the **maklak**). More recently, the sole of such a boot. Originally, a foot-covering much like the **mukluk.** (From 1870s, Russian) See also **kamik.**

luminaria

■ /LOO min AH ree uh/ n A festival light made by placing a candle in an open paper bag, usually weighted on the bottom with sand or gravel. The lights line walkways and tops of walls at various festival times in the Southwest. In other parts of the country, the practice is extending beyond just Christmastime to include Halloween or even New Year's Eve. (From 1930s, Spanish)

madrona

■ /muh DROH nuh/ n Also known as **mountain mahogany.** Any of the various arbutus evergreens found in the West and Southwest, including *Arbutus menziesii* of the Pacific Coast and *A. xalapensis,* found along the southwest border of the United States. (From 1840s, Spanish)

mahala mat

■ n Also called **squaw mat.** A dwarf creeper found in the forest of central California. The plant features dainty lavender bells that blossom in late spring. The name comes from a Yokuts word. The tribal grouping is of the Mariposan language family in California. (From 1900s Yokuts *muk'ela* 'woman')

maklak

■ n Also spelled *muckluck, mukluk.* The bearded seal found in Alaskan waters. It winters in the Bering Sea and migrates to the Arctic Ocean for the summer. The hide of the animal is especially desired in making the soles of the native-style boots. (From 1860s, Central Yupik) See **luftak, mukluk** for further information.

malamute

■ n Also spelled *malemute.* A **sled dog** of the **husky** variety. The breed was recognized by the American Kennel Club in 1935, after breeding programs had been long established by New England dog fanciers. The animal is large-boned, with a thick undercoat and coarse outer hair. The black, gray, and white markings normally include the white face with a darker mask or cap. (From 1890s, Inupiaq) See **Alaskan husky** for further information.

malibu board

■ n Also called a **chip board.** A surfboard developed in the 1950s in Southern California. The board is lightweight plastic foam (originally balsa wood) and between eight and eleven feet long. The board boosted the popularity of surfing because it was easily transportable and could be carried from parking areas far from beach access. The ride was also more suitable to the California surf. (From 1950s, after Malibu Beach, California)

malpais

■ n A rugged region of volcanic ground, with extrusions of basaltic lava, up to several square miles in size. (From 1840s, Spanish *mal* 'bad' + *pais* 'country')

manada

■ n A group of horses, or even a herd, from which saddle horses might be selected. (From 1840s, Spanish) See also **remuda.** Compare **caballada, mulada.**

mañana

■ n An undesignated time in the indefinite future. A state of mind in which any chore or task might be postponed. A rejection of rigorous punctuality. (From 1840s Spanish 'tomorrow')

mane

■ n A surfer's term for the plume of spray blown from the top of a breaking wave by an offshore wind. (From 1960s)

manga

■ n Also called **poncho.** A cape or mantle. Sometimes the garment is of a piece, with a hole through the center which the head can slip through. (From 1834, Spanish)

mangana

■ n A type of throw with a **lasso** that catches a running animal by the front feet, thereby dropping it to the ground. (From 1920s, Spanish) See also **blocker, forefoot.**

mano

■ n The upper part of a grinding stone, held in the hand, and used by Indians in the Southwest for grinding corn, seeds, and grain. (From 1890s, Spanish 'hand') See also **metate.**

manzanita ■ n Also called **mountain mahogany.** A shrub of the West that bears large, reddish berries likened to tiny apples. The shrubs include *Arctostaphylos pungens* and *A. tomentosa.* (From 1840s, Spanish 'little apple')

marine highway ■ n In Alaska, the state ferry system, formally known as the Alaska Marine Highway System, a unit of the state's Department of Transportation and Public Facilities. Local citizens and tourists alike have come to use the informal term for any water travel in southeastern Alaska. (From 1970s)

Mariposa lily ■ n Also called **Mariposa tulip.** Any of a variety of plants found in the West with tuliplike petals. The plant is of the genus *Calochortus.* (From 1880s, Spanish 'butterfly' + *lily*)

marker ■ n In grazing herds, an animal with distinctive markings used by the herder to keep track of a group. Among sheep, a black sheep. The herder knows how many black sheep are in the herd and can make a quick check, assuming that if all the black sheep are present, then few or no other sheep are missing. (From 1910s)

masru, masu ■ n See **Eskimo potato.**

maul oak ■ n See **Valparaiso oak.**

maverick ■ n 1. A cow or calf without a brand. Named after Samuel A. Maverick (1803–1870), a rancher in

Texas who did not brand the animals of his herd. Consequently, the unbranded calf belonged to whoever could put a brand on the animal (from 1860s). 2. A person who refuses to affiliate with (be "branded" by) a recognized political party. (From 1880s)

mecate
■ n Also spelled *McCarty* by folk etymology. A rope made of hair or maguey used by cowboys for tying horses, making makeshift bridles, or tying down equipment. (From 1840s, Nahuatl via Spanish)

Melchizedek priesthood
■ n The higher order of priesthood in the Mormon church. (From 1840s) See also **Aaronic priesthood, elder.**

menudo
■ n A chunky soup with a thin broth, spicy, and made with tripe, onions, tomatoes, chilis. Though a regular dish in Southwestern cuisine for generations, regular use in English dates from the 1950s. (Spanish 'little guts')

mesa
■ n Especially in the Southwest, an elevated flat-topped hill with steep sides. (From 1840s, Spanish 'table')

mescal
■ n 1. Any species of agave used for a food source (from 1830s, Nahuatl via Spanish). 2. An alcoholic liquor made from the juice of baked heads of the agave (from 1820s).

mescal button
■ n Also called **mescal button cactus.** The bud of **peyote,** especially noted for an alkaloid content that produces hallucinations in humans when ingested. (From 1890s) See also **whiskey root.**

mesquite
■ n Also spelled *masketo, musquite, mezquite, mesquit.* A deep-rooted, shrublike tree (*Prosopis juliflora*) ubiquitous in the Southwest. The hard wood makes the tree desirable for fires and barbecuing meat. The bean of the tree, which grows in a long seedlike pod, is used for food for animals and by scavenging humans. (From 1800s, Nahuatl via Spanish *mezquite*) See also **screw bean.**

mano (top), metate

metate ■ n The lower stone used by Indians in the West and Southwest for grinding corn, seeds, beans, and so on. Used in conjunction with a **mano.** (From 1830s, Nahuatl via Spanish)

Mexican banana ■ n Also called **banana yucca.** A fruit of the *Yucca baccata,* native to northern Mexico and the Southwest which bears an edible fruit. (From 1880s) See also **datil, Spanish bayonet.**

Mexican fireball ■ n A short, roundish cactus with long slender spines that are sometimes hard to see and therefore stepped on by humans and horses. See **barrel cactus** for a complete listing.

Mexican jumping bean ■ n See **jumping bean.**

Mexican saddle ■ n Also called **peak saddle.** A heavy wood-framed saddle featuring a high pommel and raised canticle, wooden stirrups, and a heavy leather skirt. (From 1840s)

Mexican spotted owl ■ n An endangered species that is causing consternation among developers and envromentalists in Arizona, Utah, and New Mexico. See also **northern spotted owl.**

Mexican spur ■ n An ornate spur with a large rowel, often with pointed spokes, and silver ornamentation designed to make a ringing noise when worn. (From 1860s)

mi casa es su casa ■ phr Literally, the phrase means "my house is your house." In other words, "you are as welcome here as in your own house." This common phrase of politeness that long signified the gentility of the Southwestern life-style has been adopted by every restaurant that uses a hint of chili powder or has potted ferns in the bars. Unfortunately, the proprietors of such establishments take a dim view of your going to their refrigerators to browse as you might at home.

mickaninny

■ n A small Eskimo child. The term was adapted from nineteenth-century whalers, whose jargon already had the word "pickaninny," itself adapted from the Portuguese diminutive form meaning "little." The Inupiaq words *miki* 'being small' or *miqliqtuq* 'child' may have influenced the Portuguese term to result in the Alaskan word. (From 1900s)

mild cure

■ n A process for preserving salmon commercially. Sides of king salmon are preserved in a light brine and cooled for several weeks until the fish can be smoked. (From 1900s)

milk the brush

■ v phr Also called **milk the bushes.** In Alaska and the Yukon Territory and other parts of the Northwest, to move a boat up a small stream by grasping overhanging brush and pulling the boat along. (From 1900s)

milpita

■ n Also called **milpa.** A small cornfield patch under cultivation in the Southwest. Also used in place-names and geographic names. (From 1840s, Nahuatl via Spanish 'little cornfield')

mining camp

■ n A temporary settlement composed of miners and the support personnel who provide everything the miners want, from equipment and supplies to liquor and gambling. (From 1860s)

mining claim

■ n Also called **mineral claim.** A patch of land that a miner can claim to be working on to extract ore. A general requirement for holding such a claim is that a specified amount of work be done on the grounds each year, usually listed as work or improvements worth one hundred dollars, a sum that has not changed in more than fifty years. (From 1850s)

mining district

■ n A specific geographic region described by particular boundaries and registered by name with a government land office. The mines and **mining claims** within that region are listed in the district's records. (From 1860s)

mining town

■ n A town that has grown beyond the temporary nature of a **mining camp.** A town has buildings more substantial than tents. But the single source of enterprise income usually marks the mining town as a transition between a mining camp and a **ghost town.** (From 1850s)

mission

■ A combining element used with a number of terms relative to or belonging to early Spanish missions in the Southwest: *mission family, ~ farm, ~ grape, ~ Indian, ~ (olive) oil, ~ school, ~ sewing school, ~ station.* (From 1850s)

mission design

■ n An architectural style characteristic of the early Spanish missions in the Southwest. The style is marked by sprawling adobe buildings with courtyards and walled enclosures, fitted overall with rounded red tiles on the roof. (From 1900s)

mission design

mission furniture

■ n A style for chairs, hutches, sideboards, rockers, cradles, and tables that features heavy dark wood, straight lines, and bulky supports and struts. Said to describe the style found in early Spanish missions of the Southwest. (From 1900s)

mission-style

■ adj Reminiscent of the structure, architecture, fittings, furniture, roofing of the (usually Franciscan) Spanish missions of the Southwest. (From 1910s)

moccasin

■ n See **dog moccasin.**

Mohave Apache

■ n See **Yavapai.**

Mohave rattlesnake

■ n A common green rattlesnake, *Crotalus scutulatus,* found in the lower regions of the Mojave Desert. (From 1930s)

Mohave yucca

■ n A yucca plant specific to biotic communities in the Mojave Desert of southeastern California and southern Nevada. The *Yucca schidigera* grows on higher slopes in the company of junipers and piñons. (From 1940s)

mole

■ /MOH lay/ n A sauce made for meats cooked in a Mexican style that features chilis and unsweetened chocolate. Other spices and sometimes peanuts are included in the sauce. (From 1930s)

money fish

■ n Among Alaskan commercial fishermen, the particular type of **salmon** caught in an area that brings the highest price at the market. (From 1980s)

money shell

■ n See **butter clam.**

Montana

■ n Nicknames: **Stubtoe State, Treasure State.** Forty-first state of the Union. Settled in 1809, it became a territory in 1864, and a state in 1889. Capital: Helena. From Latin or Spanish *montana* 'mountainous', the name was originally proposed for the Idaho Territory, but defeated. Liking the name, Representative James M. Ashley of Ohio proposed it for the largely flat territory east of the Idaho Territory. The proposal passed for want of a better suggestion. (From 1860s) See also **Jefferson Territory.**

monte

■ n 1. A Mexican card game popular in the Southwest in the latter part of the eighteenth century. The game features a pack of forty-five cards (sometimes forty), and the play is similar to faro, using a top-and-bottom layout of two cards each (from 1840s). 2. As a combining element for terms related to the playing of the game: *monte bank, ~ banker, ~ dealer, ~ layout, ~ sharp* ("cheater"), *~ table.* (From 1840s)

monte thrower

■ n A dealer of three-card monte, a scam in which the con artist puts three cards down, one usually being an ace or queen of spades. He bets that the victim cannot pick out that card, which, of course, the victim cannot, the appropriate card having been palmed by the thrower. (From 1930s)

moose hunter stall

■ n A maneuver that sometimes occurs when bush pilots in the Northwest are flying low, see something they want to check out, and stall their single engine airplanes too close to the ground to pull out safely. (From 1980s)

moose-gooser

■ n Jocular name for a train, or more specifically an engine in the deep-snow country of the Far Northwest. Moose sometimes wander along railroad tracks to avoid deep snow and are hit by the train or the snowplow on the front of an engine. (From 1940s)

Mormon

■ n A combining element relating to life, equipment, and materials frequently used or invented by the Mormons of Utah, Idaho, Nevada, Arizona: *Mormon blanket, ~ buggy, ~ elder, ~ hay press, ~ merchant, ~ missionary, ~ road, ~ station, ~ store, ~ trail.* See also **Church of Jesus Christ of Latter-day Saints.**

Mormon tea

■ n Also called **Brigham tea, canatillo, clapweed.** Any of the plants from the genus *Ephedra.* The shoots of the plant are used in making an astringent tea used medicinally. (From 1910s)

mother lode

■ n 1. Originally capitalized, the principal quartz vein running from Mariposa to Amador in California (from 1870s). 2. By extension, uncapitalized, the main vein of ore in a mine, **mining claim,** or **district.** (From 1880s)

motor musher

■ n Originally a jocular name for a person who drives a snowmobile, the term has been elevated to a formal term in Alaska and is used in the names of clubs and titles of snowmobile races. (From 1960s)

mountain

■ A combining element used for a number of alternative names for animals found in the **Rocky Mountains:** *mountain antelope,* ~ *goat* (Rocky Mountain goat); ~ *grape* (see **barberry**); ~ *grizzly* (see **grizzly bear** [found around Yellowstone National Park]); ~ *lion* (see **cougar, puma**); ~ *mahogany* (see **madrona, manzanita**); ~ *ram,* ~ *sheep* (Rocky Mountain sheep [see **bighorn sheep**]); ~ *tea* (wintergreen found in the Canadian Rockies); ~*time* (mean local time on the 105th meridian); ~ *trout* (see **rainbow trout, cutthroat trout**); ~ *man* (pioneering frontiersman adapted to surviving in the high Rockies). (From 1840s)

mouse nut

■ n A tuberous root, usually of cotton grass, collected and stored by small rodents like lemmings and voles in Alaska and on the tundra. People locate the caches of these rodents and take the small bulbous tubers, which have a sweet, nutty taste. (From 1950s)

mozo

■ n Originally, an assistant on the housekeeping staff or a domestic; more recently, a toady or overly obsequious employee. (From 1830s, Spanish)

muchacho

■ n A young boy; usually as a term of endearment. **Muchacha** is becoming more frequently used in the same way for a young girl. (From 1820s)

muckamuck

■ n Food, among natives and eventually among Alaskans generally. (From 1840s, Chinook jargon)

mudshark

■ n A long, slender, brownish fish of the cod family that is found in cool waters from Maine to the Bering Straits. It is known by many local names, "mudshark" being the Alaskan one, due to a perceived resemblance to a shark and the fact that it is a bottom-dweller. The three- to five-pound fish is delicious and available year-round as a subsistence fish and a sport fish. (From 1950s)

mukluk　　■ n Originally the sole of a soft boot made from the hide of a bearded seal (**maklak**). Later, the entire boot. Now the word has come to mean any boot made in the style of those early soft boots made by Alaskan Natives. Similar to **kamik, luftak.** (From 1860s, Central Yupik *maklak* 'bearded seal')

mukluk telegraph　　■ n Also called the **mukluk wireless.** In Alaska, the word-of-mouth system for spreading news and gossip in sparsely populated country. (From 1940s, on analogy with "moccasin telegraph," as used in Canada)

mulada	■ n A herd of mules. Compare **caballada, manada, remuda.** (From 1840s, Spanish)
mule-crippler cactus	■ n See **horse crippler.**
mule deer	■ n Also called **black-tailed deer, desert mule deer.** A long-eared deer of the West and Southwest, the *Odocoileus hemionus.* (From 1800s) See also **burro deer.**
mule skinner	■ n A driver of mule teams. By extension, any rough or uncouth person, especially one who talks loudly and irreverently. (From 1870s)
mush	■ v To travel with and by **dogsled** in the Far Northwest (from 1860s). Interestingly, the word is not used by modern dogsled travelers as a command to the dogs, as is popularly thought.
mush dog	■ n Any of a variety of dogs used to pull sleds, now mainly in the **Iditarod** race held in Alaska in the late winter. See **Alaskan husky** for a full listing.
musher	■ n Also called **dog musher.** One who travels by **dogsled,** keeps **sled dogs,** and participates in the sport of dogsled racing. (From 1900s, French *marchons* 'let's walk, go')
muskeg tea	■ n See **Alaska tea.**
mustang	■ n Also called **bronco, broomtail.** A wild horse of the West and Southwest. The horse was originally introduced by the Spanish, but now includes horses that have escaped from western herds and returned to a feral state. (From 1800s, Spanish *mesteño* 'wild horse') See also **fuzztail.**

nagoonberry　■ n Also called **wineberry, dewberry, lagoon-berry.** A raspberrylike fruit of the small *Rubus arcticus* plant found in Alaska and noted for the exquisite flavor of its juice. (From 1910s, Tlingit *neigóon*)

nanook　■ n The polar bear, or *Ursus maritimus*. (From 1940s, Inupiaq *nanuq*)

Napa leather　■ n Also called **Napa tannage.** The hides of sheep and goats prepared by a special tanning process developed in Napa, California. The area specialized in soft kid leather and suede. (From 1890s)

Navajo blanket　■ n Also spelled *Navaho*. A blanket woven in a specific style and design by Navajos. The blanket has been a popular tourist purchase for many years. (From 1830s)

Navajo ruby　■ n Also called **Arizona ruby.** A type of garnet originally found in the vicinity of Fort Defiance, Arizona. (From 1910s)

Navajo rug　■ n A rug, usually small, under four by six feet, woven with special designs by Navajos and often sold to the tourist trade. (From 1940s)

Navajo silver　■ n Jewelry, belt buckles, spoons, and other pieces worked in silver with special Navajo designs. (From 1940s)

classic design on a Navajo rug

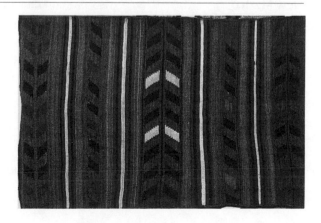

neckline

■ n Among **mushers** and **dogsled** outfitters, the line, about eight inches long, that runs from the dog's collar to the main line attached to the sled. (From 1950s)

Nephite

■ n A member of the group founded by Nephi, who brought his people to America around 600 B.C., according to the Book of Mormon. (From 1830s)

nester

■ n A person who moved west to become a home-steader or farmer or to build a small ranch in a cat-tle-grazing region of large ranches. The term was considered offensive by settlers, but in recent years has become less so with more city people develop-ing country retreats. (From 1880s)

Nevada

■ n Also called **Silver Land, Silver State, Battle-Born State, Sagebrush State, Sage Hen State.** Thirty-sixth state of the Union. Settled in 1850, it became a territory in 1859, and a state in 1864. Capital: Carson City. Named for the Sierra Nevadas that supposedly form its western border, but that are instead almost entirely in California. (From 1859; Spanish *nevada,* "snow-covered")

new ivory

■ n Walrus tusks that are not freshly harvested, but which have not been buried for a long time and are still white, but seasoned. Carvers prefer **old ivory** for carving, but will also make use of new ivory. (From 1940s) See also **green ivory.** Compare **fossil ivory.**

New Mexico

■ n Also called **Land of Enchantment.** Forty-sev-enth state of the Union. Settled in 1605, it became a territory in 1850, after the Mexican War (1846–1848) resulted in the annexation of the Mexican territories that became California, Ari-zona, New Mexico, Nevada, and Utah. Became a state in 1912. Capital: Santa Fe. (From 1850; Span-ish *Nuevo* "new" + *Mexico,* from Aztec *Mexitel,* "place of the war god.")

night herd

■ v To watch over a herd of cattle at night during **roundup** time. (From 1900s)

nooshnik	■ n Also spelled *nushnik*. In Alaska, an outhouse; a privy; a latrine. (From 1940s, Russian *nuzhnyi* 'necessary')
norteño	■ n Also **norteña.** A fast, polkalike music found mainly along the U.S./Mexican border. See also **Tejano music.**
North Slope	■ n Also called **Arctic Slope.** The northern side of the Brooks Range in Alaska, including the coastal plain to the Arctic Ocean. This is the center of oil and petroleum development in Alaska. (From 1960s)
norther	■ n Also called **blue norther.** A strong, cold wind from the north, especially blowing into Texas and the plains of the Southwest. (From 1770s, Spanish calque)
northern spotted owl	■ n A small reclusive owl found in old-growth forests ranging generally from northern California to British Columbia and east into Idaho. The Endangered Species Act of 1973 helped put this small creature in the spotlight when logging was halted to protect the habitats of the owl. (From 1970s) See also **Mexican spotted owl.**
no sabe	■ v phr Also **no savvy.** Not to understand something. (From 1850s, Spanish, generalized from the third person singular of *saber* 'to know') See also **sabe.**

ocatillo

old man cactus

oosik

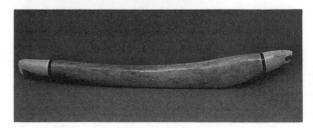

ocelot

■ n A Southwestern spotted cat, *Felix pardalis,* somewhat smaller than a jaguar. (From 1800s, Nahuatl *ocelotl* via Spanish)

ocatillo

■ /ah kuh TEE yo/ n Also spelled *ocotilla.* Also called **candlewood, coachwhip, ocatillo cactus, Saint Joseph('s) rod.** The Southwestern shrub, *Fouquieria splendens,* which is often thought to be a cactus, but is not. The long slender branches rise from a common short base and appear to bear cactuslike spines. (From 1850s, Nahuatl via Spanish diminutive for *ocote*)

old ivory

■ n Also called **fossil ivory.** In Alaska, the aged ivory from the tusks of walrus, mastodon, or mammoth. The aging makes the ivory turn yellowish and causes indelible stains. Consequently, the material is highly prized by carvers. (From 1940s) Compare **green ivory, new ivory.**

old man cactus

■ n Also called **hombre viejo, old man cholla, señita.** A cactus of the Southwest featuring long, drooping silverlike hairs at the joints and at the top of the stem. The cactus is *Cephalocereus senilis.* (From 1880s)

olla

■ /AH luh/ n A pot or container for water made from earthenware or plant fiber coated with pitch. Used by various Indian tribes in the Southwest and northern Mexico. (From 1840s, Spanish)

one-foot high kick

■ Also called the **Alaskan high kick.** One of the many games for testing strength among Alaska Natives. The competitor stands on one foot, then jumps in the air and kicks an overhead target and lands on the same foot. Other such contests involve jumping with both feet, pulling various parts of the body of a competitor, and so on. (From 1970s) See also **high kick, two-foot high kick.**

oosik

■ n The penis bone of a walrus, usually polished and carved with decorations, such as an animal head at either end. These bones are very popular with tourists. (From 1970s, Inupiaq *usuk*)

open range

■ n A cattle grazing area unrestricted by fences. Because of this, cows may wander onto roadways. Signs indicating "open range" are often provided by state highway departments, warning motorists to beware. (From 1890s)

opilio

■ n Also called **Tanner crab.** One of the crab species that became commercially important in the 1960s, after the decline of the **king crab** in Alaskan fishing waters. The *Chionoecetes opilio* is commonly called by its shorter species name. The crab is also found in the Atlantic and the name dates to the 1780s, but the frequency of use has been Alaskan since the 1960s. See also **bairdi.**

ore

■ n A combining form for describing a number of western mining terms: *ore car,* metal car in a mine or on a railroad for hauling ore (from 1870s); ~ *chimney,* a diagonal hole in the ground that circulates air in a mine shaft (from 1880s); ~ *chute,* a diagonally cut hole into a mine that sometimes ends with a shaft that goes straight down (from 1860s).

Oregon

■ n Thirty-third state of the Union. Settled in 1811, it became a territory in 1848, and a state in 1859. Capital: Salem. The origin of the name is widely disputed; perhaps the most reliable explanation is that it is a misspelling of the French word for the Wisconsin River, *Ouisconsink,* since that river was widely believed to empty into the Pacific Ocean. The name was then used to describe the Columbia River and the area around it. Jonathan Carver was the first to use the word "Oregon" to describe the territory. (From 1778) Nicknamed the **Beaver State, Hard-Case State, Webfoot State.**

Oregon

■ n A combining form for plants, trees, birds, and animals that exist in other areas, but feature species peculiar to this state; also, combined forms for self-explaining terms used in the state: *Oregon alder, ~ ash, ~ bearwood, ~ cedar, ~ chickadee, ~ corn, ~ crab apple (Malus fusca,* marked by white blossoms and tall shape, to twenty-seven feet), *~ elk, ~ finch, ~ fir, ~ flying squirrel, ~ grape* (see **barberry,** *~ jay, ~ junco, ~ maple* (see **big-leaf maple**), *~ mis-*

sion, ~ mist, ~ mytle, ~ pea, ~ pine, ~ red squirrel, ~ robin (see **Alaska robin**), *~ snowbird, ~ snowfinch, ~ sunflower, ~ towhee, ~ vesper sparrow, ~ white fir, ~ wood rat.*

Oregon boot

■ n A device originally placed on the ankle of a prisoner, made of heavy iron. Now a locking device that can be placed on the tire of a vehicle to prevent its being driven away. (From 1920s)

organ cactus

■ n Also **organ-pipe cactus.** Another form of the giant **saguaro** (q.v. for a complete listing) of the Sonoran Desert. (From 1880s)

ouija board

■ n In Alaska, a small toboggan tied between the dogs and the front of a heavy sled. The sled driver stands on this platform and pulls or pushes the **gee pole,** a long pole attached to the front of the sled like a bowsprit on a sailboat. Pushing the pole, which is attached to the right-front part of the sled, steers the sled toward the right. Pulling it steers the sled left. The name "ouija" is the result of a folk etymology, misunderstanding "gee board." (From 1930s)

outlaw

■ n A horse that is vicious by temperament or because of brutal handling while being broken. Not necessarily a **bronco,** which is trained to buck. (From 1880s)

outrider

■ n An employee on a ranch who has the job of riding to remote areas on the ranch to check fences, sheep, cattle, or other parts of the ranch operation. Nowadays the outrider usually takes a pickup truck and pulls a horse trailer to the area to be checked. (From 1870s) See also **fence rider, line rider.**

outside

■ n Also called the **Lower Forty-eight.** Any place not in Alaska. Originally most frequently used in southeastern Alaska, now used mainly adverbially to refer to comings and goings between Alaska and (usually) the rest of the United States. (From 1890s)

Outside Man

■ n Among the Aleut, a bogey-man; a wild man who represents the spirit of drowned or lost hunters; a spirit-character who rattles chimneys and scratches at doors during the dark nights trying to get in, especially to get children who have been bad. (From 1930s)

P

pachuco

■ n A young Mexican-American who flaunts a specific flashy life-style, often belongs to a gang, drives a **lowrider,** and has a particular jargon. (From 1940s, perhaps from a pronunciation of (El) Paso + *uco,* a pejorative suffix) See also **cholo.**

Pacific

■ n A combining form for terms relative to the far western part of North America. Self-explanatory combinations include *Pacific Coast, ~ diver, ~ Empire, ~ Northwest, ~ Railroad, ~ rattlesnake, ~ salmon* (see **salmon** n), *~ seaboard, ~ slope, ~ States, ~ time, ~ cod, ~ yew.*

Pacific Rim

■ n The peoples and especially the economic interests of western North America and Asia. Business people interested in trade, oil, computer parts and software, lumber, the fishing industry, and other goods and services consider the Pacific Ocean a connecting circle for common economic benefit. (From 1980s)

pack

■ v To carry something; to lug water, provisions, or supplies; to carry a concealed weapon, especially a handgun. (From 1800s)

pack

■ n A combining form for terms relative to carrying equipment and supplies. Self-explanatory combinations include *pack animal, ~ burro, ~ dog, ~ mule, ~ outfit.*

padre

■ n Originally a priest at a mission in the Southwest; now used for any priest or even an ordained minister. (From 1800s)

paho

■ n Also spelled *bahoo.* A **prayer stick** prepared by Pueblo Indians for special ceremonies. (From 1880s, Hopi *páho* 'water prayer')

Painted Desert

■ n Name of a geographical region in north-central Arizona, west of the Little Colorado River. The rocks and soils in the area have variegated colors of pink, white, red, brown, black, and other shades. (From 1860s)

= 173 =

paisano

■ n 1. A countryman, especially a fellow rustic or peasant (from 1840s, Spanish). 2. A **chaparral cock,** also called a **roadrunner** (q.v. for a complete listing). The bird is prized for ridding its hunting area of mice and vermin (from 1840s).

palo

■ n A combining element borrowed from Spanish. The element refers to white or cream colored ("pale"): plant names with the element include *palo blanco, ~ fierro, ~ verde, ~dura, ~milla.*

palo amarillo

■ n Also called **barberry** (q.v. for a complete listing). The **hollygrape** of the Southwest that has reddish bark on older stems and yellowish green bark on new growth. (From 1840s)

palomino

■ n A silver or golden-coated horse of the Southwest with a cream or white-colored mane. (From 1910s, Spanish)

pan

■ n Shortened from **panguingue.** A multiple-player card game that operates as a variation of conquian, or cooncan, the early rummy game. The game is played with six or more Spanish decks (no eights, nines, or tens) and scoring is by melding groups of cards. The game apparently originated in the Philippines and was the most popular card game among gamblers in the early West before **poker** became popular. (From 1900s)

pan

■ n In placer mining, a shallow metal dish with ridges used for washing stream gravel to extract gold flakes. (From 1840s) See also **batea, washbowl.**

parka

■ n Also called **atigi.** Also spelled *parkie, parkee, parky.* A hooded cloak pulled over the head, introduced by natives of the extreme Northwest. Originally made of animal skins, nowadays made of synthetic fabrics. (From 1860s, Russian)

pastor

■ n A sheepherder. (From 1840s, Spanish)

patio

■ n Also called **azotea.** An inner court or garden open to the sky, attached to a house or building in Spanish architecture of the Southwest. Now, any area attached to a house, and featuring chairs or

parka

benches, often a table and a barbecue. (From 1840s)

patio process
■ n In silver mining, a process of amalgamation to treat silver ore by spreading it on a floor open to the sky and treating it chemically. (From 1860s)

pay dirt
■ n Soil or gravel containing a mineral, such as gold, in large quantities. (From 1850s)

peak saddle
■ n See **Mexican saddle.**

pear burner
■ n A machine designed to singe the spines off the **prickly-pear cactus** so that the plant can be used for cattle fodder. (From 1900s)

peccary
■ n See **javalina.**

pechita
■ n Any of a variety of leguminous plants providing beans used in the Southwest for animal feed or

dried and ground for human consumption. (From 1870s, Zapotecan via Spanish diminutive of *beche*)

pedal

■ v Also called **pump.** In **dogsled** racing, to stand on one runner and repeatedly push with the other foot on the snow, helping the dogs to propel the sled forward. (From 1960s)

pedregal

■ /ped rih GAL/ n A field of lava flow, broken by erosion and nearly bare of vegetation. (From 1850s, Spanish 'stony place')

pelado

■ /pay LAH doh/ n A person of lower class, penniless and homeless and uneducated. Used as a term of contempt. (From 1840s, Spanish)

Penitentes

■ n pl Members of a religious order of flagellants among some Spanish-American natives of New Mexico and southern Colorado. (From 1830s)

peon

■ n A common laborer; a peasant. (From 1820s, Spanish) The term developed in English of the Southwest independently from the same term used in India, borrowed from French or Portuguese.

peso

■ n Originally, a Mexican dollar. Now, used colloquially in the sense of "money" generally. (From 1840s, Spanish)

petruski

■ n Also spelled *petrushki.* A form of wild parsley found in Alaska. The springtime plant grows to three feet tall, has leaves with long stalks, each leaf ending in three leaflets, shiny and rough toothed. The plant is used as greens and, either raw or cooked, is especially favored with fish. (From 1950s, Russian *petrushka* 'parsley')

peyote

■ n Also called **whiskey root.** A cactus that grows small buttons that can be used as a hallucinogenic. The cactus is *Lophophora williamsi.* (From 1890s, Nahuatl *peyotl*) See also **mescal button.**

peyote cult

■ n A branch of the American Indian Church that uses peyote in religious ceremonies. When the church was outlawed in the 1930s, the use of **peyote** became secretive in the Southwest. (From 1930s)

picacho

■ n A tall, often jagged rock or **butte,** not high enough or large enough to be called a mountain. Often a tall rock that serves as a landmark and is used by rock-climbers for day hikes. (From 1850s, Spanish 'peak, summit')

picket pin

■ n A long pointed stick, now made of metal, driven into the ground for tethering a horse or other animal at night. (From 1840s)

pigeonberry

■ n Also called **bearberry honeysuckle.** One of a variety of small fruits of the pokeweed, bristly sarsaparilla, serviceberry, or blue dogwood. As used here, pigeonberry is another term for the **western bearberry.** (From 1930s)

pigweed

■ n See **alegria.**

piki

■ n A thin bread made of corn and baked on a smooth flat stone by Pueblo Indians. (From 1850s, Hopi)

pilgrim

■ n A newcomer to the West; a **tenderfoot.** The term was popularized by John Wayne's use of it in any number of western movies. (From 1840s) See also **Arbuckle, cheechako.**

pillar cactus

■ n Another name for the **saguaro** (q.v. for a complete listing) (From 1860s)

pilon

■ n Also spelled *pelon.* A gratuitous gift put in with a purchase, in the same sense that *lagniappe* is used in Louisiana. A little extra; a small gift, such as a piece of candy given to a customer's child. (From 1880s, Spanish)

pinacate bug

■ n See **circus beetle.**

pincushion cactus

■ n One of a couple of varieties of cactus that grow low to the ground and are small and rounded. Two of the types are *Mammillaria vivipara* and *M. compressa.* (From 1910s) See **barrel cactus** for a complete listing.

pineapple cactus

■ n A low-growing rounded cactus with fishhook spines; *Echinocactus polyancistrus.* (From 1940s) See **barrel cactus** for a complete listing.

pingue weed

■ /PING way/ n Also spelled *pinguay.* A perennial herb, *Hymenoxys floribunda,* which has properties of a rubber plant. At the turn of the century, the U.S. government began a research program to investigate using the latex from this plant in rubber products. The processes were never completely successful. (From 1900s)

pink salmon

■ n Also called **humpback salmon, holia.** A food fish found along the Pacific coast from Washington to Alaska. The *Oncorhynchus gorbuscha* has the shortest life cycle of the Pacific salmon (two years), and grows to about four pounds. The male develops a pronounced hump on its back as it goes to spawn. It is a staple of the fishing industry. (From 1890s) See **salmon** n for a complete listing.

pinole

■ n A cornmeal preparation using ground parched corn and other ingredients to make **tortillas** and tamales. (From 1840s, Nahuatl *pinolli*)

piñon

■ n Also spelled *pinion.* Any of several low-growing pines of the West producing edible seeds (piñon pine nuts) and wood desired for use as fuel. (From 1830s, Spanish)

pinto

■ n 1. A spotted or piebald horse (from 1860s, Spanish 'painted'). 2. A spotted or mottled variety of a kidney bean (from 1910s).

pipe

■ n Also called **barrel, tube.** Among surfers, the inside curve of a wave that forms a hollow in which a skilled surfer can ride. (From 1960s)

pipeline, the ■ n Also called **trans-Alaska pipeline.** In Alaska, an informal name designating the oil transportation system, eight hundred miles long, from Prudhoe Bay on the **North Slope** to Valdez, operated by Alyeska Pipeline Service Company. (From 1970s)

pita ■ n The fiber from agave plants used for cordage and making ropes. (From 1760s, Spanish)

pitahaya ■ n Any of a variety of large cacti, especially those with an edible fruit. Usually the reference is to the **organ cactus,** which has a cluster of columns, each up to four inches in diameter and four to eight feet tall. (From 1760s, Spanish)

piva ■ n A homemade beer brewed in some areas of Alaska. (From 1940s, Russian)

placer ■ n 1. A deposit of sand or gravel or dirt in which gold is found in particles (from 1840s, Spanish). See **wash gold.** 2. As a combining form in terms that have to do with searching for gold: *placer camp, ~ claim, ~ district, ~ dredge, ~ field, ~ gold, ~ ground, ~ mine, ~ miner, ~ mining.*

placita ■ n Also spelled *plasita, plazita.* A small square or courtyard, often with a flower garden or fountain, built into a Spanish-style house, especially in New Mexico. (From 1840s, Spanish *plaza* 'square' + diminutive)

playa ■ /PLY yuh/ n 1. A broad, level place that accumulates rainwater or runoff, but is otherwise dry and whitish-looking because of the alkali on the surface of the ground. 2. Used in proper names and informally as a term for "beach," alongside the seashore (from 1850s, Spanish 'beach, strand').

plaza ■ n A square, public garden, marketplace, or open area in a city or as open space associated with a large, sprawling building. (From 1830s, Spanish)

plug-in ■ n In Alaska and the Northwest Territories, electric receptacles for connecting heaters on vehicle engines and batteries when the temperature drops far below zero. Receptacles are to be found in public parking lots, at public and private buildings, and at residences. (From 1960s)

pocket mouse ■ n Any of a variety of rodents of the genus *Perognathus* found in the Southwest, whose distinguishing feature is cheek pouches used to carry food. (From 1880s)

poco ■ adj & adv A little; used often in the sense of having a small amount of something, such as Spanish language, money, food. Also used with *tiempo* in the sense of 'a little while, soon,' or 'just a minute.' (From 1840s, Spanish)

pogonip fog ■ n Also shortened to **pogonip.** 1. A heavy fog in which snow or ice crystals seems to be floating in the air, cutting visibility to zero. The condition occurs in portions of the high Sierras and Rocky Mountains when humidity is very low and a powdery snow has fallen (from 1860s, Shoshonean 'white death'). 2. In a transferred sense, the term has been applied to the heavy ground fog that develops along Interstate 5 in California's central valley, causing chain accidents involving scores of vehicles (from 1970s). See also **tule fog.** Compare **high fog.**

point rider ■ n See **drag rider, swing rider.**

poke ■ n See **sealskin poke.**

poker ■ n A card game highly popular in the West after the Civil War, probably spread by soldiers. It soon replaced faro as the common card game of barroom and cow camp. The standard form was draw poker, in which each player was dealt five cards, discarded unwanted cards, and drew additional cards, never exceeding five cards in the hand. Betting took place at each stage, and the value of card combinations was strictly ranked to determine a winner at the showdown. (From 1830s)

poker chip ■ n Also shortened to **chip.** A counter used in the card game of **poker,** soon extended to all counters used in card and dice games in place of money. (From 1870s)

pollo

■ n An illegal immigrant who acts as a client of a **coyote** 3, a smuggler, and crosses the Southwestern border into the United States. (From 1980s, Spanish, literally, 'chicken')

pollock

■ n See **Alaska pollock.**

poncho

■ n See **manga.**

poorga

■ n An especially violent Arctic blizzard. (From 1860s, Russian *purga*)

post cedar

■ n See **incense cedar.**

potlatch

■ n 1. A gift-giving celebration among various tribes of the Pacific Northwest from Washington State through British Columbia and Alaska. Elaborate preparations are made by the family of the person giving the potlatch, sometimes taking two or three years to assemble. The time of the festival lasts several days and serves as a gathering of clans and a social event for the entire region. Attendees will travel several hundred miles to be present. For a time during the early twentieth century, missionaries and government officials attempted to ban the potlatch, having misunderstood the social and cultural function of the event. Wiser heads prevailed and excluded the missionaries (from 1860s, Nootka via Chinook Jargon). 2. In the Pacific Northwest, and extending to Montana and Alberta, a social gathering in which participating families bring a prepared dish of food; a potluck dinner; a covered-dish supper (from 1940s). The term is also used as a verb.

potrero

■ n A meadow or pastureland. Used frequently in place-names in the West and Southwest. (From 1840s, Spanish)

pozo

■ n A well or spring, especially one that is fifteen to twenty feet in diameter and shallow, with about two feet of water. (From 1850s, Spanish)

powder

■ n Among skiers in the high mountains of the West, a fine, light snow covering , usually several feet deep. The fine and fluffy snow results from snow falling in areas of low humidity and cold

temperatures. The condition is highly desirable for skiers and particularly photographers who like to take pictures of skiers sweeping through the drifts. (From 1950s)

prayer stick

■ n Also called **paho.** A special stick or small board prepared by Pueblo Indians for ceremonial purposes. These devices are intricately carved and decorated. (From 1860s)

praznik

■ n In Alaska, a festival day or feast or party featuring special foods and influenced by the festival days of the early Russian settlers. (From 1860s, Russian *prazdnik* 'public or religious holiday')

preacher

■ n In Alaskan rivers and navigable waters, an uprooted tree with roots still attached that floats at an angle, with the lighter end sticking out of the water. Currents make the hazard bow and bob up and down. (From 1970s)

prickly pear

■ n Also called **prickly pear cactus, coyote cactus.** A flat, jointed cactus that features red blossoms in the spring that produce an edible fruit. (From 1850s)

primary ditch

■ n In **irrigation,** the main ditch that runs from the canal to the highest point on the section. All other **irrigation ditches** are fed from this source by means of gates, now electrically controlled. (From 1890s) See also **corrugate.**

prospect

■ v To search or hunt for gold or silver or other precious minerals. (From 1840s)

prospecting	■ Also as **prospect.** A combining form for terms relative to searching for gold or silver in the West: *prospecting camp, ~ diggings, ~ horn, ~ pan, ~ party, ~ operations, ~ shaft, ~ trip, ~ work.*
prospector	■ n One who searches for gold or silver. Nowadays, also one who searches for oil, especially on the **North Slope** in Alaska. (From 1840s)
proxy	■ n Among Mormons, a person who substitutes for another in a Mormon temple marriage, or other ceremony for the living or dead. (From 1880s) See also **seal.**
puchki	■ n See **wild celery.**
pueblo	■ n A Southwestern Indian village made up of a series of adobe or stone buildings, or a multitiered, terraced building serving the needs of the entire community. (From 1800s, Spanish 'village')
pulk	■ n Also spelled *pulka.* Also called **ahkio.** A type of sled adapted from the Lap reindeer sled, shaped like the front of a small rowboat with runners. Nowadays made of aluminum or fiberglass and pulled by a snowmobile or even dogs. (From 1890s, Lap)
pulling the badger	■ n See **badger fight.**
pulque	■ /PULL kay/ n A thick, fermented drink made from various species of agave. The thick, pulpy liquid can be drunk as is or distilled into tequila. (From 1830s, Spanish)
pulqueria	■ /pull kay REE uh/ n A place where **pulque** is fermented and sold. Found especially along the border from El Paso westward. (From 1840s)
puma	■ n Another word for **cougar,** the large southwestern cat that can bring down a deer, calf, sheep, or other medium-sized animal. The animal often lives a solitary existence and has a wide-ranging territory. (From 1780s, Quechua via Spanish) See also **mountain lion.**
pump	■ v See **pedal.**

punch

■ v To drive cattle. Nowadays to work on a ranch around cattle generally, roping cows, branding, fixing fences, and working as a cowboy. (From 1890s)

puncher

■ n Also **cowpuncher.** A cowboy; one who works on a ranch, riding horses, herding cattle, fixing fences, branding calves, and so on. (From 1870s)

pupfish

■ n pl Any of a variety of small (one to three inches) fish of the genus *Cyprinodon* found in brackish or fresh water in arid parts of the West. In many areas, the fish are an endangered species, and some of the earliest arguments for protected environments raged over pumping water from the habitats of these fish in Ash Meadows in the Amargosa region near Death Valley. Prior to this time, Ash Meadows was most famous for its brothel. (From 1940s)

Q

qagri

■ n Also spelled *qasgiq, kashgee, kashim.* The community house or men's house for many Alaska Natives, especially Yupik and Inupiaq. The structure serves as a working area for the men and the center for ceremonies. (From 1860s, Yupik)

qantaq

■ n Also spelled *kantak.* The traditional wooden bowl used originally by Alaska Natives, now collected by tourists. (From 1860s, Yupik)

qaspeq

■ n Also spelled *kuspuk, kashbuk, koshbrook, kashbruk.* Originally a hooded, cloth garment worn over heavy clothing by Alaska Natives. Nowadays a pullover made of modern fabrics and often shaped as a dress or jersey. (From 1920s, Yupik)

quakenas

■ n See **trembling aspen.**

quaking aspen

■ n Also shortened to **aspen, quaking asp.** A deciduous, white-barked tree that grows in proximity to pine trees, making a striking contrast of fall colors in the mountainous areas of the West. The leaves of *Populus tremuloides* quiver in the slightest breezes, making alternately silver and green flashes during the summer and red, brown, and yellow flashes during the autumn. (From 1900s) See also **aspen** for additional names for the tree.

queen crab

■ n The name developed for commercial purposes for the **Tanner crab** that is now better known in western Canada as the **snow crab.** Alaskan fishermen use "queen crab," and restauranteurs in the western United States use either term. (From 1970s) See also **Alaska king crab, bairdi, opilio.**

querida

■ /keh REE duh/ n A term of endearment used for a female; darling, sweetheart. (From 1840s, Spanish 'dear, sweetheart')

quien sabe

■ phr Literally, Spanish for 'Who knows?' Occurs regularly with a shrug of the shoulders in the Southwest. May have been the source for Tonto's regular reply to the Lone Ranger in a generation of radio programs and movies. (From 1840s)

quinnat

■ n Shortened from **quinnat salmon.** Another name for the **Chinook salmon,** the large *Onchorhynchus tschawytscha.* (From 1870s, Salish *t'kwinnat*) See **salmon** n for a complete listing.

quisutch

■ n Another name for the **coho,** the middle-sized salmon that grows to about nine pounds. See **salmon** n for a complete listing.

quirt

■ n A short-handled whip with leather thongs, used to whip a horse on the flank while riding to increase speed. (From 1840s, Spanish *cuarto*) Used also as a verb.

quorum

■ n In the Mormon church, a group of men who share a specific rank of priesthood as Quorum of the Seventies and Quorum of the Twelve, who have specific duties and privileges within the hierarchy. (From 1840s)

quyana

■ excl The word for 'thanks' or 'thank you' in several Alaskan Native languages. The term is becoming more frequently used in the far Northwest, as **gracias** is frequently used in the Southwest. (From 1960s)

R

rabbit ears

■ n pl In **keno,** a type of blower used to select the twenty balls drawn for the game. Two clear plastic tubes, about eighteen-inches long, jut from the blower at upward angles. Ten balls are blown into each tube. (From 1970s) See also **keno goose.**

rag city

■ n Originally, in the days of the gold rush in the 1850s, this was a town consisting mainly of tents. Now, it is any quickly assembled conglomerate of aluminum house trailers and campers at the site of a boomtown. Nowadays every western state has a rag city or two, depending on the state of the mining industry or military defense contracts.

railroad belt

■ n Also called **railbelt.** Originally the area along the railroad line (but not the track itself) connecting Anchorage, Fairbanks, and Seward in Alaska. The line was built with federal funds in 1922 and turned over to the state of Alaska in 1985. Nowa-

modern keno goose, or "rabbit ears"

days the area referred to is along both sides of the line between Anchorage and Fairbanks. (From 1920s)

railroad hyacinth

■ n See **camas.**

rainbow cactus

■ n A cactus featuring red and white spines. The *Echinocactus rigidissimus* has a large red flower. (From 1890s)

rainbow trout

■ n Also called **mountain trout.** A trout that thrives between four thousand and six thousand feet in the western mountain ranges. *Salmon iridius* or *S. shasta* is marked with iridescent reds and blues around the gills. Lower than this elevation lives mainly the **brown trout.** Above this elevation is found the favored **cutthroat trout.** (From 1880s) See also **speckled trout, steelhead, Yellowstone trout.**

ramada

■ n An arborlike structure, open on all four sides, constructed of four poles with a cover to ward off sun or rain, sometimes with reed sides that can be rolled up or down; a shelter. The term is from the Spanish, but the modern hotel chain sporting the name is a far cry from the early rough shelter. (From 1860s)

ramrod

■ n By extension, this term for the stiff wire or metal rod used in loading old-fashioned guns came to refer to the foreman or supervisor on a ranch. By 1900, owners of large ranches had foremen for the various crews working on the ranch. A foreman had to be firm in dealing with rowdy cowboys, and soon came to be known as "stiff as a rod."

ranch

■ n In the West, an extensive area of land with buildings that serves as the scene of a business operation, raising cattle, horses, sheep, or even orchards of specific kinds of fruit (*orange ranch, pecan* ~). The term is often preceded with a descriptive modifier: *milk* ~, *chicken* ~, *hay* ~. (From 1800s, Spanish *rancho*) See also **spread.**

range

■ n A combining form for terms relative to wide-open spaces or wild and uncultivated country areas: *range boss, ~ cattle, ~ fire, ~ horse, ~ rider, ~ war.*

ranger

■ n 1. A member of a body of armed men employed to protect a wide area by patrolling on horseback, maintaining order, rounding up stray animals, and serving as a law enforcement officer (from 1830s). 2. Short for **Texas Ranger.** Usually capitalized. One of a famous group of law-enforcement officers with wide-ranging legal powers and a reputation for integrity and tenacity (from 1860s).

rawmane

■ n Also called **rummish, romaine.** In Alaska and the Northwest, a leather thong made from strips of caribou or moose hide. The thong may vary in length and thickness, depending on the intended use for it as a lashing line, material for snowshoes or **dogsleds,** or other purposes. (From 1900s, Russian *remen,* but frequent since 1950s, formed on folk etymology with *raw*hide, bab*iche*)

rebozo

■ n A long shawl or scarf that is draped over the head and around the shoulders of a woman. Once considered a sign of the peasant class in the Southwest, but more recently a stylish fashion. (From 1820s, Spanish *revosa*) See also **serape.**

reclamation engineer

■ n An engineer engaged in reclamation projects in the West, developing arid areas or alkali regions; an employee of the Reclamation Service, a bureau in the Department of the Interior charged with development of arid land. (From 1910s)

red

■ adj A combining form for describing certain subspecies of birds peculiar to the West: *red-breasted sapsucker, ~-breasted woodpecker, ~-headed woodpecker, ~-shafted flicker, ~-shafted woodpecker, ~-tailed blackhawk.*

red cedar

■ n Any of the western junipers, including **western red cedar, incense cedar.**

red king crab

■ n Also called **Alaska king crab** (q.v. for a complete listing). The largest of the three species of anomuran crabs taken in Alaskan waters by commercial fishermen. *Paralithodes camtschatica* measures up to five feet across and can weigh up to fifteen pounds. (From 1980s)

red salmon

■ n Also called **blueback salmon.** Another name for the **sockeye salmon.** The *Ochorhynchus nerka,* the flesh of which is deep red in color, is a favorite salmon for hot dishes and salads. It grows to about six pounds. (From 1880s) See also **jack salmon.** See **salmon** n for a complete listing.

redwood

■ n Also called **California redwood, giant redwood, giant cedar, sequoia.** 1. A very large and valued tree, the *Sequoia sempervirens* found in Northern California and Oregon. The great trees grow to more than one hundred feet in circumference and several hundred feet high (from 1830s). See also **big tree, Washington cedar.** 2. A combining form for terms relating to growth and locations of the tree: *redwood belt, ~ canyon, ~ cutting, ~ Empire, ~ forest, ~ grove, ~ mountains, ~ shanty, ~ tree.*

remuda

■ /ruh MOO duh/ n Also called **caballada, cavvy.** In the 1840s, cowboys, then called **buckaroos,** learned from the Mexican cowboys. On long trips or arduous jobs during **roundup,** each cowboy kept a string of horses so that he could trade mounts frequently and always have a fresh horse. Both the group of horses and the place he kept them were called the "remuda." Compare **manada, mulada.**

riata

■ /ree AH tuh/ n From the 1840s, California cowboys had many uses for this short rope made of leather or rawhide. It was not, like the **lariat,** used for catching cattle from horseback because it was much shorter. But both words come from the same Spanish root. The difference is that "lariat" preserved the article *la* before the word *reata.* The word was so widely used in the West that Oregonians jocularly called cowboys "Knights of the Riata," and a cowboy who "coiled up his riata" was one who had died.

riffle

■ n This was a device used by the forty-niners who chased the elusive flecks of gold in the streams around Sutter's Mill. It was a small bar or slat placed crosswise on the inside channel of a **sluice box.** Several of these, spaced a few inches apart, turned the sluice box into a **riffle box.** Riffle boxes, or **rifflers,** are still used by weekend gold seekers.

riffle under a sluice

right limit

■ n The downstream, right side of a creek in a **mining claim** in Alaska and the Yukon Territory. See also **left limit.**

rincon

■ n This term was borrowed from Spanish in the 1840s and referred to a small nook of land, usually a nice piece on which to build the ranch house and corrals. It so often referred to a pleasant little corner of land that the term is used as a place-name frequently from California to Texas.

rio

■ n This Spanish word for 'river' occurs frequently in the names of rivers and plants and animals in the Southwest. In fact, it is so frequent that a certain redundancy is found in reference to the "Rio Grande river," that is, "the Great River river."

road agent

■ n This term for the highwayman came into English in the West during the Civil War. Former Confederate soldiers, shying from the battlefields in the East, moved west to practice their nefarious arts on stage lines and their patrons.

road brand

■ n When large herds of cattle were being moved to railheads in the 1870s, a road brand was lightly burned into the hide of each cow to distinguish one herd from another when there were meetings and intermingling of herds near watering holes or near towns along the trail. This brand was different from the "ranch brand," which was seared into the hide of a young animal. See also **counterbrand, cross-brand.** Compare **burnt brand.**

roadrunner

■ n Also called **chaparral cock, ground cuckoo.** Jocularly called **Arizona peacock, California peacock.** This long-tailed bird can fly for short distances and then only high enough to get onto back fences and walls in newly developed housing areas in western cities. The roadrunner of cartoon fame is depicted as being much faster than the normal run-of-the-mill runner. But the bird does move faster than one might expect. It likes open space for running, so it gravitates to roads or pathways where it won't be slowed by brush or undergrowth. It has inhabited the deserts of the Southwest for many years, though it wasn't noticed enough to be named until the 1850s. See also **paisano,** 2.

roaring camp

■ n This term was first put into print in 1871, when Bret Harte published "The Luck of Roaring Camp." But the term was currently used for a mining camp where drinking, gambling, and prostitution were rampant. The term has been preserved in all the romantic tales and faux histories of western lore.

roble

■ n This Spanish word for 'oak' became English in the 1870s and was used as a descriptor in many place-names, such as Paso Robles. For some reason, the sound of the word has made it a popular addition to many songs and poems about peaceful and quiet California valleys.

Rockies

■ n pl The **Rocky Mountains** became so famous so quickly after English-speaking explorers encountered them that by the 1820s they were familiarly known as simply, "the Rockies."

Rocky Mountain(s)

■ This western mountain range is so much a part of the land and language of the West that, in its singular form, it has become common as a first element for fauna and flora found in western North America: In the names of animals and insects such as the *Rocky Mountain chipmunk, ~ dormouse, ~ elk, ~ flying squirrel, ~ goat* (known as **white buffalo, white goat**), *~ grasshopper, ~ ground squirrel, ~ hare, ~ locust, ~ rat, ~ trout, ~ whitefish, ~ wood rat, ~ wood tick;* also, the *Rocky Mountain sheep* is known as the **bighorn sheep,** also as the **white buffalo, white goat;** in the names of birds, such as the *Rocky Mountain antcatcher, ~ bluebird, ~ blue jay* (see **camp robber**), *~ chickadee, ~ flycatcher, ~ goldeneye, ~ screech owl, ~ song sparrow, ~ swallow, ~ warbler* (see **Virginia's warbler**); in the names of trees and plants, such as the *Rocky Mountain barberry, ~ bean, ~ bee plant, ~ cornflower, ~ gentian, ~ juniper, ~ pine.* More than thirty common vocabulary terms indicate the influence that the Rockies have on western language.

Rocky Mountain oyster

■ n The testis of a deer, bull calf, ram, or other male animal used as food. Usually roasted in the campfires of hunters, sheepherders, and cowmen. So called because when roasted the testis forms a hard crusty shell on the outside, but is soft on the inside.

Rocky Mountain spotted fever

■ n This term needs an entry of its own. Although it has been in English since the 1930s, the more recent outbreaks of this febrile disease have made tourists pay attention and avoid the ground squirrels that carry the wood tick which transmits the disease through its bite. Though the disease was discovered in the Rocky Mountains, it is rarely found there. The disease is most prevalent in the Southeast and Appalachian regions, where it is transmitted by the common dog tick. The tick requires a blood meal to advance from the larval stage to the adult stage. And the female tick likes a human blood meal to move to the egg-laying stage. The tick carries the disease from birth. The disease is debilitating to humans, but fatalities result in only about 3 percent of the cases, usually from heart or kidney failure.

rodeo

■ n In the 1840s, when this term was borrowed into English from Spanish, a rodeo was the **roundup** of cattle held once a year on ranches. The cattle were to be counted, branded, treated for any ailments. The gathering usually brought together cowboys who rarely saw one another on the range. In spare time, they naturally liked to show off their skills in horsemanship, bringing down dogies, riding unbroken horses, and even daring to get onto the occasional range bull for a spectacular feat of daring. As the activity attracted more and more people to watch the antics of the cowboys, the games began to acquire rules and finally became formalized into the public exhibitions now viewed miles from the range, in Madison Square Garden even, for loads of cash as well as bragging rights. (Spanish 'cattle ring' from *rodear* 'go round')

roe-on-kelp

■ n In the 1980s, a food that had been gathered by the occasional fisherman became commercialized. The cold waters of bays in Alaska provided kelp beds in which herring spawned. Alaskan fisherman learned that the seaweed covered with roe was considered a delicacy in Japan, rather like smoked salmon. Soon entrepreneurs had set up pens of seaweed dangling from floats. The pens were surrounded by nets, and herring about to spawn were released into the pens. The roe-covered seaweed was then processed in brine and the bulk of it shipped to Japan. Western palates used to sushi and sashimi are developing a taste for roe-on-kelp, or **spawn-on-kelp,** as it is sometimes called. See also **kazunoko, sac roe.**

rope

■ v Originally, in the 1840s, to capture an animal on the range with a **lariat.** But by the 1870s, the verb was used figuratively to catch unwary gamblers and bring them into gaming establishments for fleecing. The person who did both, as either cowboy or shill, was known as a "roper" or a "roper-in."

Rose City

■ n Easterners might think of Pasadena, California, when they hear this appellative, but they would be wrong. The City of Roses is a latecomer with the Rose Parade and Rose Bowl every New Year's Day on every TV. Actually, Portland, Oregon, has been the "Rose City" since the last century.

Ross's goose ■ n This small white goose is a migratory bird found mainly in the Sacramento and the San Joaquin valleys in California. The *Chen rossi* is less famous than its far-ranging and much larger cousin, the Canada goose.

rough lock ■ n This term shows the versatility for English to shift meanings as conditions shift in the surrounding world. In the 1850s, the form was used in the mountainous West to refer to a method for slowing down wagons while descending steep hills. A chain or rope would be tied from the front axle to a back wheel, causing the back wheel to stop turning and thus act as a brake. By the 1900s, the term was being used by **mushers** in the area that was to become Alaska. To slow a sled, the musher would wrap a rope or chain around the runners. The chain would dig into the packed snow or ice and keep the sled from running away on a slope.

roughrider ■ n Teddy Roosevelt, before he became President Theodore Roosevelt, was the first to use this term. In a magazine article in 1888 he said, "The roughrider of the plains, the hero of rope and revolver, is first cousin to the backwoodsman of the Southern Alleghenies." Cowboys were strongly recruited for the regiment that Roosevelt organized during the Spanish-American War. And the distinction was soon made by Mark Twain between the cowboy roughrider, lower case, and the Roughrider, capitalized, of Roosevelt's First United States Volunteer Cavalry, famous for its charge up San Juan Hill in Cuba.

roundup ■ n By the 1870s, the collecting and shipping of cattle had become big business. Twice a year the cowboys on a large **ranch,** or on several ranches collectively, would gather the cows. In the spring the cattle were counted and calves were branded. In the late summer, the cattle were collected and shipped to slaughterhouses in population centers. Both collections were called "the roundup." Before the end of the decade, the noun became a verb. Soon after it took on an extended meaning, referring to the collecting of a band of suspicious characters, or criminals. The term was cemented into the language by means of a popular song about the death of a cowboy, "heading for the last roundup," or judgment day.

row, the

■ n Also called **the line.** From the gold-rush days in Alaska, every mining camp had a string of establishments in one section that featured prostitution, drinking, gambling. The area was called "the row." But propriety kept the term from print until the 1930s.

ruffed grouse

■ n See **willow grouse.**

run money

■ n In the early 1900s, the Alaskan canneries needed to keep fishermen from abandoning the work load once the fishing season ended. The "run" was the time that the cannery operated, from before the opening of the fishing season until all the cans had been loaded on freighters a couple of weeks after the end of the season. To keep the fishermen-become-longshoremen on the job, a bonus was given to those who stayed throughout the "run." This bonus was the run money.

running iron

■ n In the 1880s, when cattle collecting and shipping became big business, some cowboys carried a straight piece of iron that could be heated and used to brand a stray cow that had no brand. The cowboy used the hot iron like a pencil to put the brand of his ranch on the cow. Oftentimes, the brand obliterated an already existing brand on the hide of the cow. Such running brands soon came to be frowned on, and by the 1890s, any cowboy caught with a running iron was likely to be dealt with swiftly and immediately on the range. See also **brand artist, burnt brand.**

Russian pie

■ n In Alaska, Russian *piroq* 'pie, tart' has been adapted to the foods of the regions. A dish made of layers of salmon, canned cabbage, spices and topped with biscuit dough is baked and served. The dish has been traditional for many years as "pirok," but generally as Russian pie since the 1940s.

rustler ■ n Although this word was in the language long before there was a Wild West, the romance of the range and the ubiquitousness of the cattle thief made this a favorite western word since the 1880s. At that, the first rustlers were admired as men who eked out a living by rounding up strays and abandoned cattle. The term even extended to wild horses that are successful at finding food on marginal range. It wasn't until the 1890s, when stock management programs became more efficient, that rustlers began collecting animals that clearly belonged to someone else, thereby besmirching their own reputations. See also **wide loop.**

S

sabe

■ n Also **savvy.** Knack, understanding, practical knowledge. Although this word was found in England as a borrowing from French, the American form was borrowed from Spanish in the 1850s. As a verb it means to understand or comprehend. See also **no sabe.**

sacahuista

■ n A southwestern plant, also called **bear grass,** sometimes chopped and used as cattle feed or silage in emergencies. In English, the word is from the 1890s. It is from Nahuatl via Spanish *zacahuiscle.*

sacaton

■ n Also **sacaton grass.** A coarse perennial grass, *Sporobolus wrightii,* found in the Southwest. In English, the word is from the 1840s. It is from Nahuatl via Spanish *zacatón.*

Sacramento

■ n The name of the river and the capital city of California is also the first element in *Sacramento perch,* a freshwater fish, *Archoplites interruptus,* similar to the perch and found in rivers along the Pacific Coast; ~ *pike,* the squawfish or yellowbelly, *Ptychocheilus oregonensis;* ~ *Chinook salmon* (see **Chinook salmon**).

sacred fire

■ n A ceremonial fire used by the Pueblo Indians of New Mexico as part of their rites. Various Indian ceremonies have been part of the Southwest tradition in English from the earliest time of contact. This term dates from 1840.

sac roe

■ n The eggs harvested from female herring that are still in the ovarian membrane. The membrane is the sac. Ultimately from Latin by way of French. And roe 'fish eggs' has been in English for centuries. However, only in the 1980s did sac roe become important in western English. At that time, Alaskan fisheries began catching herring just before spawning and preparing the herring eggs for a Japanese delicacy called **kazunoko.** See also **roe-on-kelp, spawn-on-kelp.**

saddle mat ■ n The name for the heavy pad used when horses are required to carry a heavy load, as when packing into the mountains. It takes the place of the lighter saddle blanket. Used since the 1880s. See also **salea.**

saddle train ■ n A train of animals carrying packs or passengers. Though the term dates from the 1860s, it is used today mainly in reference to such trips as leading tours down the narrow trails of the Grand Canyon.

safety ■ n There are many kinds of safeties, including condoms and the guards on guns and pistols to prevent accidental discharge, not to mention a special score in football. But the safety of the Northwest, Alaska and the Yukon is a special fitting around a stovepipe where the pipe protrudes through the roof of a cabin or tent, preventing surrounding material from getting too hot and starting a fire elsewhere than in the stove. The meaning has been regular since the 1950s.

sage ■ n A shortened form of **sagebrush.** The term is used as the first element in combinations: 1. *sage bush,* a bush of sage. 2. Pertaining to landscape where sagebrush is prevalent: *sage country, ~ desert, ~ hill, ~ hillock, ~ plain, ~ prairie.* 3. Of animals found in the sagebrush plains of the West: *sage chicken,* a prairie chicken; *~ chipmunk (Tamias minimus pictus); ~ cock,* a large grouse *(Centrocercus urophasianus),* also called *~ fowl, ~ grouse, ~ hen; ~ hare, ~ rabbit,* any one of various western rabbits thought to be related to the eastern cottontail; *~ sparrow,* any one of various sparrows found in the West; *~ squirrel (Citellus mollis mollis); ~ thrasher,* thrush *(Oreoscoptes montanus).*

sagebrush ■ n The ubiquitous plant that defines the western landscape in the minds of many easterners. The word refers to any of several species of *Artemisia,* especially *A. tridentata,* that grow wild on the western plains. It is used in combinations pertaining to landscape where sagebrush is prevalent: *sagebrush country, ~ desert, ~ flat, ~ land, ~ plain,*

~ *range* (from 1800). See also **white sage.** One interesting historical bit is that the term once referred to a spurious process of refining gold and silver ore, where the ore is treated with a strong brew of sagebrush to amalgamate the gold and silver. Many an unwary investor was taken in by the scam in the 1870s.

Sagebrush Rebellion   ■ n A movement by certain westerners concerned about the degree of federal control over lands that westerners feel should be under state or county control. The goal is to increase the degree of local control over federal lands. This attempt has led some counties to challenge federal ownership of land in western states. The movement began in Nevada, Utah, and Arizona, but soon spread to the rest of the West. (From 1970s)

Sagebrush State   ■ n A nickname for **Nevada** since the turn of the century. Also **Silver Land, Silver State, Battle-Born State, Sage Hen State.**

sage hen   ■ n 1. A native of Nevada. 2. Many states claim to raising the best-looking young women in the country. In the South, she was a Georgia peach; in the West she was a sage hen, at least from the 1860s until recently.

Sage Hen State   ■ n A nickname for **Nevada,** from the beginning of statehood in 1864. Also **Silver Land, Silver State, Battle-Born State, Sagebrush State.**

saguaro   ■ /sa WHA roh/ n A tall cactus, usually with several upraised arms, each ranging from six to twelve inches in diameter. *Carnegiea gigantea,* found in the deserts of the Southwest. Since 1850 this magnificent cactus has served for the image of the western desert. It is featured in most cartoons and in many minds as the quintessential plant of the desert, even though it occurs only in the Sonoran Desert. See also **Carnegiea, giant cactus, organ cactus, pillar cactus.**

saguaro woodpecker   ■ n Also called **Gila woodpecker.** The woodpecker, *Centurus uropygialis,* that makes its home in the **saguaro.** Observers marvel that the bird is

saguaro

able to fly around the sharp spines of the cactus with apparent immunity.

saint
■ n The Mormon term for members of the **Church of Jesus Christ of Latter-day Saints** (or Mormons). The Mormon pioneers that settled the West have called themselves such since the 1830s. Before long, all their neighbors had picked up the term and it is commonly used in states surrounding Utah. See also **carrot eater, cricket stomper, Latter-day Saint.**

Saint Joseph('s) rod
■ n Another name for **ocatillo** (q.v. for a complete listing), though admittedly of small regional occurrence, mainly around southern Utah, southwestern Colorado, and eastern Nevada. First encountered in the 1850s. See also **candlewood.**

sala
■ n Since the 1830s in English, this word borrowed from Spanish refers to a large hall.

salal
■ n Also **salal berry.** The berry of the *Gaultheria shallon,* a small shrub found on the Pacific Coast, is about the size of a grape. The purple fruit, a sweet favorite food of both humans and blue

grouse, was first noted in the journals of the Lewis and Clark expedition in 1805. The explorers took the name from the Chinook Jargon *shele wele.* The term also refers to the shrub or its wood.

salea

■ n An undressed sheepskin, used for padding on pack horses. As might be expected, the aroma is rank in hot or wet weather. (From 1890; Spanish *zalea*) See also **saddle mat.**

sale brand

■ n See **vent.**

saleratus lake

■ n Also **saleratus pond.** An alkaline body of water. As a western word, saleratus originally referred to the baking soda that was so important to the biscuit-making of the trapper and frontiersman. The transferred sense came to refer to any alkaline substance, which is endemic to basins in the Southwest. By the 1850s, the term was common for any small, alkaline pond. (From Latin *sal* + *aeratus,* 'aerated salt.')

salina

■ n Also called a **salinera.** A salt lick, salt spring, salt pond; a salt pit or mine. The term dates from the 1840s, when ranchers borrowed the term from Spanish.

Salish

■ n Indian tribe of the western Montana and Columbia River basin areas. The term was borrowed in the 1840s. It is the native word for "people." For many years, other people called the members of this tribe "flatheads," because the practice of using cradleboards flattens the back of the head. In fact, one of the more beautiful lakes in Montana is called Flathead Lake.

salmon

■ n It is fitting that this entry should be the longest one in the book. The word has been in English since the 1300s, and salmon have been prized as food in England and Europe; even Pliny knew of the delicacy. This mother lode of various types and the cornucopia of salmon known to northwestern North America have made it one of the special words of the West. Between the Sacramento River and the coast of Alaska, salmon have defined the subsistence, the industry, and the very culture of the people. There are five general types of salmon in this huge region: 1. **King/Chinook,** flesh white to light red in color, good in salads, *Onchorhynchus tshawytscha,* grows to about twenty-two pounds. 2. **Red/sockeye,** flesh deep red in color, good in hot dishes, salad, *O. nerka,* grows to about six pounds. 3. **Silver/coho,** flesh light red, good in all dishes, *O. kisutch,* grows to about nine pounds. 4. **Dog/chum,** flesh light/white color, *O. keta,* grows to about eight pounds. Originally called "dog" or "chum" salmon because it was thought best suited for dog food or being chopped up and used to attract other fish. 5. **Pink/humpback,** flesh pale pink, *O. gorbuscha,* used in entrees, soups, sandwiches, grows to four pounds.

There are so many types and so many names that overlap, depending on the specific region and the knowledge of the person catching the specific fish, that the following are listed separately: **Arctic trout, black salmon, blackmouth ~, blueback ~, calico ~, California ~, Chinook ~, chum, coho, Columbia River ~, dogfish, dog ~, dog tooth ~, fall ~, fall chum, feeder king, holia, hookbill, hooknose, hoopid ~, keta** (a dog salmon), **king, kokanee** (a sockeye), **pink ~, quinnat, quisutch, Sacramento ~, silver ~, skowitz, sockeye salmon, spring ~, summer chum, tschawytscha, tyee ~.** See also **money fish.**

salmon

■ Used as a combining element for a variety of terms related to the salmon fishing industry: *salmon bellies,* from the 1860s, the abdominal wall of the **king** was preserved by salting or pickling; *salmon cache, ~ cannery, ~ chuck* (a fishing area), *~ house, ~ jerky* (see **squaw candy**), *~ killer* (the stickleback fish), *~ pirate, ~ season, ~ strips* (see **squaw candy**), *~ wheel* (see **fish wheel**).

salsa

■ n This word is borrowed from Spanish and means 'sauce'. The mixture is made from chili peppers, spices, and tomatoes. Since the 1970s, salsa has taken the English-speaking palate by storm. It now outsells ketchup in supermarkets. Compare **chili sauce.** Another kind of salsa, referring to the peppy music that is a combination of traditional Mexican, Cuban, Puerto Rican, and rock 'n' roll, did not originate in the Southwest, but was introduced nationally by Mexican bands.

salt

■ n The first element in combinations describing areas of a salt or alkaline nature found in the West: ~ *desert,* ~ *flat,* ~ *lake,* ~ *plain,* ~ *prairie.* In plants found in saline or alkaline regions of the West: *salt grass,* any of various grasses, including *Distichlis spicata* (see **alkali**); ~ *sage,* a variety of **greaseweed;** ~*weed,* a variety of *Atriplex;* ~*wood,* a shrub, *Purshia tridentata,* used as winter forage.

salt

■ v To scatter or bury gold dust, ore, or precious stones to make someone believe a mine or property is valuable. The scam dates from the 1850s, but practitioners of this type of fraud still take in gullible investors even today.

salt chuck

■ n See **chuck,** 2.

sand

■ The first element in combinations designating features of desert landscape: *sand butte,* ~ *creek,* ~ *desert,* ~ *field,* ~ *prairie,* ~ *wash;* in the names of plants and animals indigenous to the West: *sand cricket;* ~ *dock,* a wildflower, *Rumex venosus;* ~ *lily,* a white-flowered lily, *Leucocrinum montanum;* ~ *lizard;* ~ *puff, Abronia solsa;* ~ *strawberry, Fragaria chiloensis;* ~ *sucker,* the California whiting, a fish found along the coast of California; ~ *verbena,* a plant of the genus *Abrona,* resembling the verbena.

sand painting

■ n A sacred representation created by medicine men of the Hopi and Navajo tribes. On a flat patch of prepared sand, various colored grains of sand and ground or crushed charcoal, corn, flowers, and berries are carefully poured by hand to make designs in the sand as part of the medicine man's healing ceremony. Since the 1890s the general public has been allowed to watch the creation of certain of the designs.

sand spout

■ n Also called **sand auger, sand whirl.** A small whirlwind occurring in the deserts of the Southwest. (From 1900) See also **dancing devil, dust devil.**

sandia ■ n A watermelon. Also used in place-names. (From 1840, borrowed from Spanish)

Santa Ana ■ n Also spelled *Santa Anna.* A windstorm from the north, northeasterly, or easterly mountains in southern California, in which the wind is very strong and hot and dry. Originally, around 1900, this type of wind was so called only when blowing from the Santa Ana Mountains. But soon the term was being used for any hot, dry wind in the Southwest. The mountains themselves were named after the Mexican general Antonio López de Santa Anna. Reportedly, many Californians pronounce the name /san TAN uh/.

Santa Fe ■ n The capital of **New Mexico.** As the first element in combinations pertaining to the history of the area: *Santa Fe expedition,* a military-commercial expedition by the Republic of Texas to claim the eastern part of New Mexico in 1841; ~ *town,* settlements founded in that area; ~ *road,* also ~ *trail,* a road from St. Louis to Santa Fe, used for trade; ~ *trader,* one who traded along this route; ~ *wagon,* a wagon used on the trail. *Santa Fe tea* is a tea made from the leaves of a local plant.

Santa Lucia fir ■ n The bristlecone fir, *Abies venusta,* found in the Santa Lucia Mountains of southwestern California. (From 1900)

santo ■ n A small idol or image of a saint. (From 1830; Spanish)

Sasquatch ■ n Since 1929, stories have been told in the Pacific Northwest and western Canada about a large, hairy humanlike creature. The beast is said to stand between six and fifteen feet tall and leave a footprint about eighteen inches long. A bit farther south, stories are told of **Bigfoot.**

savvy ■ n See **sabe.**

saw-kwey ■ n See **Chinook salmon.**

scad

■ n Early in the 1800s, this term was slang for "dollar." But after the forty-niners' gold rush in California, it came to mean a fleck of gold found in a gold **pan.** The plural form always meant "a great many," whether of dollars or gold flakes.

scallyhoot

■ v To run, especially to run off quickly in any direction; to skedaddle. This slang term appeared in the 1860s, and may have been imported to the West by runaway Confederate soldiers or in reference to them.

scarlet

■ A combining form for a variety of brightly colored wildflowers found in desert regions from California to Utah: *scarlet bugler, ~ gilia, ~ paintbrush.*

Scotch lovage

■ n See **wild parsley.**

screw bean

■ n Also called **screw mesquite, screw wood, screw-pod mesquite.** A hardwood tree that grows in a gnarly and twisted fashion. The long seedpod of the tree is coiled, or screw-shaped. The wood burns hot and completely and is a favored wood for cooking fires. The bean pod is nutritious food for grazing animals. See also **mesquite.**

seaborgium

■ n The name given to element 106 on the periodic table of elements. The most recent elements were created by using nuclear accelerators. The name honors Dr. Glenn T. Seaborg, codiscoverer of plutonium and nine other man-made elements. Dr. Seaborg won the 1951 Nobel Prize in Chemistry. The term came into English in March 1994 at Lawrence Berkeley Laboratory, California.

seagull wireless

■ n In every sparsely settled region, information and rumors spread very rapidly over great distances. This phenomenon is known by various terms in different parts of the world. The Australians have their "bush telegraph"; for many years, inhabitants of the Yukon have had the "moccasin telegraph" or, more recently, the **mukluk telegraph.** The seagull wireless of Alaskans probably has a reasonable explanation. Every settlement and small village has a radio to stay in touch with neighbors miles away. The term has been in use since the 1950s.

seal

■ v In the Mormon religion, marriage in an LDS temple seals a couple for "time and eternity." In another temple ceremony, one can be married, by **proxy,** or be sealed to one's ancestors. The word stems from the beginning of Mormonism in the 1840s, so there is a possibility that the word was used as a noun and verb in some New England denominations before the Mormons brought it West, where it thrives today.

seal hook

■ n A wooden float shaped like a gourd, with three or four sharp hooks extending from the larger end. The narrow end of the float is attached to a leather thong, which in turn is tied to a length of cotton line. Native Alaskan hunters shoot a seal, then drag the body to the boat or shore by throwing the seal hook beyond the carcass and drawing in the line, thereby snagging it and bringing it in. First used in English in the 1950s.

sealskin poke

■ n Also called **seal poke** or just **poke.** A sack or bag, made by pulling the whole, unsplit skin of a seal backward beginning at the mouth. The skin of the seal, thus turned inside out, makes an airtight bag that can be used as a float or a watertight bag for carrying things. This word is a good example of what lexicographers call a folk etymology. The Yupik word *puuq* refers to a sack or bag, especially one that floats in the water when filled with air. When English speakers encountered the Yupik word in the 1880s, they thought it sounded like "poke," a term used often in the southern and rural United States for a tote sack or bag. So, the error was made and the confusion between *puuq* and "poke" was perpetuated.

sego

■ n Also **sego lily.** A perennial plant with a showy, trumpetlike flower. The word is Shoshonean and was borrowed into English in the 1850s. The bulb is edible, as the Indians showed the early Mormon settlers in Utah. The Mormons found the bulb palatable and a worthy food in times of duress. The plant was named the state flower of **Utah.**

señita

■ n See **old man cactus.**

señor

■ n A title of respect or address, equivalent to "mister." Originally, a señor was a Spanish gentleman, and the word was used before the surname. But in the Southwest it has become a standard form of address when the surname is not known. When used by strangers who are not obviously of Mexican descent, it has the force just a shade nicer than "bud" or "mac."

señora

■ n A title of respect, equivalent to "Mrs." Used mainly by people of Hispanic descent who are using English in daily affairs. The form **señorita** is used in the same fashion as "Miss" in direct address. When used referentially, the term usually indicates a young and attractive woman and is more formal than **chica.**

sequoia

■ n The giant **redwood** of northern California. The genus was named by the Hungarian ethnologist Stephan Ladislaus Endlicher in the 1840s. He was honoring the memory of the famous Cherokee Sikwaya, or Siquoya, who devised a syllabary of the Cherokee language. See also **big tree, giant cedar, Washington cedar.**

serape

■ n The shawl or rough-woven blanket draped from the shoulders and worn for warmth. As the word has been used more and more in English, it has lost its connotation of being a wrap for men. The female version was the **rebozo,** which has nearly been supplanted in usage by "serape."

shanghai

■ v Originally, to kidnap sailors and press them into service for long voyages, often to China. Now, to press anyone into service in a devious manner. In San Francisco in the 1850s, captains of the greyhounds of the sea, the China Clippers, often found themselves short of crew members. Waterfront toughs were employed to "secure the ship's personnel." Many a tar took a free drink (laced with knockout drops) in a waterfront dive, and woke up after two days at sea with the choice of working or swimming.

sharp-tailed grouse	■ n See **willow grouse.**
Shasta	■ This term has been used as a combining element for a number of plants found in the vicinity of Mount Shasta, such as *Shasta daisy, ~ fir, ~ lily.* The word itself refers to an Indian tribe of that name. And the California mountain was named in the 1820s by the explorer Peter Skene Ogden, who in turn left his name on a number of places in the West.
sheefish	■ n Originally called a **shee** in 1900, this large whitefish is a favorite sport fish in Alaska. It grows from thirty to sixty pounds in different habitats. The word was borrowed from the Athapaskan language at a very early time in Canada. It may have been borrowed into Eskimo languages, and then again into English by settlers in Alaska during the early part of this century. See also **cony.**
shell ice	■ n Also called **drum ice.** In northern Canada and Alaska, the thin layer of ice that is formed when a lake or river freezes over and then the water recedes, leaving an air space under the ice several inches or several feet deep. People and **dogsleds** have accidentally broken through such ice and dropped as much as seven or eight feet onto a rocky shoreline or a clutter of tangled brush and logs.
shelter cabin	■ n In Alaska and the Yukon, a small, one-room building erected along a long **dogsled** trail. Since the 1920s, such structures have provided a haven for cold **mushers.** The building has a small stove and a supply of wood. Before leaving such a shelter the next morning, the traveler must replenish the wood supply, since the next occupant might arrive late at night. Unable to collect wood in the darkness, that traveler would freeze to death.
shoulder holster	■ n In the 1880s, a **shoulder scabbard** was a leather holster for a pistol that could be worn under the coat, near the armpit, and well out of sight. By the 1940s, this invention of the Old West was being used by a variety of evildoers as well as do-

gooders. By the 1940s, it had also acquired the name **shoulder draw.**

sideline

■ v A method for hobbling a horse by tying a front leg to the back leg on the same side of the animal. Texas cowboys began this practice in the 1860s while camped out to prevent their horses from running off during the night or from being stolen by **rustlers** sneaking into camp. The sideline hobble was soon being used by cowboys all over the West.

sidewinder

■ /SIDE wine der/ n 1. A pale-colored desert rattlesnake, *Crotalus cerastes* that grows to about thirty inches long. So called because of its looping, lateral progressive motion (from 1870s). See also **horned rattlesnake.** 2. Also called the **sidewiper.** Any of several small rattlesnakes that propel themselves in a looping, sideways motion. They were first named in Arizona during the 1870s, but are found throughout the arid regions of the West. In spite of its fierce reputation, the snake will not strike until practically stepped on. As long as the snake, which grows up to three feet long, is seen a few feet away, it is easily dealt with, avoided, or gently moved to another location by picking it up with a long stick. The sidewinder will wrap itself around the stick, and can thus be carried a distance away from a camp or a trail. 3. By an extended meaning, an untrustworthy, unpredictable person (from 1900s). 4. In logging, a tree knocked down unexpectedly by the fall of another (from 1900s).

sierra

■ n This word has been used in English since the middle of the eighteenth century. It comes from Spanish and means, literally, 'saw, sawtooth'. It was used to describe any ridge of sharp mountain peaks encountered in the West. By the middle of the nineteenth century, the word was frequently capitalized and used to describe many plants and animals in the environs of the Sierra Nevada range. Now, it is used in both upper and lower case as a combining element for many terms, from "Sierra bighorn" to "Sierra Club."

Silicon Valley

■ n A part of the Santa Clara Valley, southwest of

San Francisco, near San Jose, where many of the high-technology semiconductors used in computers are designed and manufactured. Refers to the silicon wafers used in the semiconductors. The term for the region was first used by Don C. Hoefler in a series of articles in *Electronic News* in the early 1970s. Hoefler, in turn, said the name was suggested to him by Ralph Voerst.

Silver Land

■ n A nickname for **Nevada.** Also **Silver State, Sagebrush State, Sage Hen State.** In the 1860s, Nevada was producing tremendous amounts of silver from mines in the territory. To help finance his costs for the Civil War, Lincoln wanted to have the revenues that statehood would provide. He pushed for Nevada to be declared a state. It was, and he received the revenues he needed (the source of another nickname, **Battle-Born State**).

silver pine

■ n A pine that grows in the West, partly because it thrives at a height not found throughout most of the rest of the country. *Pinus monticola* grows at about 8,000 feet above sea level, a height that is found with any consistency only in the **Rocky Mountains.** John Muir, in 1869, was the first to record the name.

silver salmon

■ n Another name for the **coho,** *Oncorhynchus kisutch.* This is a sport fish, growing from six to twelve pounds and has a light-red flesh. It is a favorite eating salmon for cookouts. Though known throughout the West since the 1870s, the name is not in many dictionaries. See **salmon** n for a complete listing.

silversides

■ n See grunion.

Silver State

■ n The most common nickname for **Nevada.** The reference is to the enormous amount of silver mined in the Territory and later in the State just before, during, and after the Civil War. Also **Battle-Born State, Sagebrush State, Sage Hen State, Silver Land.**

silvertip

■ n A color phase of the **grizzly bear.** Since the 1880s, people have noted a variety of large bears in the Far Northwest. But it was not discovered until later that the **brown bear, Kodiak bear,** and silvertip were all variations of the same bear, *Ursus horribilis,* which is, one must admit, a perfect and descriptive scientific name for the beast.

siwash

■ This term is used as noun, modifier, and verb. It is both capitalized and noncapitalized. Some uses of it have taken on a pejorative meaning over the years. The term originally came into Chinook Jargon from a folk pronunciation of the French voyageurs term *sauvage* 'savage', their term for Indians, especially the Indians of the Far Northwest. In the 1840s, the term, capitalized, was used to refer to any Indian in the Far Northwest, but the reference to people is now rare or even obsolete.

As a modifier, the term often carries a connotation of something cheap or trashy: so a *siwash dog* was a **sled dog** that had undesirable traits; a *siwash harness* was a simple rope around the breast of a sled dog; a *siwash coat* was a simple garment pulled over the head while working in water or with messy material; *siwash candy* was narrow strips of salmon, cut lengthwise, salted, dried, and smoked (see **squaw candy** for a listing of other names for this treat). Finally, the modifier was generalized in the 1940s and used to refer to a mythical college, usually the equivalent of "Podunk U."

As a verb, the term meant to camp out without a tent or many of the usual amenities used in camping. It came into use around the turn of the century.

skidoo

■ /SKEE doo/ n A small, one-person machine with a single ski on the front used for traveling over snow. A snowmobile. The term came from the brand name *Ski-Doo,* a trademark of Bombardier Ltd. in Canada, first sold in 1959. By the 1970s the term was being used in lower case to refer to any open, one or two-person snowmobile. See also **snow machine.**

skid road

■ n In logging, a path along which logs are dragged. The path is constructed of small logs laid perpendicular to the roadbed in the form of a trough, along which teams of oxen pulled the logs. Compare **skid row.** (From 1880s)

skid row

■ n An area in a city frequented by laborers out of work or petty criminals, where cheap lodgings, church missions, soup kitchens, and the like can be found. A corruption of **skid road.** Originally, loggers gathered at the terminus of such logging roads for lodgings and entertainment. When their money was gone, they waited to be rehired and taken back to work in the logging areas. Soon the term came to refer to any run-down section of a city. (From 1940s)

skijor

■ v Also called **skijogging** in the Northwest. To ski along a level surface, being pulled, originally by a horse, later by automobile. **Skijoring** as a noun dates from 1910, and was borrowed from Norwegian *skigjøring* 'ski-doing'. The activity has been especially popular in Colorado. Compare **bizzing, hookey bob.**

skookum

■ /SKOOK um/ adj This modifier is from the Chinook Jargon of the Northwest and dates back to the 1840s in its earliest occurrences. It has various, connected meanings, including "strong, brave, good, excellent, fearsome, ghostly (or mysteriously powerful)." Common uses of the forms include *skookum breakfast,* a good or hearty meal; *skookum chuck,* a strong current of water in a fishing area, as near an inlet (see **chuck,** 2); *skookum house,* a strong enclosure, that is, a jail.

skookum

■ /SKOOK um/ n 1. A disease, especially one brought on by an evil spirit. 2. An evil spirit, ghost, or demon. (Chinook Jargon, 1830s)

skowitz

■ n Another name for a **coho.** See **salmon** n for a complete listing.

skunkberry

■ n Another name for the **bearberry honeysuckle.** It is unclear whether the name comes from the odor of the plant or because it is a favorite food of the polecat.

sled dog

■ n Also called **Alaskan husky** (q.v. for a complete listing). Any of a variety of dogs trained to pull sleds. The working sled dog has been replaced by the snowmobile, but the animals are still used for racing and hobbyists. The term is now most common to the Far Northwest, though it did not originate there.

sleeper

■ n Nowadays, a wager that has been left on the crap table in a casino after the roll of the dice has decided a bet. If the rightful owner of the wager does not claim the money, someone else will. Originally, in the 1850s, the term referred to a wager left on the faro table. But faro, once the most popular of western betting games, is not found in modern casinos. In the popular imagination, **poker** is depicted as the card game of choice in the Old West. But that notion was created by moviemakers.

Slope

■ n A short form of **Arctic Slope,** the **North Slope** of the Brooks Range, reaching across the coastal plain to the Arctic Ocean in northern Alaska. The term became widespread in the 1970s as the oil fields of the region were developed.

slow elk

■ n A facetious reference to a cow that has been stolen and slaughtered. The practice was first named in 1910, but continues to the present day in rural areas of the West, where cattle are often on the open range and hunters and poachers can act without interruption.

sluice

■ This term did not originate in the West. Indeed, it has been in English since the thirteenth century, referring to a constructed channel, usually made of wood, to let water flow from one place to another. But "sluice" as noun, adjective, and verb became so important to the gold-mining interest of the West after 1850 that it spawned dozens of terms related to gold mining. Most of these terms are still used by prospectors and independent miners. A few of the obvious ones are *sluice box, ~ fork, ~ head, ~ mine, ~ mining, ~ process, ~ robber, ~ robbing, ~ tailing, ~ trough.* As a verb, the word means "to mine."

smooth mouth

■ n Since the 1940s, this term has referred to an old horse. Since horses' teeth wear down to a smooth surface as they age, a prospective buyer always looks at the animal's teeth to determine its merits. Although when one is given a horse, it is not polite to look in its mouth.

snake

■ adj As a modifier, "snake" has a long history in the West. Various tribes of Shoshone Indians were known as **Snakes** or **Snake people** as early as the 1770s. They were reputed to be able to glide and disappear quietly and quickly from prying eyes. Naturally enough, large portions of the West came to be called **Snake country** in reference to the inhabitants. The **snake dance** dates from about the same time, but referred to a portion of the rain dance performed by the Hopi Indians. Some said the dancers used snakes as part of the ceremony, others said that the line of dancers moved about the dance area single file in a snakelike motion. Many of the terms referred to aspects of the Shoshone or Hopi people: *Snake horse,* ~ *kiva,* ~ *nation,* ~ *priest,* ~ *squaw,* ~ *tribe,* ~ *warrior.*

snake cactus

■ n A low-growing cactus that puts out shoots along the ground. *Pediocactus simsoni,* or brain cactus, has been noted since the 1910s in the Southwest.

sno-go

■ n Plural: **sno-gos, sno-goes.** Also called a **sno-traveler.** A snowmobile or **skidoo.** Used almost exclusively in rural Alaska, Klondike, and the Yukon. The term dates from the 1960s and was, from the beginning, used as noun and verb. See also **snow machine.**

snow anchor

■ n Also called **snow hook, ice hook.** A curved piece of metal attached with a rope to the harness of **sled dogs** or to a **dogsled,** used to keep the sled from moving or the dogs from pulling the sled when they are not supposed to. The term dates from the 1960s, and replaced **ice anchor,** which had been used since the 1940s.

snow berm

■ n In the Far Northwest, the ridge of snow and gravel pushed lengthwise along the side of a road by a snowplow. The term dates only from the 1970s in print.

snowbird

■ n A person who travels to southern climes during the winter. The term was first used in the 1960s to describe people who traveled from Minnesota and various points in Canada to dwell in the Phoenix area during the wintertime. Soon, the term spread all over the Southwest, then finally to Florida and the rest of the country.

snow crab

■ n Also called **bairdi, opilio.** After the **king crab** had been mightily harvested, Japanese fishermen began harvesting the **Tanner crab** and selling it in the United States as the snow crab. So the word may have been invented by the Japanese for the American market. The snow crab began appearing on American and Canadian menus in the 1970s. Finally, Alaskan fisheries began harvesting it.

snow hook

■ n See **snow anchor.**

snow machine

■ n Another name for a **skidoo.** Since the 1960s, this has been the most frequent term used in rural areas of Alaska and the Yukon. The snow machine is built for one or two persons, and usually has no cover.

snowshirt

■ n A light cloth covering, usually cotton or canvas, pulled over the outer fur **parka** worn in the Far Northwest. The snowshirt acts as a windbreaker and keeps blowing snow and dirt off the fur linings of the parka. The sleeves and hems are often embroidered and decorated with native designs. In English since the 1920s, though in use longer.

snowshoe rabbit

■ n A western hare first found in the **Rocky Mountains** in the 1890s. The animal has large feet for moving over snowfields and has a white winter coat.

snub line ■ n Usually shortened to **snub.** A rope tied to a boat, floating log, **dogsled,** or animal, then tied closely to a tree or post to keep it from floating, drifting, or running away. The term came into use in the 1890s as a method for keeping a boat in check, but is used throughout the West by cowboys, **dog mushers,** and loggers. The verb came into use almost at the same time.

soap plant ■ n See **amole, soapweed.**

soaproot ■ n See **camas, soapweed.**

soapweed ■ n Also called **soap apple, soap bulb, soaproot, soapwort.** Any of a variety of western plants that can be lathered when water is added to the various chopped parts of the plant. From the 1840s, this sudsing property was discovered in a number of alkaline-loving plants found in the arid parts of the Southwest. See also **amole.**

sockeye salmon ■ n A red-fleshed salmon (*Oncorhynchus nerka*), that attains an average weight of five pounds. A major resource of the streams and rivers of the Pacific Northwest, British Columbia, and Alaska, it is an elongated fish, with a metallic-blue back and silver color on the sides and underneath. Called **red salmon** in Alaska. The name is borrowed, with a process of folk etymology, from the Salish *sukkegh* 'red fish'. (From 1880s) See also **salmon** n for a complete listing.

soda ■ Used as a combining element relative to western phenomena featuring alkaline soil. Thus, *soda butte* is a bluff or hill that is white or whitish-colored because of the alkali; likewise, ~ *mound* and ~ *mountain;* ~ *grass* grows in an alkaline area; ~ *fountain* is a spring of mineral water with soda bubbles.

sodbuster

■ n Slang term for a western farmer. The term first appeared in the early 1920s and may have been created by a fanciful writer. There is no early record that ranchers called farmers by this name, either in jest or derision. It would be a book-learned word to most westerners seventy or eighty years ago.

Soledad pine

■ n Also called **Torrey pine.** A pine tree that grows in scattered, open groves on the highlands near the sea in southern California. The name comes from Spanish *soledad* 'solitary', because the tree is often by itself in the open hillside. Both words, "Soledad" and "Torrey," are frequently found in the West in place-names, town names, street names, and names of housing subdivisions, often far inland from the coast.

sombrero

■ n Any of a variety of large, wide-brimmed hats worn in the Southwest, especially as protection against sun, rather than from rain or for warmth. From the 1820s the word has been used in English. As with all articles of clothing borrowed from Mexican culture, the sombrero can be highly decorative, with designs, silverwork, and beads. From Spanish *sombra* 'shade'.

Sonoran

■ adj Relating to the **Sonoran Desert** of the Southwest or the Mexican state of **Sonora.** Certain plants are found only in that region. But the most common use of the adjective is relative to the winds and rain that come from the south at certain times of the year and flow northward into Arizona, California, Nevada, and New Mexico. As early as the 1870s, the adjective was being used to describe the zoogeographical zone of the region bordered by northern Mexico, southern California, Colorado, and west Texas.

sopapilla

■ /SOPE uh PEE uh/ n A fried yeast bread served with honey. In New Mexico, often prescribed to cut the fiery effects of some chile dishes. (Spanish, 1930s)

sourdough

■ n A person who spends a great deal of time in rural, open areas, especially as a prospector in Alaska. More generally, a prospector in the West (see also **alkali,** 2). The name, from the 1890s, is taken from the container of sourdough, a part of which is saved over each day to continue the fermentation process for new batches of bread or biscuits.

Spanish bayonet

■ n Also called **banana yucca, datil,** or **Spanish dagger.** The pointed, stiff leaf of the *Yucca bacata* or *Y. aloifolia,* the fruit of which is banana-shaped and roasted for food. Most yuccas are elevation specific, growing in biotic communities at elevations between three and six thousand feet only. (From 1840s)

Spanish dagger

■ n A stiff, short-trunked plant of the *Yucca* genera (especially *Y. gloriosa*) found in the Southwest. The rigid, spiny leaves grow perpendicularly to a height of seven feet or more. (From 1850s) Often confused with **Spanish bayonet** and **Spanish sword.**

Spanish sword

■ n Any of a variety of stiff, short-trunked plants of the *Yucca* genera found in the Southwest. The name is used generically by the public to refer to any spiny plant that ends in a point sharp enough to draw blood when bumped into. (From 1950s) See also **Spanish bayonet, Spanish dagger.**

Spanish Trail

■ n Any of a variety of roads used in early days in the Southwest. But two main routes carry the name today: the road from Santa Fe to Los Angeles and the road from Salt Lake City via Cedar City and Las Vegas to other Mormon settlements in San Bernardino. It has become commonplace in the names used by land and subdivision developers in the Southwest.

spawn-on-kelp

■ n The eggs of herring that were attached to seaweed, then harvested and pickled in brine. A favorite of Alaskan and Japanese palates since the 1980s. See also **kazunoko, roe-on-kelp, sac roe.**

speckled trout

■ n Also called **speckled brook trout, speckled**

mountain trout, speckled rainbow trout. Any of the varieties of trout found in mountain streams in the West. At about three thousand feet are found the **browns,** darkly speckled with a soft flesh, usually to twelve or fifteen inches long and thick in appearance. At about five thousand feet are found the **rainbows,** with lighter backs and smaller speckles, pink tinge around the gills, with a bit firmer flesh, growing ten to twelve inches in length. At about eight thousand feet are found **cutthroats,** with very dark backs, small speckles, firm to hard flesh, scarlet around the gills, growing seven to eleven inches in length, with narrow bodies. Considered the finest fresh fish for eating over a campfire.

spider crab
■ n Also called **Alaska king crab** (q.v. for a complete listing). This large crab can have a leg-spread of twelve feet or more. It was a staple of the Japanese fishery in the 1920s and canned commercially as **Japanese spider crab.** As the Alaskan fishing industry increased its share of the commercial market, the name was shortened and in the 1940s was regularly called by its present name. See also **bairdi.**

spillionaire
■ n Facetious name used for Alaskans who took excessive profits from the Exxon Valdez oil spill disaster in Prince William Sound in 1989. Blended from *spill* + m*illionaire.*

spread
■ n A ranch or large farm with all appurtenances pertaining thereto: buildings, rangeland, livestock, rolling stock. The term has been so used in the West since the 1920s, but probably was a semantic shift from an earlier regional term from Dutch *sprei* or British English, meaning 'covering a broad, flat space', which gave rise to earlier terms such as "bedspread," "spread on a billiard table," "covering of jam or jelly on a slice of bread," and such other uses. See also **ranch.**

spring salmon
■ n Also called **tyee salmon, Chinook salmon.** The earliest salmon to arrive at the spawning grounds. So called since the 1850s. See **salmon** n for a complete listing.

squaw

■ A combining form used with a number of western words, usually relative to plants and fish that Indian women used, or might have used in the minds of observers: *squawberry, ~ carpet, ~ currant, ~ grass, ~ mash, ~ weed,* all plants; a *squaw man* used to refer to a white man who had married a Native woman; *squaw wood* refers to twigs and small dead branches from the lower parts of trees that can be used to start a fire easily.

squaw candy

■ n Narrow strips of salmon salted, dried, and smoked, a delicacy original to Alaskan Natives, but now covering a multitude of palates. The treat is known by a number of names: **Alaska candy, Eskimo ~, siwash ~, Yukon ~; fish strips, strips.** There is even a movement to cash in on the jerky craze, with **salmon jerky.** (From 1940s)

squaw mat

■ n See **mahala mat.**

staghorn cactus

■ n Also called **staghorn cholla.** A low-growing, jointed cactus with arms about three inches in diameter and segments one or two feet long, covered with dense spines, giving the cactus a furry appearance. In use since the 1920s. See also **cholla.**

stake house

■ n The building serving as the center for the region or division of a Mormon community. A "stake" is a region made up of several **wards,** each headed by a bishop, somewhat similar to several parishes making up a "bishopric" in other religions.

stampede

■ n A wild, headlong rush of cattle, buffalo, horses, or other animals. Borrowed from Spanish *estampida* in the 1840s. Consequently, applied to any group that rushes, from gold seekers to dancers, from rodeo participants to conventioneers at an open bar. The verb entered English simultaneously, there being a general need to describe the actions of such groups.

starved rat

■ n See **coney.**

steelhead

■ n A large-sized trout, *Salmo gairdneri*. It is not clear whether the fish was so named in the 1880s because of its color or the hardness of its head. Both possibilities have been offered. See also **rainbow trout.**

Steller

■ A combining form for a variety of wildlife found in the West. G. W. Steller was a German naturalist who lived a short life, from 1709 to 1746. But in his brief life he gave his name to numerous western fauna, including the *Steller* (or *Steller's*) *duck*, ~ *eider*, ~ *jay*, ~ *sea cow*, and ~ *sea lion*.

Stetson

■ n The trademark of a hat designed by John Batterson Stetson; the ubiquitous cowboy hat found in every country-western dance hall from Long Island to Long Beach. He designed the hat in 1865, just in time for the western expansion after the Civil War. By the time he died in 1906, he had seen his hat worn for every social occasion from cattle roundups to society balls. Richard Slatta notes that many cowboys now wear baseball caps rather than cowboy hats so they won't be mistaken for truck drivers. See also **ten-gallon hat.**

stinky head

■ n Also called **stink fish, stinky,** or simply **stink.** A fermented fish dish prepared by Alaska Natives. The term came into English in the 1950s, but the practice is much older, and the process is used not just with fish heads, but also fish eggs, and other parts of fish or even walrus meat. The preparation of fish heads, particularly, is similar to the preparation of Korean kimchi in that both feature burial in the ground while fermentation takes place.

stock

■ A combining form used in a number of self-explanatory compounds dealing with ranching life and cattle or horses: *stock corral* (see **corral**), ~ *country,* ~ *raiser,* ~ *ranch* (see **ranch, spread**), ~ *ranching,* ~ *range,* ~ *region,* ~ *roundup* (see **roundup**), ~ *saddle,* ~ *water.*

storm porch

■ n On houses in Alaska and the Yukon, a small enclosure framing the door to the house. The space can be as small as two by three feet or as large as ten by twelve feet. The purpose of it is to provide a buffer between the interior of the house and the elements outside. Formerly, the structure was called a **storm shed,** and could be a crude affair built of rough-cut lumber and even covered with animal skins. But by the 1940s, gentility was setting in. Modern storm porches have well-set doors, rubber mats, and rods for hanging wet outer clothing.

strawberry cactus

■ n A low-growing cactus of the Southwest that has a strawberrylike fruit. *Echinocereus enneacanthus* is squat and regularly lumped into the category of **barrel cactus** (q.v. for a complete listing).

striped fish

■ n Also called **Alaskan mackerel** (q.v. for a complete listing). A greenish fish with dark blue bands across the back. The fish has been confused with the Atlantic mackerel, but is an entirely different fish. Confusion of this sort is more common than might be imagined. When English-speaking peoples go into new areas, they often apply the names of birds, animals, and fish they knew back home to new species because of a slight similarity in appearance.

strips

■ n Also called **Alaska candy, siwash candy.** Narrow strips of salmon, cut lengthwise, salted, dried, and smoked. Long a favorite of Alaska Natives, the delicacy has become a palate pleaser around the country, sometimes by the name of **salmon jerky.** The name "strips" has been used in English since the 1920s. See **squaw candy** for a complete listing.

Stubtoe State

■ n A nickname for **Montana.** As early as the 1890s, the region was called the "stubbed-toe state" because of the craggy mountains in the western part of the state, in contrast to the flatlands of the eastern part.

subsistence fish

■ v To catch fish for eating, as opposed to catching fish for commercial gain. It is used in contrast to "commercial fish." Both verbs were formed in the 1980s by the language process of back formation from the nouns "subsistence fishing" and "commercial fishing." The terms came about in Alaska, where strict regulations govern fishing rights of all the citizens, whether such fishing is for sport, commerce, or survival. On analogy with the term, the verb "subsistence hunt" is now in use also, although there is no corresponding verb for commercial hunting.

Suckley

■ A combining form for certain wildlife found in the West, named after naturalist Dr. George Suckley, 1830–1869. Two of the more notable creatures are *Suckley's gull* found in the Puget Sound, and *Suckley's salmon trout,* first found on the east slope of the Coeur d'Alene Range in the 1860s.

sugarberry

■ n Also called **anaqua.** A half-evergreen tree (*Ehretia anacua*) that is found along the Texas-Mexico border. The multiple-trunk tree has a yellow-orange sweet fruit that is considered edible.

summer chum

■ n A salmon that spawns in the lower 500 miles of the Yukon River in the early part of the season, as opposed to **fall chum.** See **salmon** n for a complete listing.

sunfish

■ v In a **rodeo,** to buck and bend sideways, making an arc of the body. The horse that so bucks reminds one of a sunfish flopping on a fishing line. (From 1960s)

Sunshine State

■ n A favorite nickname of state boosters, though not especially original, considering that it is applied to New Mexico, California, Florida, and even South Dakota. Perhaps boosters from other states are already using the name for their neck of the woods.

surf

■ A combining form for wildlife and activities along the West Coast. Examples of wildlife: *surf-bird,* from 1830s; *surf fish,* any of the members of the family Embiotocidae, from 1880s; *surf perch* and *surf smelt,* both from the 1880s.

Also for activities and phenomena related to surfboard riders along the West Coast, beginning in the 1950s: *surf band, ~ beat, ~ art, ~ music* refer to music and murals found near beaches in California celebrating surfing; *surf bum, ~ bunny, ~ cat, ~ chick, ~ dog, ~ doggie, ~ dude, ~ nazi, ~ punk, ~ rasta, ~ rat, ~ rebel* refer to types of people who ride surfboards; *surf bumps,* calcium deposits that form below the kneecap and on the arch of the foot from kneeling on a surfboard for long periods of time, similar to "housemaid's knee."

Swainson's

■ A combining form used to honor William Swainson, 1789–1855, a naturalist born in England who worked mightily to identify western birds: *Swainson's buzzard, ~ cliff swallow, ~ hawk, ~ swallow, ~ thrush, ~ warbling vireo.*

swamp sego

■ n See **camas.**

swamp tea

■ n See **Alaska tea.**

sweeper

■ n In the Northwest, a tree that has been undermined by the current of a river so that the tree leans over into the river while still being moored by its roots. Since the 1880s such hazards have been noted by boatmen plying the rivers of the Yukon and Alaska.

swing rider

■ n Since the 1900s, moving cattle herds from the rural areas of the West to the railheads was a major undertaking. A large herd was composed of the "point," or the cows at the front of the herd, the "swing," or the main body of the herd, and the "drag," the cows toward the end of the herd. The cowboys who rode at different points alongside the herd were called, appropriately, **point rider,** swing rider, and **drag rider.**

T

taannaq

■ n Alcohol in various forms, especially cheap bootleg liquor. The Inupiat word came to national attention in 1995, when residents of Barrow, Alaska, voted to revoke the one-year-old ban on liquor in any form.

taco

■ n A fried **tortilla** filled with meat, lettuce, tomato, cheese, and **salsa.** The Spanish word was borrowed into English in the 1930s, but did not become widespread outside of the Southwest until the 1970s.

Taku

■ n Shortened from **Taku wind.** A particularly strong and cold wind that blows into Juneau, Alaska, by way of the Taku River Valley. This is just one of the more famous of a number of winds named by the location in the West, beside the famous **chinook.** Some of these winds are named the "Knik," "Matanuska," and "Stikine." The Taku and chinook, like the **Santa Ana** of Southern California, blow in more populated areas, so are known to more people.

tamale pie

■ n Although the word "tamale" was borrowed from Nahuatl in the early 1600s and used from the beginning of English-speaking settlement of North America, "tamale pie" was not established in the English-speaker's cuisine until the 1910s in the Southwest. The pie consists of a lining of cornmeal mush in a pie pan, and a filling of meat, peppers, tomato, and **chilies.**

Tanner crab

■ n Also called **Alaska king crab, queen crab.** In Alaska, the catch-all name for either the **bairdi** or the **opilio.** Zera L. Tanner, whose name was given to the crab, died in 1906. But the name became generally applied to the different crabs only in the 1940s as commercial crabbing increased in Alaskan waters.

tapadera

■ n When cowboys encountered the rough **chaparral** of the Southwest, they discovered their feet and legs were scraped and scratched by the rough brush. In the 1840s, they adopted not only the leather stirrup covers used by Mexican **vaqueros** but also the name.

tapajo

■ n An eye cover or blinder used on pack animals while loading them or adjusting their packs. The name comes from Spanish *tapar* 'to cover' + *ojo* 'eye'. It came into English in the 1840s.

team dog

■ n In **dogsledding,** the term for any dog hitched between the **lead dog** and the **wheel dog.** Like horse teams of old, the dogs of a team are named by the position they occupy in front of the sled. The first dog is the "lead," the second is the "swing," and the one just in front of the sled is the "wheel." All others in between are called "team" dogs.

Tejano

■ /tay HAH no/ n The Spanish word for "Texan," used in English since the 1920s.

Tejano music

■ n A type of music produced initially along the Mexican/U.S. border. It contains elements of **salsa, norteño,** and the snappy polka rhythms of the region. Originally, "Tejano" referred, beginning in the 1920s, to the cultural life and tastes of people of Mexican descent living along the border. But as the music became a hallmark of that culture, the term became wider spread in English. With the death of one of the music's most popular singers, Selena, the term immediately became a nationally recognized English term. (From 1980s)

ten-gallon hat

■ n A high-crowned, broad-brimmed cowboy hat. It is so called, not because it holds a large amount of water, but because of the number of braids (Spanish *galons*) that circled the hat in place of a hatband. Folk etymology changed the Spanish *galon* 'braid' into English *gallon* 'measure of liquid' in the 1920s. See also **Stetson.**

tenderfoot

■ n A newcomer to the West, especially one inexperienced in worldly ways and notably naive. The term arose with the influx of newcomers during the great gold rush of 1849. See also **Arbuckle, cheechako.**

Teton

■ /TEE ton, tee TAHN/ n The form of a mountain suggestive of a woman's breast, which the word means in the original French. Since the 1850s, the term has been used as a descriptor for many peaks, and figures as a place-name for an entire range in Wyoming.

Texas

■ The word comes from Spanish, but ultimately was used by some native tribes to mean "friends, allies." A combining form used in relation to many plants and animals found in Texas, most of them self-explanatory: *Texas armadillo, ~ ash, ~ blue-bonnet, ~ bluegrass, ~ cattle, ~ cow, ~ ebony, ~ fever tick, ~ hare, ~ herd, ~ longhorn, ~ millet, ~ moss, ~ oak, ~ persimmon, ~ pony, ~ sparrow, ~ star, ~ steer, ~ thrasher, ~ umbrella tree, ~ white oak, ~ woodpecker.* As the first element in compounds: *Texas cattleman; ~ dialect; ~ hat, ~ norther* (see **blue norther, norther**); *~ Panhandle; ~ Ranger* (see **ranger,** 2); *~ saddle,* a heavy Mexican-style saddle; *~ style; ~ trail; ~ wagon; ~ yell.*

Tex-Mex

■ n The customs, language, culture, dress, foods, and so on that mark the regional flavor of the people who live along the Mexican/U.S. border, especially those things influenced by Mexican culture in contact with the U.S. English-speaking culture. (From 1940s)

Thompson seedless grape

■ n A light-colored grape developed in California in the 1890s, originally as a sultana variety of the raisin grape. But popular now as a table grape.

tilicum

■ n Also spelled *tillicum, tilikum.* Friends; the common folk. This Chinook word has been in English since the 1840s and is used in the Pacific Northwest in the same sense as in Chinook Jargon: people, friends, folks, relations. As opposed to people of some rank. It has the same force as "paisan" or "paisano" in other parts of the country.

tinaja

■ n An earthenware jar used for storing water. Originally this Spanish word came into English in the 1830s and referred to depressions carved in flat rocks by the Indians of the Southwest for catching rainwater. But since the 1880s the word has re-

= 229 =

ferred to the red clay jars manufactured by the Pueblos or other Indians.

tobacco root

■ n See **kooyah.**

tomatillo

■ n A small tomatolike vegetable grown with a leafy covering around the fruit. The word came into English in the 1930s from the Spanish diminutive for "tomato," itself from the Nahuatl Indian language, *tomatl.*

tong

■ n A club, social organization, or secret society among Chinese in the United States. The Chinese word *t'ang* or *t'ong* means 'meetinghouse, hall'. The word came into English in the 1880s in San Francisco, where the societies first formed themselves for mutual protection and aid. By the 1920s, **tong war** was being used by newspapers to describe the feuds between and among some of these societies.

top hand

■ n The best cowboy in an outfit. Also called the **top waddy.** The term dates from the 1910s. By extension, it has come to mean anyone who is among the best at what they do.

top off

■ v To finish breaking a horse to a saddle, after the initial bronc-busting has taken place. The word came into English in the 1920s, and later came to refer to finishing up any sort of business or small chore, such as filling up a tank that is nearly full of gas or filling a glass of liquid that is already more than half full.

tornillo

■ n The screw bean from the **screw-pod mesquite.** This Spanish word came into English in the 1840s. In Spanish it meant, literally, 'little screw'.

toroso

■ n A **greasewood** shrub. The word comes from the Spanish adjective meaning "strong, robust" and refers to the fact that there is so much resin in the plant that it will burn even when wet and green. The word came into English in the 1910s. Only a greenhorn would actually try to cook or get warm by burning the plant, however. The thick and sticky black roiling smoke that the burning plant gives off coats everything around with a greasy black film. See also **creosote bush, hediondilla.**

Torrey pine

■ n A California pine, *Pinus torreyana,* that is the distinctive tree growing along the West Coast. Where the cliffs are windswept, the pine grows as a low, crooked, and sprawling tree about twenty-five or thirty feet high. It is the picturesque tree shown in so many photographs of the Monterey area. When the tree is found away from the wind-swept cliffs, it is straight and fifty to sixty feet tall. It was named in the 1840s for American botanist John Torrey, 1796–1873. His name is prominent in a number of plant names and place-names in the West. See also **Soledad pine.**

tortilla

■ n A thin, flat, and round griddlecake, originally made of masa, or cornmeal, in the 1830s, when it was borrowed from Spanish into English. Now, it might be made of masa or wheat flour. The tortilla made of wheat flour is usually ten to twelve inches in diameter, whereas the corn tortilla is usually five or six inches in diameter.

towline

■ n In **dogsledding,** a long rope or line between the dog and the sled. See also **bridle, gangline, neckline.**

Townsend

■ n A combining form commemorating J. K. Townsend, 1809–1851, an American naturalist who identified a number of birds in the West, including *Townsend's flycatching thrush,* ~ *fox sparrow,* ~ *solitaire,* ~ *sparrow,* ~ *warbler.*

trail

■ A combining form referring to the movement of cattle from the range to the railheads, especially between 1880 and 1940. The time and the process has been romanticized in song and story so that few people realize how few **waddies** or cowboys actually participated in such drives. Many of the terms that developed had ranching counterparts: *trail cattle,* ~ *crew,* ~ *herd,* ~ *herder,* ~ *outfit,* ~ *rider,* ~ *rope,* ~ *steer,* ~ *wagon.* Some terms were specific to the trail, but self-explanatory: *trail drive,* ~ *driver,* ~ *drover,* ~ *man,* ~ *work. Trail broke(n)* referred to a herd that had been moving for a few days and had settled into a routine.

trans-Alaska pipeline ■ n See **pipeline, the.**

trap pirate ■ n See **fish pirate.**

trap robber ■ n Also called **fish pirate.** In the days before Alaska statehood, commercial fishermen used large net corrals to control the **salmon** in rivers and streams. Salmon rustlers were a common problem.

traveler's friend ■ n A squat, rounded cactus found in the Mojave Desert. The flesh of the plant contains moisture that can be sopped up with a cloth and placed in the mouth. The traveler cannot eat the flesh of the plant itself because the cells of the plant are absorbent and would further dehydrate the traveler. See **barrel cactus** for a complete listing.

Treasure State ■ n A nickname for **Montana** since the 1930s because of the vast mineral wealth still buried in the state, in spite of the fact that billions of dollars of mineral have already been extracted.

tree cholla ■ n See **cholla.**

trembling aspen ■ n Also called **aspen, quakenas, quaking aspen.** The birchlike tree covering the higher slopes of the **Rocky Mountains.** A deciduous tree with brilliant autumn leaves.

tremblor ■ n An earthquake, usually a light one, less than 4.5 on the Richter Scale. The word has been in English since the 1910s and is the result of the confusion of two words. Spanish *temblar* 'to shake' and English "trembler."

tripas ■ n A euphemism for "entrails, guts." In the 1930s, the Spanish word was adopted by the queasy. Never mind that it comes from the same word as "tripe."

tshawytscha ■ n Also called **Chinook salmon.** The large (up to twenty pounds) salmon that became the foundation for the commercial fisheries of the Northwest. See **salmon** n for a complete listing.

tube

■ n Also called **barrel, pipe.** The inside of a curled wave breaking on the shore. The accomplished surfer tries to ride inside the leading edge of the wave as it topples over. Used since the 1960s along the West Coast.

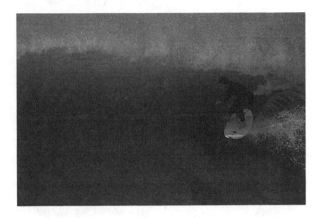

tule

■ /TOO lee/ n 1. Either of two types of large bulrushes found in overgrown and swampy areas. The word is from Nahuatl by way of Spanish and has been used since the 1830s. 2. A region considered desolate and forbidding. In the West "the tules" is used frequently to describe an out-of-the-way place, as "Podunk" or "Flatbush" might have been used by vaudeville comedians. See also **Bush,** 2. 3. As a combining form, the word has been attached to aspects of such a terrain: *tule balsa, ~ boat, ~ bottom, ~ elk, ~ farm, ~ gnat, ~ hut, ~ lake, ~ land, ~ marsh, ~ potato, ~ root, ~ raft, ~ sail, ~ swamp, ~ wren.*

tule fog

■ n A ground fog that develops in a large region, as opposed to fog from the sea or moisture in the air. The most famous tule fog develops in the Imperial Valley of California, along most of the length of Interstate 5 from Bakersfield to just south of Sacramento. The fog has hidden some of the longest chain collisions in the history of driving. Every few months, from 30 to 200 cars are involved in an enormous accident along that stretch of interstate highway. See also **pogonip fog,** 2. Compare **high fog.**

tumbleweed

■ n Any of a variety of branching plants whose globe-shaped tops break free from the roots and are pushed about in the wind, especially true of **sagebrush.** The metaphorical image of the drifter helped to create the romanticized notion of the West as a place for people to move around, rarely settling down.

tumtum

■ n Affection, mind, opinion. Literally, the word comes from Chinook Jargon in the 1860s and means 'beating heart'. The transference in meaning is to anything that makes the heartbeat change or any emotion that speeds it up.

turban cactus

■ n A short, bulbous cactus of the Southwestern deserts. See **barrel cactus** for a complete listing.

turkey buzzard

■ n See **vulture.**

turk's head

■ n Another name for **turban cactus.** See **barrel cactus** for a complete listing.

twenty-mule team

■ n A group of twenty mules harnessed together, once used to pull large wagons of borax from the collection areas in Death Valley around the turn of the century.

two-foot high kick

■ n Same as **Alaskan high kick.**

tyee salmon

■ n Another name for **spring salmon, Chinook salmon.** See **salmon** n for a complete listing of names.

twenty-mule-team wagon train

uintaite

■ n A glossy black hydrocarbon first found in the Uintah Mountains in Utah, and so named after them. The pure form of this asphalt serves in the manufacture of certain varnishes and paints. (From 1890s) *Uintah* is a tribal name from Ute, a language in the Shoshonean family.

ulu

■ n Also spelled *ooloo*. Called a "woman's knife," this cutting tool is favored by women in Alaskan Eskimo culture. The curved, crescent blade has a shape like a slice of pie. At the apex, where the point of the pie slice would be, is a palm-sized handle made of wood or bone. Women favor the tool, whereas men prefer a hunting knife or a jackknife for similar chores. (From 1890s, the current spelling is from Inupiaq; other spellings include central Yupik *uluaq* and Alutiq *ulukaq*)

umiaq

■ n Also spelled *oomiak*. Also called **bidar, angyak.** A large open boat used by Aleuts to carry up to thirty persons or large amounts of cargo. The frame of the boat is similar to a canoe and is covered with the skin of sea lions or seals. (From 1870s, Inupiaq) See also **bidarka.**

ulu

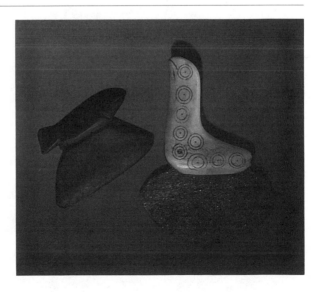

Upper Sonoran

■ n A biogeographical zone covering mainly an area in the Southwest. The zone is determined by both latitude and altitude. It is marked by dominant plant forms in biotic communities that grow at specific altitudes at different latitudes. The biogeographical zones of North America were determined on the basis of principles worked out by biologist Clinton Hart Merriam (1855–1942). Specific plants and birds are found dominant in different biogeographical zones. The Upper Sonoran borders the Transition Zone. (From 1910s)

upraise

■ n Also **uprise.** A vertical shaft drilled upward in a mine. (From 1870s)

Urim and Thummim

■ n phr Two stones set in silver bows, which in turn are mounted on a breastplate. Joseph Smith used the stones to translate plates containing the Book of Mormon. Apparently the stones resembled spectacles, because Smith referred to them as "Seers." Prior to the time of Joseph Smith, Urim and Thummim are found only in the Bible. In Exodus 28 are detailed instructions for making the priestly garment that is to be worn when approaching the Tabernacle. There, Urim and Thummim (verse 30) are described as lots worn inside the breastplate, close to the heart. In I Samuel 14:41, Urim and Thummim are lots to be cast to determine the source of guilt among the Israelites. (From 1830s)

Utah

■ n Also spelled *Youta, Eutah, Utaw.* Forty-fifth state of the Union. Settled by Mormon pioneers in 1847, it became a territory in 1850, and a state in 1896. Capital: Salt Lake City. The name of the Ute Indian tribe was suggested by John C. Frémont, and adopted over the Mormons' own choice, **Deseret,** which Congress opposed, both because it came from the Book of Mormon and because it sounded too much like "desert." Nicknames: **Basin State,** also **Great Basin State,** because the state lies almost entirely in the Great Basin; **Beehive State.** (From 1720, *Ute,* 'people')

Utah juniper

■ n A tree reaching twenty feet in height, twelve inches in circumference. *Juniperus utahensis* thrives especially at altitudes above four thousand feet. (From 1900s)

Utah mullet ■ n A chub fish, *Squalius atrarius,* found particularly in Utah Lake. (From 1880s)

Utah route ■ n This name for the immigrant's pathway from the Midwest to California fell into disuse in the 1850s, in favor of the now common "Mormon trail."

Utah War ■ n The hostilities between the federal government and the Mormons in 1857 threatened to become a shooting war. (From 1940s)

Ute ■ n A Shoshonean tribe that inhabited large areas of Utah, Colorado, and New Mexico. Also, the language family of several different groups of Indians, known collectively as Uto-Aztecan. (From 1770s)

Ute Diggers ■ n A name once applied to the Piute Indians of the **Great Basin.** (From 1870s)

uthlecan ■ /YOOTH luh kun/ n A small freshwater fish once found regularly at the mouth of the Columbia River. (From 1830s, thought to be from a language of a local coastal Indian tribe)

V

V-flume

■ n This now-obsolete term referred to the wedge-shaped trough that was found in every mountainous region of the Pacific Coast where gold was mined. (From 1890s)

vaca

■ n A cow. Also used as a place-name in California. (From 1840s, Spanish)

vacher

■ n See **vaquero**

valley cottonwood

■ n Any of a variety of species of cottonwood found in the Southwest and the West, especially New Mexico, Texas, Arizona, Utah, and Nevada. (From 1910s)

valley oak

■ n A white oak, *Quercus lobata,* found along the coast in northern California. Sometimes called **weeping oak.** (From 1890s)

valley quail

■ n Originally this bird was thought to be the same as the **California quail.** But ornithologists make a distinction between the larger California quail and the smaller valley quail, which is also found in Arizona and parts of southern Nevada. The California quail is considered a diner's delight, whereas the valley quail, in addition to being smaller, is less tasty. (From 1850s)

valley tan

■ adj Originally, this term applied to the leather made in the Salt Lake Valley, Utah Territory, to distinguish it from leather and leather goods imported from eastern states. In time, the term came to refer to any goods that were homemade, including such things as tools. By the 1940s, the term was used derisively for things that were homemade and judged therefore inferior to manufactured goods. (From 1850s)

valley tan whiskey

■ n A homemade whiskey from stills originally built in and around the Salt Lake Valley. As the existence of local, hidden stills spread westward, the brew developed a reputation similar to that of the white lightning found in the hills of the Southeast;

that is, it was sometimes found to be good, sometimes terrible, but always consumed when available. (From 1860s)

Valparaiso oak ■ n An evergreen found along the coast of California, also known as the **canyon oak.** Sometimes called the **maul oak.** (From 1880s)

vamoose ■ v Sometimes *bamanos* (Spanish). To go; to leave, usually with the sense of leaving quickly. In Spanish, the word *vamos* carries the sense of 'let us now depart', without the same sense of urgency that the term has acquired in English. (From 1840s, Spanish)

vapor barrier boot ■ n Also called a **bunny boot.** A boot originally developed by the army as cold-weather gear. The white, rubberized lace-up boot became very popular in Alaska and the Yukon Territory. The boot is constructed with heavy insulation in the sole and around the foot. Between the insulation and the inside layer of felt is a protective barrier made of plastic or a mylar substance which prevents moisture from penetrating to the inside of the boot. The vapor barrier was developed for insulation in the building trades during the Second World War. By 1950, the process was being used in boots which in turn began showing up in army surplus stores. The original boots were white, to serve as camouflage against the snow and ice. That, plus the fact that the boots kept feet warm and cozy led to the nickname "bunny boot." (From 1940s) See also **breakup boot.**

vaquero ■ n Also **buckaroo.** A cowboy, especially in the Southwest. Nowadays the term is used for cowboys of Mexican extraction, while other cowboys are called "buckaroos," an anglicized pronunciation. (From 1830s, Spanish)

vara ■ n Originally, this term was borrowed into English in the 1830s as a Spanish term of measurement, a bit shorter than the thirty-six-inch yard. Soon the term was used for the measuring device, similar to "yardstick." By the 1860s, the "vara stick" was often decorated with designs. Among

= 239 =

the New Mexico pueblos, a specially decorated vara was used as an emblem of authority. Each pueblo had a silver-mounted vara with both the name of the pueblo and the name of President Lincoln. (The use of Lincoln's name or likeness was not restricted to the Southwest. In the Pacific Northwest, Indians carved at least one totem pole with the likeness of President Lincoln at the top.) (From 1830s, Spanish)

vega

■ n A plain or an extensive valley. The term appears to be obsolete, but lives on in place-names in New Mexico and Nevada. (From 1850s, Spanish)

vent

■ n A special brand used on an animal to show that the animal has been legally purchased. Sometimes called a **sale brand.** When used as a verb, the term carries the same sense as the verb "brand," with the special understanding that such branding represents a legal sale. A "vented" horse is a legally sold horse. (From 1840s, Spanish)

verdin

■ n A small titmouse marked by a yellow head and darker body, found in the arid regions of the Southwest. (From 1880s)

viga

■ n A beam or log used as a ridgepole for a roof or as a supporting rafter in some Indian and Spanish-style houses in the Southwest. Such poles are usually six to ten inches in diameter, sixteen to twenty feet long, and made from undressed pine logs. (From 1840s, Spanish)

vigilante

■ n A member of a group of people who take the law into their own hands, usually to avenge what they see as a crime. Vigilance committees were themselves outlawed in most states. Ironically, a vigilante breaks the law in trying to enforce it. Although this term originated in the eastern states and was most closely identified with the South after the Civil War, generations of writers of the western novel and the cowboy movie associated the term with the Old West. Consequently, many people think of vigilantes as members of a mob, lynching **rustlers** and other ne'er do wells. (From 1860s)

village ■ n In Alaska, a community inhabited by Alaska Natives, as opposed to a community inhabited by white people, which is called a "town," even though the populations of both may be about the same. Tabbert (*DAK*) offers the example of the town of Eagle and the neighboring Eagle Village; the first is inhabited by whites, the second is inhabited by Alaskan Natives. Hence, a **villager** is specifically an Alaska Native. (From 1930s)

vine maple ■ n A small, scrubby tree that has leaves resembling a maple. After a fire or clear-cutting in the coastal Northwest, this scraggly brushlike tree pops up, along with thickets of scrub oak. (From 1850)

vinegarroon ■ n A large whip scorpion of the Southwest. The insect got its name from the vinegarlike odor emitted when it is startled. The vinegarroon is popularly presumed to be poisonous. It is not. It is commonly confused with the matavenado, which *is* a large poisonous ant. (From 1850s, Spanish)

Virginia's warbler ■ n Also called **Rocky Mountain warbler.** A warbler whose range is the southern **Rocky Mountains.** Named by ornithologist Spencer F. Baird to honor Mrs. W. W. Anderson. (From 1860s)

viva ■ excl A shout of approval, common to the Southwest. (From 1830s, Spanish)

vomito ■ n A form of yellow fever initially found mainly in the Southwest. It is marked especially by black vomit, and so sometimes is called **vomito negro.** (From 1830s, Spanish)

vulture ■ n A common abbreviation for the **California vulture,** which is found throughout the West, not just in California. The resemblance of the bird to others of both the Old and the New worlds have resulted in the bird's being called also **turkey buzzard, vulture buzzard,** and even **vulture eagle.** (From 1800s)

W

Waco

■ n Tribal name for one of the divisions of the Tawakoni. The main village of the tribe was at the present site of Waco, Texas. The tribe was involved in a number of recorded battles with other Indian tribes and federal soldiers. Finally, in 1902, after making a series of treaties, the members of the tribe received land allotments. (From 1820s)

waddy

■ n Originally, a cattle **rustler.** Later, the name was expanded to include any cowboy. The implication of the term is that a waddy is rough-hewn, drinks hard, and is ready to take advantage of any situation. The origin of the term is unknown, though a few outrageous etymons have been suggested. (From 1890s)

wagon boss

■ n This now historical term designated the man in charge of a **wagon train** that specifically carried people and their goods westward from Kansas and Nebraska. The driving of the golden spike at Promontory Point, Utah, linked the East with the West, and rapidly brought to an end the profession of wagon boss. (From 1870s in print, but wagon trains were moving across the country earlier than that)

wagon mound

■ n Now historical, except as a place-name. The term refers to a hillock in the shape of a covered wagon. (From 1840s)

wagon train

■ n This now-historical term designated a group of wagons assembled for the purpose of transporting people and goods, especially westward between the 1840s and 1880s. (From 1840s)

walk-down

■ n A method for catching wild horses by following them in relays, keeping them moving and unable to graze or rest until they are exhausted enough to capture. The pursuers may be on foot or on horseback. By spelling one another, usually across a valley or up a canyon, the pursuer who finally gets close enough has an easy time roping the entire herd. (From 1900s)

Wallawalla	■ n A tribe of the Shahaptian family that once inhabited the area of a tributary of the Columbia River. The tribe was moved to the Umatilla Reservation in Oregon. The name is used for a river and a city in southeastern Washington, home of a state penitentiary. (From 1800s, *wallawalla* 'little river')
wall-eye	■ n A saltwater surf fish with large eyes. This wall-eye, *Hyperprosopon argenteus,* is not to be confused with the more famous freshwater fish of the upper Midwest. (From 1880s)
Walrussia	■ n One of the names suggested for what is now **Alaska.** When the United States became interested in the territory, a number of names were suggested, from the bizarre to the poetic. In addition to "Walrussia," the list included "American Siberia," "Icebergia," "Polario (or Polaria)," and "Zero Island." Charles Sumner's suggestion of the Aleutian word *Alaska* was finally adopted. (From 1860s)
wanigan	■ n Although the origin and etymology of this word is eastern, it has come to have a special significance in the Northwest. Originally, the word was used in lumber camps to refer to a small chest, later to a small shed used as an office or temporary refuge. By the time lumbering became big business in Alaska, the vocabulary of the lumber camp had spread into the general population. Since the 1950s, the term has regularly referred to an addition built onto a house trailer or cabin. (From 1840s, Ojibwa 'pit' or 'dig a hole') See also **add-on.**

wanigan, at the end of train

wapatoo

■ n A term used for any of various edible roots in the Northwest. (From 1800s, Chinook Jargon)

ward

■ n A territorial subdivision of a **stake** in the Mormon church, for purposes of ecclesiastical government. The executive head is called a bishop. Though the term is found in England, Scotland, and the eastern United States, it is used in those areas to designate a political subdivision or region. In some areas with a very high concentration of Mormons, the ward is *ipso facto* both an ecclesiastical and a political unit. (From 1850s)

Warm Springs Apache

■ n An Indian tribe originally from southwestern New Mexico, near the headwaters of the Gila River. The springs there were called Ojo Caliente ('hot water'). The members of the tribe were shipped to the Mescalero Reservation in New Mexico in the early 1900s. (From 1880s)

Warm Springs Indians

■ n pl Collective name for the tribes sharing the Warm Springs Reservation in Oregon. The tribes include Piute, Tenino, Tyigh, and Wasco. (From 1910s)

Wasco

■ n The name of a tribe originally from around The Dalles, Oregon. The tribe subsisted mainly on fish, but changed dietary habits when transferred to the reservation for the **Warm Springs Indians** in the early 1900s. (From 1850s)

wash

■ n Also called **arroyo.** The erosion of soil and upper layers of earth by flash floods brought on in arid regions by sudden cloudbursts that dump a lot of water on a small area in a short time. The water rushes quickly through the wash, making it deeper. The washes have sharply vertical sides rather than sloping banks. (From 1830s) See also **gulch.**

wash gold

■ n Gold that is found in the detritus of alluvial fans, or other eroded features such at those found in glaciated areas or scattered in **washes,** as opposed to gold that is found in lodes or veins. (From 1870s) See also **placer.**

washbowl

■ n A prospector's **gold pan.** Used somewhat facetiously now, although prospectors have always

talked of "washing gold." (From 1840s) See also **batea, pan.**

Washington

■ n Nicknames: **Evergreen State, Chinook State.** Forty-second state of the Union. Settled in 1811, it became a territory separate from the Oregon Territory in 1853, and a state in 1889. Capital: Olympia. The settlers' suggestion, "Columbia," after the Columbia River, was turned down by Congress, who instead adopted the name "Washington" in honor of the first president, despite the already pervasive use of it as a place-name. (From 1853)

Washington cedar

■ n Another name for the giant **sequoia** of California. (From 1880s) See also **giant cedar.**

Washington clam

■ n See **butter clam, gaper, horse clam.**

Washington lily

■ n A large lily first described by John Muir in his journals of travels in the West. The *Lilium washingtonianum* is common to the northwest Pacific Coast. (From 1860s)

Washington navel

■ n A type of orange that became the foundation for the citrus production of southern California. From first experiments with the orange in the 1880s, the fruit was found to thrive in what is now Orange County, south of Los Angeles. The large groves of oranges that became the foundation of citrus production that would rival Florida, were nearly all Washington navels. (From 1880s)

Washington palm

■ n Also called the **Washington fan palm.** A type of fan palm that grows well in arid environments. It has been planted in many areas of the Mohave Desert, and can be found even in Death Valley in California. (From 1900s)

Washoe

■ /WAH show/ n An Indian tribe that inhabited the area along the Truckee River, through what is now Reno, Nevada. The tribe constituted a unique linguistic family, not related to the Paiute languages of the region. The region became known as "Washoe," and consequently many terms associated with the area use Washoe in the name. The Comstock Lode at nearby Virginia City, during the 1850s, spawned many now-obsolete mining terms using the regional name: *Washoe canary,* a facetious nickname for a **burro** (q.v. for a list of other names); ~ *diggings,* the mining area; ~ *excitement,* ~ *fever,* gold-fever; ~ *mine;* ~ *pick,* a short-handled pick; ~ *process* (also called "wet-silver mill"), extracting silver by grinding ore and washing it with mercury or other chemicals like blue vitriol and salt; ~ *Seeress,* a local spiritualist in the 1870s; ~ *silver mine;* ~ *wagon,* a large ore wagon; ~ *weather,* unsettled weather that frustrates forecasting.

Washoe zephyr ■ n A strong west wind that blows through the Truckee River Valley in the spring and fall. (From 1860s)

water dog ■ n The western name for any of a variety of salamanders, most commonly used as fish bait on large western lakes that support bass. (From 1850s)

watermaster ■ n In the Southwest and arid regions of the West, especially, the person in charge of controlling the water used in **irrigation** or the water levels in reservoirs. (From 1850s)

wavy oak ■ n Another name for the common scrub oak of the Southwest. (From 1880s)

wawa ■ n, v Talk, speech; to talk, to speak. (From the 1850s, Chinook Jargon)

Webfoot State ■ n A nickname for **Oregon,** reflecting a common perception about the wet climate of the state. Hence, **Webfoot, Webfooter,** a citizen of Oregon. (From 1860s) Also **Beaver State, Hard-Case State.**

weeping oak ■ n See **valley oak.**

West ■ n The region generally comprising that area from the eastern slopes of the **Rocky Mountains** to the Pacific Ocean. See Introduction for more details. (From 1840s)

West Coast ■ n That section of North America bordering on the Pacific Ocean, especially the western sections of California, Oregon, and Washington. (From 1850s)

West Coast jazz ■ n A type of smoothly flowing, harmonic ensemble jazz popularized especially in nightclubs of North Beach in San Francisco in the 1950s.

Western ■ n A novel or motion picture depicting places, characters, and events related to the Old West, or cowboys of earlier days. (From 1920s)

western

■ A combining form that makes compound nouns of many terms that are especially associated with the West. 1. Plants that have certain characteristics or variations peculiar to the western regions: *western azalea; ~ bearberry* (see **pigeonberry**); *~ black ash; ~ chinquapin,* a shrub oak of the Sierra Nevadas and Cascade Mountains; *~ iron weed; ~ larch; ~ pennyroyal; ~ red cedar* (see **red cedar**); *~ sugar maple,* marked by leaves that have furry undersides; *~ white pine; ~ yellow pine.* 2. Birds or animals of wide distribution that have certain characteristics found only in the western varieties: *western black pewee; ~ bluebird; ~ duck; ~ flicker; ~ grass bunting; ~ gull; ~ meadowlark; ~ mockingbird; ~ nightingale,* a facetious nickname for a **burro** (q.v. for a list of other names); *~ palm warbler; ~ red-tail hawk; ~ robin; ~ snowbird; ~ turkey; ~ warbling vireo; ~ wood peewee.*

Westerner

■ n One who lives in the West or was born in the western section of North America. (From 1830s)

Westernism

■ n A word or expression peculiar to the West, originating in the West, or regularly associated with the West. (From 1830s)

western saddle

■ n A heavy saddle having a high cantle and pommel. The pommel horn and fork are leather-covered steel. Wide leather flaps protect the riders legs. Heavy wooden or steel stirrups mark this as working equipment. (From 1910s)

Western Slope

■ n The west side of mountain crests, especially west of the Continental Divide, of the Rocky Mountain and Sierra Nevada ranges. (From 1850s)

wet

■ adj Of or relating to livestock or goods brought across the border from Mexico, especially illegally. Early references were to "wet ponies," "wet dogies." (From 1920s)

wetback

■ n An illegal alien from Mexico who enters the United States illegally. The term is used in a derogatory fashion and refers to a person's swimming the Rio Grande, although the term is applied to any Mexican national who swims, walks, wades, or drives across the border illegally. (From 1940s)

wet diggings

■ n Areas of gold mining found near running water, usually along the banks of streams. (From 1850s)

whale

■ n An Alaska fisherman's term for a very large halibut, over eighty or ninety pounds. As distinct from a "chicken" halibut weighing in under ten pounds. (From 1960s)

wheel dog

■ n Also called **wheel, wheeler.** The **mush dog** attached closest to the sled. The dog is supposed to be more powerful than average. (From 1900s, on analogy with "wheel horse," a term from the 1700s) See also **lead dog, team dog.**

whipsnake

■ n Also called **coachwhip snake, coppery whipsnake.** A slender snake that grows to five feet in length and has a long tail resembling a braided whip. It is found in the Southwest and Mexico. (From 1760s)

whiskerino

■ n A competition usually held in towns in the West when a festival or local celebration is coming in a couple of months. Men show themselves clean-shaven on entry day, usually a month or six weeks before the festivities, then a judging contest is part of the celebration to determine longest, most unusual, ugliest, and so on of the various beards. (From 1920s)

whiskey root

■ n An old term for **peyote.** (From 1870s) See also **mescal button.**

whispering bells

■ n pl California yellow bell flowers, which dry on their stems, while keeping their color and shape, and make a soft rustling sound in a light breeze. (From 1910s)

whistler

■ n Also called **whistling marmot.** A type of western marmot, squat and round, that communicates danger or anything else with a sharp whistling cry. (From 1900s)

white alder

■ n The western version of the sweet pepperbush,

which is found widely in the eastern states. (From 1850s)

white-barked pine

■ n Also called **white-stemmed pine.** A pine that marks the timberline in the Rocky Mountain and Sierra Nevada ranges. It is marked by whitish scales on the bark. It is not sought for timber. (From 1900s)

white bear

■ n A western name for the **grizzly bear.** Now rare. (From 1790s)

white brant

■ n The western term for the snow goose found all over North America. (From 1800s)

white buffalo

■ n Also called the **white goat.** The **Rocky Mountain goat,** or **sheep,** of the Northwest. (From 1800s)

white fir

■ n A long conical fir with relatively soft wood. It is used mainly for pulp, plywood, boxes. (From 1880s)

white fox

■ n The winter-coated version of the Arctic fox. (From 1900s) See also **blue fox.**

white goat

■ n See **white buffalo.**

white-headed woodpecker

■ n A woodpecker found especially among the yellow pines of California, Oregon, and Washington. (From 1850s)

white king salmon

■ n Also shortened to **white king.** The **Chinook salmon,** whose meat runs from white to pale pink. See **salmon** n for a complete listing. (From 1950s)

white loco

■ n Also called **crazy weed.** A Rocky Mountain type of **locoweed,** marked by white blossoms and dark green foliage, which makes it stand out. (From 1900s)

white maple

■ n See **big-leaf maple.**

white pelican

■ n A large pelican inhabiting the coastal waters of Oregon. (From 1810s)

white sage

■ n One of two main western plants marked by whitish leaves. One, also called **greasewood,** is a member of the mint family, *Salvia apiana,* and is marked by spiky white or pale lavender flowers. It is found in southern California. The other, *Artemisia mexicana,* is a type of **sagebrush** whose leaves have a hairy white underside. (From 1860s)

white-stemmed pine ■ n See **white-barked pine.**

white-tailed grouse ■ n A particular grouse found in the **Rocky Mountains,** distinguished from other grouse because of its tail. (From 1850s)

white-tailed hawk ■ n A particular hawk found in the Southwest, distinguished by its tail. (From 1850s)

white-tailed ptarmigan ■ n A ptarmigan specific to the higher ranges of the **Rocky Mountains,** distinguished because of its tail. (From 1850s)

white weasel ■ n A Pacific Northwest type of ermine. Once called the "genuine ermine." (From 1800s)

wickiup ■ n In Nevada, Arizona, Idaho, especially in the Paiute and Gosiute areas, a dwelling or hut made of brushwood, perhaps covered with mats. In more recent years, the word has taken on the meaning of a crude, temporary shelter. The origin of the word is in some dispute, but it appears to be a corruption of the Algonquian (perhaps Fox, Sauk, or Kickapoo) term for 'lodging' *wigwam,* a term used in the East. Perhaps explorers brought the term west and the name was applied to a certain type of dwelling in the Southwest. To confuse even more, the Abnaki and Delaware Indians had a similar term that referred to stringy bark, the kind that would be used in constructing such a dwelling. (From 1850s)

wide loop

■ Descriptive of the act of rustling. To accuse a man of "swinging a wide loop" is to accuse him of cattle rustling or horse stealing. The allusion is to the size of the loop in the lariat. A loop that is too large may catch more than legal cattle. May be a literary concoction adopted by writers of Westerns. (From 1920s) See also **rustler.**

wild and woolly (West)

■ phr This term was originally used to describe anything crude or unrefined that might be suggestive of the lawless frontier of the West. It was apparently in the air, because the earliest use of it was in the Southwest, but it was almost immediately spread across the country. (From 1880s)

wildcat claim

■ n Also called **wildcat ground.** A speculative **mining claim** filed in a region that has successful mining operations in place. Shares in the claim are then sold by means of a written prospectus that sings the praises of the region and implies tremendous returns on investments. Sometimes a pyramid scheme is constructed: by returning some of the later money invested to earlier investors, the operator of the scam can entice additional and larger investments by the earliest investors. Using the news of payoffs to earlier investors, new investors can be lured into the scheme. (From 1860s, but probably in use much earlier)

wildcat mine

■ n Often shortened to **wildcat** in context. A mine of dubious value, often **salted** with high-grade ore to lure potential investors. (From 1860s)

wild celery

■ n Also called **puchki, cow parsnip.** In northern Alaska, a wild plant growing sometimes three to five feet tall that is eaten like celery. (From 1940s)

wild hyacinth

■ n A wild flower of the West whose bulb is much sought as a food staple. Many Indians whose tribal names were known only to them were called "diggers" or "camas eaters" by outsiders because the Indians depended on the bounty of the wild hyacinth for sustenance. (From 1840s) See **camas** for further information.

wild Indian

■ n Originally, an Indian who refused to move to a

reservation and was therefore regarded as a roving savage, especially in the Southwest. Later, any person exhibiting unruly behavior and unwillingness to settle in one place. (From 1840s)

wild onion ■ n Also called **death camas.** A root resembling that of the **wild hyacinth,** but poisonous. (From 1930s)

wild parsley ■ n In Alaska, a name applied to a type of plant found along the coast, more commonly named after the European lovage, often **Scotch lovage** or **beach lovage.** Used as greens in soups and salmon recipes. (From 1950s)

wild West ■ n phr The western part of the United States, especially as it is regarded as rough, uncivilized, even lawless. The term is eastern in origin, coined by persons who never visited the West, but did not let that stop them from creating images of their worst fears. (From 1850s)

Wild West Show ■ n A presentation that is part pageant, part circus, part **rodeo,** featuring cowboys and Indians performing feats on horseback. The term originally applied to the spectacle created by William F. Cody. Buffalo Bill opened his traveling show on May 17, 1883, in Omaha, Nebraska. Soon after, other entrepreneurs opened similar traveling shows, employing real cowboys and Indians, ex-scouts and buffalo hunters, trick riders and trick shooters, the most famous of whom was Annie Oakley. (From 1880s)

Williamson's sapsucker ■ n Also called **Williamson's woodpecker.** A sapsucker or woodpecker found only in the **Rocky Mountains** that has no red feathers on its head. Named after Lt. R. S. Williamson (1824–1882), a topographical engineer on the Pacific Railroad survey. One source reported that Lieutenant Williamson had bright red hair, but went bald at a young age. (From 1850s)

williwaw ■ n Also called **wooly.** A sudden, sharp and cold wind that blows from high mountains seaward. Found specifically in northern Alaska, the Aleutian

Islands, and the Alaska Peninsula. Tabbert (*DAK*) reports that the same wind is found in the southern hemisphere at high latitudes, such as the Straits of Magellan. He accounts that "wooly" is a pronunciation variant. The term was well known to whalers. Both forms have a high frequency of use in Alaska and among Alaskan fishermen. (From 1840s)

willow goldfinch

■ n A Pacific Coast variety of goldfinch. (From 1910s)

willow grouse

■ n Any of a variety of grouse or ptarmigans found in the mountainous regions of British Columbia, the Yukon Territory, and Alaska. Variously also called **willow ptarmigan, ruffed grouse,** and **sharp-tailed grouse.** (From 1820s)

Wilson's phalarope

■ n A large phalarope found in Oregon. Named after Alexander Wilson (1766–1813), a Scottish-born ornithologist who tracked many of America's birds. A number of American birds were named after Wilson, but just two are found only in the West: Wilson's phalarope and Wilson's petrel, a type of petrel found in the West from Mexico to high northern latitudes. (From 1830s)

Winchester

■ n A code name for an IBM research project in San Jose, California, in 1969 for a high-speed, large capacity, fixed-disk storage system. The plan was to place two 30-million character drives (called "files" by IBM) into a single storage system, which would be enclosed and dustproof. The phrase "30-30" reminded the engineers of a popular model of the Winchester rifle. The system came out with 70-million characters, called the "33-40." But the Winchester name stuck. The term is now historical, indicating the speed with which times and products change in the computer world.

wineberry

■ n See **barberry, nagoonberry.**

winter range

■ n In the **Rocky Mountains,** cattle and sheep grazing grounds that are at a lower altitude than the summer range, to avoid the worst of the snow and make the livestock more accessible to the rancher and sheepherder. (From 1870s)

winter road

■ n A route in Alaska that is used only when the ground is frozen in the wintertime. Such roads often lead to timber areas for loggers. (From 1920s)

winter saint

■ n A term coined by Brigham Young, perhaps bemusedly, for people who came into the Salt Lake Valley and decided to spend the winter there among the Mormons rather than hazard crossing the Sierra Nevadas. Such people often did not meet the standards of morals, ethics, and devotion of full-time **Saints.** Perhaps these temporary residents were the first **snowbirds** on record. (From 1850s)

winter salmon

■ n See **Chinook salmon.**

winter trail

■ n In the Far Northwest, a **dogsled** trail that is marked for winter travel only. (From 1900s)

Wintun

■ n A collective name for the two divisions of the Copehan family of Indians found originally in northern California along the upper Sacramento River and below Mount Shasta. The name means 'people, human beings'. (From 1870s)

wipeout

■ n Originally a surfer's term for being thrown unceremoniously off a surfboard by a wave. The term soon came to mean the act of being immobilized by any number of causes: drugs, alcohol, broken heart, lack of gasoline for one's car, and so on. (From 1950s)

wire cutter

■ n Although the term did not originate in the West, it took on a particular meaning during the range wars among ranchers and farmers. The development of barbed wire led to a rebellion by cowmen over closed land. A person (wire cutter) who cut barbed wire to open up rangeland or let out cattle was often technically breaking the law, but usually saw himself as protecting a former, simpler, and more logical way of life. (From 1870s)

wobbly

■ n Often capitalized. A nickname for a member of the union of Industrial Workers of the World (I.W.W.). Though unconfirmed, the traditional explanation is that the term derives from a Chinese speaker's distortion of I.W.W. to "I Wobble, Wobble." (From 1910s)

wo-haw

■ n Now a historical term, the word was apparently coined by Indians who heard drivers of ox teams calling "whoa" and "haw" to their teams. When the Indians asked for cattle, they used the term. It was picked up by Texas cowboys, who spread the term for a time. (From 1880s)

wokas

■ n A great yellow water lily of Oregon, or its seeds. The seeds are gathered by Indians, dried, and roasted for food. The particular Indian language from which the word is derived is unknown. (From 1870s)

wolf eel

■ n Also spelled *wolf-eel.* A long eel-like fish found along the California coast. Different sources give *Anarrhichthys ocellatus* or *Anarhichthys felis* for the fish. It is definitely not an eel, but has an elongated body. (From 1880s)

wood ranch

■ n A place where trees are cultivated for timber, Christmas trees, or pulp. Different from forest land in which large-scale logging takes place. (From 1860s)

woodsman

■ n Also called **brushman.** In the Far Northwest, the creature of stories and tales who lives alone in the wilds, steals babies, and harasses people. The equivalent of other wild men, like **Bigfoot** and **Sasquatch** in the Pacific Northwest, the hairy man of Louisiana, the bogeyman elsewhere. (From 1960s, though "brushman" is decades earlier)

woolly, wooly

■ n See **wild and woolly, williwaw.**

wrangler

■ n This term is traced back to the sixteenth century in England with the sense of "disputant." William Shakespeare has Henry V refer to himself as a "wrangler" for the throne of France. But the word developed a new sense in the American West in the 1880s, first as **horse-wrangler,** probably a conflation of the English "wrangle" and a translation of the Spanish *caballerango,* then as a cowboy who worked with livestock on a ranch. The *OED* has a separate entry for it as a word from the "American West."

wrestle   ■ v To throw a steer or calf to the ground and hold it down for branding. (From 1880s)

Wyoming   ■ n Also called the **Equality State,** because it was the first state to enfranchise women. Forty-fourth state of the Union. Settled in 1834, it became a territory in 1868, and a state in 1890. The capital is Cheyenne. "Cheyenne" was the name proposed for the state, which would have been inappropriate because the Cheyenne Indians originally lived in central Minnesota and North and South Dakota. They were then shipped to Montana and Oklahoma. None of the Cheyenne wound up in Wyoming, at least officially. Although the name "Wyoming" comes from the Delaware Indians and is used as a place-name in the East, Representative James M. Ashley of Ohio proposed it over "Cheyenne" because of what he thought was the appropriateness of the name to the territory's landscape. Much of it is high desert, but the **Rocky Mountains** could hardly be considered "flat." (From 1868; Delaware *Meche-weami-ing* 'at the big flats')

Yakima

■ n Originally a tribe of the Shahaptian group that inhabited both sides of the Columbia River from Long Rapids to the confluence with the Lewis River. Also the name of the language of the tribe, and now a place-name in Washington near the same area. The tribal reservation is near Wapato. (From 1880s, native *iakooma* 'runaway')

Yamel

■ n Originally a tribe living along a river in the Willamette Valley in Oregon. Unlike the **Yakimas,** the Yamel did not fight the earliest settlers. Consequently, they were simply displaced and became extinct. It is unknown what the word *yamel* meant. The tribe numbered five in 1910. (From 1840s)

yampa

■ n A plant of the genus *Atemia* that has a tuber similar to a potato. Sought after as a food staple by various Shoshonean groups. Just as certain Indians in Oregon were called "camas eaters" by their neighbors, so too a group of Comanches were called *yamparika* 'yampa eaters' by their Shoshonean neighbors. (From 1840s, Ute)

yarner

■ n A pronunciation corruption of **llano** as in Llano Estacado, also called the Staked Plain, a plateau of forty thousand square miles situated in Texas and New Mexico. The region is high desert, arid, and appears bleak to those who must cross it. (From 1900s)

Yavapai

■ n Also spelled *Yampai.* A Yuman tribe also known as **Mohave Apache.** Also a place-name found several times in the Southwest. There is some confusion about the origin of the term. One view is that the term is from a native Indian phrase meaning 'children of the sun'. Another view holds that interpretation to be a romantic concoction, preferring a Spanish origin. (From 1850s)

yedra

■ n Poison ivy or poison oak, especially *Rhus diversiloba,* which seems to affect some people worse than others. (From 1830s, Spanish *hiedra*)

yellow
■ n A term for gold, especially gold dust or nuggets. (From 1900s)

yellow-backed rockfish
■ n The *Pteropodus maliger,* a rockfish that inhabits Pacific Coast waters from Monterey, California, northward to the Puget Sound. (From 1880s)

yellow-bellied marmot
■ n A type of marmot marked by a yellowish underside, found in west Texas, New Mexico, and Arizona, northward on the eastern range of the **Rocky Mountains.** (From 1910s)

yellow-billed magpie
■ n A type of magpie found in the area of the San Joaquin and Sacramento valleys westward to the Pacific Coast in California. Marked by its yellow bill. (From 1850s)

yellow fir
■ n Another name for the **Douglas fir** of the Pacific Northwest. (From 1880s)

yellow fish
■ n Also called the **Atka mackerel.** *Pleurogrammus monopterygius* is found along the Aleutian Islands and the Alaskan Peninsula. In early years, it was thought to be the same as the Atlanta mackerel, but is an entirely different genus. (From 1880s) See **Alaskan mackerel** for a complete listing.

Yellowstone trout
■ n A type of **cutthroat trout** found in the headwaters of the Yellowstone River, which rises in Yellowstone National Park. It is larger than most high-altitude cutthroats, but has the same firm flesh and succulent taste. (From 1870s) See also **mountain trout, rainbow trout.**

yerba buena
■ n Any of a variety of medicinal plants found around the San Francisco Bay area. Capitalized, it once referred to the area of San Francisco, and still exists as a place-name. (From 1830s Spanish, 'good herb')

yerba del vaso
■ n Also spelled *yerba del bazo.* Also called **brittlebrush.** A small shrub found in the Southwest. The gum from the plant is applied topically to relieve pain in the *vaso,* the left side of the body, below the ribs. (From 1910s, Spanish 'herb of the artery')

yerba santa

■ n Also called **bearweed.** Any of several plants of the genus *Eriodictyon.* The shrubs grow two to five feet high and are used in pulmonary remedies. (From 1880s, Spanish, 'holy herb')

Yokaia

■ n An Indian tribe, a division of the Pomo group, inhabiting the region around the northern end of the Redwood Range in California. Ukiah, California, is named for the tribe. The name means 'down in the valley' or 'lower valley'. (From 1850s)

Yokut

■ n An Indian tribe, a division of the Mariposan group, originally found in the San Joaquin Valley in northern California. The remnants of the tribe now are found to the south of Yosemite National Park. (From 1870s)

Yosemite

■ /yo SEM uh tee/ n A glaciated valley of the Merced River in east-central California on the eastern slope of the Sierra Nevada range. (From 1850s, Miwok *uzumaiti* 'grizzly' or 'killer')

Yukon boat

■ n A type of rowboat with a square end, first introduced by prospectors and miners on the Yukon River. Such boats were cheap to make and not very durable. (From 1850s)

Yukon candy

■ n Strips of salmon salted, smoked, and dried. The delicacy was introduced by Alaska Natives, and has become as popular as beef jerky in convenience stores in the West, though somewhat more expensive. (From 1930s) See **squaw candy** for a complete listing.

Yukon sled

■ n A broad utility sled made of a flat platform mounted on runners. Runners and platforms of various sizes can be purchased, then assembled by the buyer. No stanchions protrude above the platform, so oversized loads can be carried. The sleds are used mainly for freight or large items like boats or logs. (From 1890s)

Yukon stove

■ n Originally a small sheet-iron box with an oven at the back and a telescoping pipe to lead the smoke out of the tent or cabin in which it was used. By the 1940s, the term was used for a stove built from a fifty-five-gallon steel drum, split lengthwise, and fitted with sheet metal top. A door is cut into the end of the half barrel and four legs are welded to the bottom circumference. A stationary stove pipe leads through the roof. (From 1890s) See also **barrel stove.**

Yukon tea

■ n See **Alaska tea.**

Yuma

■ n Originally a reference to a division of Indian tribes centered along the Colorado River in what is now Arizona. The languages of the group are called "Yuman." Eventually, the term was applied to a prehistoric people who had inhabited the area and left traces of themselves by the distinctive arrowheads, called **Yuma points,** found concentrated in the region, but with a distribution larger than the **Folsom points** of northwestern New Mexico. The term survives as a place-name in Arizona. (From 1830s)

Yurok

■ n An isolated Indian tribe that inhabited a region of the lower Klamath River and Pacific Coast area of northwestern California. The people were taller than their neighbors, and may possibly have once been belonged to the Algonquian group from farther east. (From 1850s, 'downward', 'downstream')

Z

zaguan

■ /suh GWAN/ n The vestibule or long entryway in a **hacienda,** 1, of the Southwest. It serves as a buffer to outside weather, helping to maintain coolness within the house. (From 1850s, Spanish)

zanja

■ /SAWn juh/ n Also called **acequia.** A man-made ditch for **irrigation** or for carrying water that might be used for more than irrigation. (From 1860s, Spanish)

zanja madre

■ n The "mother ditch." The main irrigation canal of a region. It may run twelve to fifteen miles in length. The regular zanjas run off at right angles. (From 1870s, Spanish)

zinfandel

■ n A dry red wine made in California from black vinifera grapes. (From 1890s)

Zuni

■ n The name of an Indian tribe and the pueblo in which they live in western New Mexico. Also, the language they speak. (From 1830s)

Bibliography

Adams, Ramon F. *Western Words.* Norman: University of Oklahoma Press, 1968.

Albuquerque Journal. 7777 Jefferson NE, Albuquerque NM 87109.

Anchorage Daily News. PO Box 149001, Anchorage AK 99514.

Arizona Republic. 120 E. Van Buren, Phoenix AZ 85004.

Avis, Walter S., ed. *Dictionary of Canadianisms on Historical Principles.* Toronto: Gage, 1967.

Barnhart, David. *Barnhart Dictionary Companion.* Cold Spring, N.Y.: Lexik House Publishers, 1982–1991.

Beck, Warren A., and Ynez D. Haase. *Historical Atlas of the American West.* Norman: University of Oklahoma Press, 1989.

Book of Mormon. Salt Lake City: Church of Jesus Christ of Latter-day Saints, 1982.

Bright, Elizabeth S. *A Word Geography of California and Nevada.* University of California Publications in Linguistics, vol. 69. Berkeley: University of California Press, 1971.

Cassidy, Frederic G., and Joan H. Hall. *Dictionary of American Regional English,* vols. 1 and 2. Cambridge, Mass.: Belknap Press, 1985 and 1990. *DARE*

_____. Unpublished files for *Dictionary of American Regional English.* Madison, Wisconsin. Consulted summer 1984 and by correspondence since.

Clark, Thomas L. *Dictionary of Gambling and Gaming.* Cold Spring, N.Y.: Lexik House Publishers, 1987.

_____. Nevada Language Survey Oral Collection. File at the University of Nevada, Las Vegas, 1972–1991.

Cralle, Trevor. *Surfin'ary: A Dictionary of Surfing Terms and Surfspeak.* Berkeley: Ten Speed Press, 1991.

Daily Spectrum. 275 E St. George Blvd., PO Box 1630, St. George UT 84771.

Denver Post. 1560 Broadway, Denver CO 80202.

Espenshade, Edward B., Jr. *Goode's World Atlas.* 13th ed. Chicago: Rand McNally, 1970.

Flexner, Stuart Berg. *The Random House Dictionary of the English Language.* 2d ed., unabridged. New York: Random House, 1987.

Frémont, John C. *The Exploring Expedition to the Rocky Mountains, Oregon, and California.* Buffalo: Derby Press, 1851.

Fresno Bee. 1626 E St., Fresno CA 93706.

Gove, Phillip. *Webster's Third New International Dictionary.* Springfield, Mass.: G. & C. Merriam, 1961.

Idaho Statesman. 1200 N Curtis Rd., Boise ID 83706.

Kobayashi, George. Curator, California Room, Martin Luther King, Jr., Public Library, San Jose, Calif. Words and terms from Asian languages.

Knowles, Elizabeth. Lexicographer, Oxford University Press. Frequency and source of selected terms.

Las Vegas Sun. (University of Nevada)

McConnell, R. E. *Our Own Voice.* Toronto: Gage, 1979.

McCulloch, Walter F. *Woods Words: A Comprehensive Dictionary of Loggers Terms.* Portland, Or.: Champoeg Press, 1958.

Mathews, Mitford M. *A Dictionary of Americanisms on Historical Principles.* Chicago: University of Chicago Press, 1951.

Mish, Frederick C. *Webster's Tenth New Collegiate Dictionary.* Springfield, Mass.: Merriam-Webster, 1993.

New English Bible. New York: Oxford University Press, 1976.

The Oregonian. 1320 S.W. Broadway, Portland OR 97201.

Oxford English Dictionary. 2d ed. Oxford: Clarendon, 1989.

Sacramento Bee. 2100 Q St., Sacramento CA 95816.

Salt Lake Tribune. 143 S. Main St., SLC UT 84111.

San Diego Union Tribune. PO Box 191, San Diego CA 92112-4106.

San Francisco Chronicle. 901 Mission St., San Francisco CA 94103.

San Jose Mercury News. 750 Ridder Park Dr., San Jose, CA 95190

Seattle Post-Intelligencer. (University of Washington)

Seattle Times. PO Box 70, Seattle WA 98111.

Shreve, Forrest. *The Cactus and Its Home.* Baltimore: Williams and Wilkins, 1931.

Shreve, Forrest, and Ira L. Wiggins. *Vegetation and Flora of the Sonoran Desert.* Publication no. 591. Washington, D.C.: Carnegie Institution of Washington, 1951.

Slatta, Richard W. *The Cowboy Encyclopedia.* Santa Barbara: ABC-Clio, 1994.

The Sun. 399 N. D St., San Bernardino CA 92401.

Tabbert, Russell. *Dictionary of Alasakan English.* Juneau: Denali, 1991. *DAK*

Tahoe Daily Tribune. 3079 Harrison Ave., South Lake Tahoe CA 95705.

Tucson Citizen. 4850 S. Park Ave., PO Box 26767, Tucson AZ 85726.

Winick, Charles. *Dictionary of Anthropology.* Totowa, N.J.: Littlefield, Adams & Co., 1970.

Illustration Credits

Alaskan malamute: Alaska Division of Tourism
atigi: Alaska Division of Tourism. Ernst Schneider,
    photographer.
atlatl: Nevada State Museum
barrel cactus: Jeanne W. Clark
basket, basket sled: Alaska Division of Tourism. Ernst
    Schneider, photographer.
batea: Jeanne W. Clark
beavertail cactus: Jeanne W. Clark
bidar: Anchorage Museum of History and Art,
    B72.27.93
bighorn sheep: Nevada State Museum
billiken: Anchorage Museum of History and Art,
    70.103
blanket toss: Anchorage Museum of History and Art,
    B70.28.111
bronco: Cragin Collection, University of Nevada, Las
    Vegas
burro: Davis Collection, University of Nevada, Las
    Vegas
butte: Rockwell Collection, University of Nevada, Las
    Vegas
chaps: Courtesy of Jeanne W. Clark
chuckwalla: Sasha Tate-Clark
coho: Alaska Division of Tourism
concha: Margaret Brandner
creosote bush: W. E. Niles
dead man's hand: Thomas L. Clark
diamondback: Thomas L. Clark
dog driver, dog musher: Alaska Division of Tourism
downwinder: Manis Collection, University of Nevada,
    Las Vegas
fish camp: Anchorage Museum of History and Art,
    24541. Steve McCutcheon, photographer.
Folsom point: from Riley, *Rio del Norte,* University of
    Utah Press, 1995
Gadsden Purchase: Nathan F. Stout, Department of
    Geoscience, University of Nevada, Las Vegas
ghostflower: W. E. Niles
Great Basin: Nathan F. Stout, Department of
    Geoscience, University of Nevada, Las Vegas
hoodoo: J. Poon
horned toad: Sasha Tate-Clark
humpback salmon: Alaska Division of Tourism

igloo: Alaska Division of Tourism. Ernst Schneider, photographer.
keno goose: Nevada State Museum
kiva: from Riley, *Rio del Norte,* University of Utah Press, 1995; after Lister and Lister, 1987
mane: John Lyman. All rights reserved.
manzanita: W. E. Niles
mano, metate: Jeanne W. Clark
mission design: Nevada State Museum
mukluk: Alaska Division of Tourism. Ernst Scheider, photographer.
Navajo rug: Jeanne W. Clark
ocatillo: W. E. Niles
old man cactus: W. E. Niles
oosik: Alaska State Museum
organ cactus: Jeanne W. Clark
parka: Alaska Division of Tourism. Ernst Schneider, photographer.
pipe: John Lyman. All rights reserved.
powder: Deer Valley Resort
pupfish: Jack E. Williams
rabbit ears: Nevada Palace Hotel and Casino
riffle: Heritage Museum
saguaro: Jeanne W. Clark
sidewinder: Thomas L. Clark
snow machine: Anchorage Museum of History and Art, 24330. Steve McCutcheon, photographer.
sockeye salmon: Alaska Division of Tourism
sourdough: Anchorage Museum of History and Art, B64.1.842
Spanish bayonet: Jeanne W. Clark
squaw candy: Alaska Division of Tourism. Ernst Schneider, photographer.
tube: John Lyman. All rights reserved.
twenty-mule team: Manis Collection, University of Nevada, Las Vegas
ulu: Alaska State Museum
wanigan: Anchorage Museum of History and Art, B72.32.292
washbowl: Alaska Division of Tourism
Washington palm: Thomas L. Clark
wickiup: Heritage Museum